Staying Close

Staying Close

A POSITIVE APPROACH TO
DYING AND BEREAVEMENT

MICHAEL WATERHOUSE

CONSTABLE • LONDON

Constable & Robinson Ltd
3 The Lanchesters
162 Fulham Palace Road
London W6 9ER
www.constablerobinson.com

First published in the UK by Constable,
an imprint of Constable & Robinson Ltd, 2003

A copy of the British Library Cataloguing in
Publication data is available from the British Library

ISBN 1–84119–681–9

Printed and bound in the EU

For Tessa

In memory of
Margaret Waterhouse and
Simon Houghton

Contents

Acknowledgements   ix
Introduction   xi

1 Why We Think as We Do   1
2 Terminal Illness   43
3 The Gift of Hospice   95
4 Dying at Home – the Future of Palliative Care   133
5 The Need for Ritual   163
6 Dealing with Grief   195
7 Conclusion   263

End Notes   283
Recommended Reading   291
Useful Contacts   295
Index   299

Acknowledgements

In the course of writing this book, I have been very privileged to meet a large number of brave and generous people, who have given their time and talked freely to me. Their stories reveal how painful and disturbing the effects of death can be, but they also give evidence of the courage and resilience of which human beings are capable when faced with the greatest trial of their lives. In particular, I would like to thank the following for their help: Anita Binns, Glenn Binns Jr, Paul Coli, Donald Dean, Laurie Didham, June Harding, Jeremy Howe, Clare Houghton, Janice Hunt, Dina McCullough, Helen Neocleus, Jo New, Bev Sage, Sue Smith and Loris Thurston.

I have also been greatly assisted by those who work with the dying and the bereaved, in particular: Caroline Anson, Lynn Barclay, Claire Barracliffe, Ellie Bennett, Julian Bond, Denise Brady, Maggie Brain, Margaret Brennan, Valerie Chillis, Richard Cowie, Paula Rainey Crofts, John Ellershaw, Marcie Gibbons, Vincent Gordon, Kerry Grant, Josie Hickmott, Richard Higgs, Richard Hillier, Martin Hughes, Michael Illston, Peter Jupp, Matthew Kestenbaum, Andrew Knight, Martin Ledwick, Margot McAfee, Gerry McGregor, Sara Miller, Gill Oliver, Ian Palmer, Sarah Rowland-

Jones, Catherine Russell, Cicely Saunders, Molly Sherwood, Linda Smout, John Stroud, Angela Walton, Dorothy Waterhouse, Sue Weatherell, Julia Wootton and Jayne Wythe.

Introduction

Let us learne to stand, and combat her with a resolute minde. And begin to take the greatest advantage she hath upon us from her, let us take a cleane contrary way from the common, let us remove her strangenesse from her, let us converse, frequent, and acquaint our selves with her, let us have nothing so much in minde as death . . .

Michel Eyquem de Montaigne

Throughout the 1980s, and especially from 1984 onwards, my mother suffered from intermittent and often very severe back pain. Sometimes the muscular discomfort would spread into her legs and her neck and during one spell she also had a 'frozen' shoulder, which left her able to do very little by herself. She sought help initially from her GP, and then from a series of alternative or complementary therapists. She tried osteopathy, acupuncture and reflexology. None of them seemed to make a jot of difference. She would improve slightly and then relapse. She set great store by rest and avoiding sudden movements that might trigger a

further bout or worsen the current one. She believed firmly
that her back pain was characterized by a number of crises,
which wouldn't have happened if she hadn't stepped out of
the bath awkwardly last Tuesday or sat in that draught at
the concert.

My mother was not a hypochondriac. She was certainly
vigilant in the care she took of herself, but prior to the onset
of her back problems, she had been a lively and physically
active woman, who enjoyed walking, swimming and what
seemed to me gruelling coach tour holidays across great
stretches of western Europe. Back pain transformed her.
She remained a highly resilient personality, but physically
she became timid and although never reconciled to a life of
semi-confinement, she gradually surrendered her autonomy, allowing my father to do more and more for her.

The failure of the treatments to make her significantly
better was puzzling, especially when I put her in the hands
of an extremely effective osteopath, who had cured the
rest of my family's backaches and those of many of my
friends. It did occur to me that there might be a psychological component, that in some part of my mother's
psyche there was a resistance to the idea of being fully
well again. I chased around a number of quack theories –
self-evidently wrong now – that she was trying to secure
my father's attention now that both of their children had
grown up and left home. I never managed to get anyone
to listen very seriously to these speculations, rightly as it
later proved.

The possibility of a psychological element, together with
my mother's own theories about her poor treatment,
blinded me, I think, to the real changes in her behaviour
which started towards the end of the 1980s. To begin with,
she had odd moments of silence on the phone, when she
could find nothing to say. At other times, she would cut
across what I was saying and make some quite unrelated
remark. It was irritating, but then that's part of the function
of mothers: mothers *are* irritating. I decided that she was

getting older, that there was no point in shouting at her, and that it was I who would have to adapt, not she.

On one occasion, my uncle, then a high court judge, was sitting at Maidstone and he invited my mother and father to stay with him at the judge's residence. My wife and I joined them one evening for dinner. We were having drinks, and in the middle of a lengthy discussion about Thatcherism, my mother suddenly interrupted: 'Do you like my dress, Ronald?' she said. Ronald was a bit taken aback, but he recovered and mumbled something about it being very nice, and the Thatcher chat resumed. A few minutes later my mother cut in again, this time rather loudly, 'You've always liked the way I dress, haven't you, Ronald?' Grenades of this kind were lobbed into the conversation throughout the evening. I began to think, for the first time, that either she was mad or easily affected by drink.

There were many episodes of this kind over the next few years. I wondered whether my mother had become a secret drinker and that the drinks she had in public were merely topping up what she'd put away in private. Although there was no hard evidence to support this, it was obvious that alcohol was having an instant and powerful effect on her. I think it odd now that we let things go on for as long as we did. When I eventually pressed my father for his opinion, he agreed that my mother had become, on occasion, 'embarrassing'. She had, he admitted, passed out one Burns Night at a friend's house and been carried home unconscious.

There was also a new problem with the mobility of her hands. We decided that whatever was wrong, it needed to be diagnosed, and in the autumn of 1992 she went for tests at the Brook Hospital in Woolwich. They decided she was suffering from Motor Neurone Disease, a diagnosis later confirmed by the National Hospital for Nervous Diseases in London. The news was both shocking and surprising, because although there was some relief in finding out that her condition had a name, I was not convinced that it fully explained all her symptoms. The causes of MND have yet to be discovered, and so it remains unclear whether her earlier back problem was related to it or even precipitated it.

Then there was the matter of her aberrant behaviour. MND, it is said, does not damage the brain. When I asked the consultant at the National Hospital to explain my mother's patent intellectual deterioration, he said that her mind was intact; it was simply that MND makes the patient much more emotionally excited. At the time, I found this answer thoroughly unsatisfactory, but I suspect that I was in denial and casting around for any argument that would refute the consultant's opinion. After all, I reasoned, MND usually affects younger people and predominantly men. Why should my mother be one of the very few older women to contract it?

The consultant didn't pull his punches. He said Mum might have two or three years to live, during which she would become completely disabled. At the end, she would be lucky if she had a coronary. Otherwise, pneumonia or the collapse of her respiratory system would probably finally kill her, or, if she were particularly unfortunate, she might choke to death. He went on to say that he had not told my parents about her likely life expectancy and he strongly advised that I shouldn't do so either. I believe now that that was the wrong advice to have given me. I wrestled with it for some time and then decided to tell my sister. We debated what we should say to my father, but as it turned out, he knew all there was to know. The consultant at the Brook Hospital had described the natural development of the disease in much the same detail as I had been given. I couldn't imagine how he'd kept it to himself.

The next dilemma was whether we should tell my mother. On one side, the argument ran: ignorance is bliss, enjoy your present health without worry, keep positive about the future, avoid fear. On the other, there was the value of having time to prepare for death, to settle accounts, to say and do things not yet said and done, to squeeze the best out of what remained of life and to say goodbye at the end. It was also naïve to imagine that fear and worry might be kept at bay. The physical deterioration ahead of her would be terrifying in itself, informed or not. Overwhelming all the reasons for silence, I came to believe that however upsetting it might be for her and even if at some level she didn't *want* to know, it was her inalienable *right* to know. It was, after all, *her* life, and she should be empowered by the knowledge of her death to make choices about the time that was left. My sister and I agreed that it was my father's prerogative to tell her or not. We argued with him long and hard, but I don't believe he ever disclosed the full truth to her.

My mother was saved the worst extremities of this awful disease by her death in June 1993. In the months following the diagnosis, we had lived with the knowledge that, in a short time, she would be physically trashed. Her body would be mangled and she would be left a twitching, choking wreck. This prognosis was not in the least melodramatic. It was a reasonable expectation, because that is what MND does to the body. It is a slow process of destructive torture. In my mother's case, although the disease began to take its course throughout the early part of 1993, she succeeded in remaining mobile. The utility of her hands deteriorated and by the time we were holidaying in Lanzarote in February, she had a developed a serious difficulty with swallowing. There were a number of occasions during that fortnight when I thought she would die in front of us, choking on a piece of meat or a crust of bread.

She also had a major fall in the second week of the holiday. She tripped on uneven pavement and struck her head as she went down, cutting it open in several places. A local doctor provided her with a wimple-like head bandage, which she wore with great dignity; it made her look like Katherine Hepburn in *The Lion in Winter*, an image that kept us amused and warded off some of our mounting anxiety. We all knew that this was to be our last sustained period together, at least the last in which Mum would be halfway coherent and physically comfortable, so we treated the whole thing as lightheartedly as possible. It wasn't easy.

One characteristic of MND is that the sufferer begins to behave in an uninhibited and instinctual manner. This had both good and bad manifestations. Mum could be affectionate and contradictory in equal measure. She could be sensitive to your every feeling or disregard everyone around her. We began to look on her as a mental invalid. Her pleases and thank yous disappeared and were replaced by a matter-of-fact peremptoriness. She was unaware of it, as indeed she was unaware of her cheerful stubbornness. On holiday, her liking for routine became comic. Each morning we had breakfast on a sunny patio. Someone had to peel an orange for her, prepare her cereal and make her coffee, and woe betide anyone who was busy doing something else when she was ready to eat and drink. In the evening, there would be the ritual of the whisky tasting. The proportions of whisky to ginger ale had to be exactly right. She drank more than was good for her and alcohol had the effect of further weakening her muscles so that she had alarming coughing fits, but the doctor had said that there were few enough pleasures remaining to her and she should be allowed to drink as much as she fancied. So we mixed her whiskies carefully and she drank them with a smile.

In May 1993, she went on a two-week holiday with my father to California. It might seem astonishing that she managed it, but I firmly believe she put every last ounce of her remaining energy into that trip. By Tuesday 1 June, she was back home and in hospital with pneumonia. She had been admitted during the night after she'd failed to throw off a cold she'd caught from my father. She'd woken in the early hours troubled by her breathing. Once in hospital, she was put on oxygen and a liquid feed and they injected antibiotics into her from time to time. When I went to visit her on Wednesday afternoon, the prognosis was said to be good. She was expected to respond to the drugs in twenty-four hours and to be sent home on Friday or Saturday.

My mother was clearly doubtful. I found it very difficult looking at her in all her discomfort, plastic tubes up her nose and into her arms. She could hardly speak – scarcely above a whisper – and I struggled to understand much of what she was saying. She seemed to have realized her death was imminent. She said, 'I may die soon', then suddenly, 'Be warned'. I was taken aback and had no idea whether she meant in months or years or something sooner. I now think she knew it was only a few days away. I asked her if she was frightened to die and she said no. 'I'd much rather die young than old,' she remarked, to which she might have added '. . . and suffering', but it was difficult to hear.

I returned to the hospital on Friday morning to find that they had already taken Mum off the oxygen supply, ostensibly to reduce the carbon dioxide in her blood. She was unconscious and breathing in rough, jerky, inward gasps, followed by quiet exhalations. Dad didn't seem to realize how bad she was. All he'd been told on the phone was that she'd 'worsened overnight'. I set about trying to establish exactly what state she was in. The nurses were sympathetic, but didn't know. Shortly after my sister arrived, I contacted the ward sister and she confirmed that Mum was 'very poorly'. (You learn in such situations that the word 'poorly', which throughout my childhood was synonymous with being slightly out of sorts, means something very different and grave for the medical profession.)

The ward sister drew the curtain around Mum's bed and a young woman doctor appeared to inform us that my mother was, indeed, very ill. She didn't seem able to say 'dying'. I asked, 'Are you saying that we must face the fact that my mother is dying?' 'Yes,' she replied. My father asked, 'In a few hours?' For several vital minutes, we received no answer and then the sister chipped in. 'I think it could be a lot sooner than that,' and she looked rather intently at Mum in bed. The fact was, they could tell that she was dying in front of their eyes, but we couldn't. Eventually, the sister said, 'I think she's going now.' But for that warning, my mother might have died without our knowing it. Later I wrote:

> She went very quiet and died about ten minutes later. We all had a chance to kiss her and say our goodbyes. Of course, it's better this way. Her life would have been wretched if it had continued – mangled by MND, paralysed, rendered silent. We all know that. But we cried – little choking bursts. The sister gave us a cup of tea; Dad signed some forms; we collected some of her effects, kissed her goodbye again and left. I'm so glad we had Lanzarote, that they had California, that I learnt from Mum that she wasn't afraid of death, that I held her hand on Wednesday and told her I loved her and, lastly and most importantly, that we were there when she died. It was a beautiful, sunny, warm morning, one Mum would have loved.

From the moment of diagnosis, my mother had survived only eight months, nothing like the two to three years predicted. Nonetheless, much of my grieving had already been done. I'd had many tearful episodes of anticipatory bereavement. Driving home from the hospital, I did let out a yell and beat the steering wheel, but there was also in my grief a profound gratitude that she had not had to go through the full tearing savagery of a disease which robs people of their bodies, their personalities and their dignities.

Over the next few days, we went through the bureaucratic rituals of death, arranging the funeral, registering for the state that she had left the company of the living. When we collected the remainder of her things from the hospital, there was an odd pair of green trainers in with her clothes. God knows whose they were. Perhaps there were other, grieving relatives who missed those trainers. We had more tea, thanked the nurses, signed off.

My mother's was the first dead body I'd seen. In some respects, it was unremarkable. Her complexion, almost immediately after her death, was a shade too pale, and her skin was soft, cool and moist as I kissed her. But the crucial point I realized was that she was no longer there. People who routinely work with the dying, in hospitals and hospices, speak of a moment when they can see that the soul is clearly departing. I was not conscious of such a moment, but I was very aware, after she died, that whatever constituted my mother, whatever combination of energies defined 'Mum', had left, gone away or – harder to accept – disintegrated. I decided not to go and see her when she was laid out and having seen a number of bodies in funeral parlours since, I think I made the right decision. My sister regretted going and my aunt found it very disturbing to see her sister 'made nice'.

The funeral was held on my mother's birthday, 10 June, when she would have been sixty-six. My father spoke, so did I, and my sister played Mozart on the church piano. I emphasized how Mum had been made exceptionally loving by this disease. Despite its cruelties, MND seemed to release her from her usual social inhibitions. Her nature was, in any case, kind and affectionate and so, for all her peremptoriness, those characteristics were generally to the fore in her declining months. She told me frequently that she loved me and was not above telling a restaurant waitress, whom she'd never met before, how pretty she was and how well she'd served.

For me, the funeral was a memorial service. We celebrated her life and mourned her going. But I no more thought of *her*, the essence of my mother, as being held within the coffin that sat below the altar than I later thought of her as buried six feet down in the churchyard. Mum had moved on. I never visit the grave now. That might sound callous, but the grave itself has no meaning for me. It is not where my mother is and I am much more likely to reflect on her strolling the Kentish hills than taking flowers to that corner plot.

One of the striking features of my grief, perhaps of all grief, was the sense of expectation it engendered. It was surprising to me, and paradoxical, that my mother's long-awaited end seemed not so much a finality as a prelude. I kept thinking: 'This must lead to something.' I sensed the approach of a grand event, something which would change our lives, lurking just around the corner. Of course, it never came because it had already happened.

I suppose it's inevitable that grief, particularly the first time around, will have its surprises. I hadn't expected such lasting tiredness, nor that so many people would treat it like a bout of flu. *If you're not over it in a fortnight, you jolly well ought to be.* Not everyone behaved like that, by any means. Some of the taciturn became articulate. I received one very touching letter, which said: 'You get to be very adept at blocking it out. You learn to be very gentle with yourself and relook at life.' That was from a friend who does not say much about her feelings in general conversation, but she knew from her own experience that a death needs to be marked, to be responded to. The bereaved need to know that they are not alone.

In the months following the funeral, I came to understand that there is a real value in openness and intimacy when someone dies of a terminal illness. It was something I'd begun to grasp right at the start, when I was agonizing over what I should tell my father of my interview with the consultant at the National Hospital. In those days, I was the series producer of the BBC1 television series *Heart of the Matter*. I felt so passionately about this question of who should tell what to whom that we made a programme about it, which I worked on during my mother's illness. *Tell Me the Truth, Doctor* was transmitted on Sunday 7 February 1993. If I had had any doubts before, the making of the programme convinced me that irrespective of the emotional and intellectual strengths of the patient, he or she has a right to know the truth about what is happening in his or her life. It can afford people who have loved each other a unique opportunity.

Above all, in the relationship with my mother I discovered how precious the last phase of life can be, for both the dying and for those who are about to be bereaved. During those eight months that she survived, we grew closer and although the conversation in which she revealed that she was not afraid to die was very brief, it played a crucial and beneficial part in her eventual death and the bereavement of her family. It reduced our anxiety about what she was going through and helped us to accept the inevitable. We stayed close to the end and that, paradoxical as it may sound, has made it much easier to live with her loss. My mother's death was, in these terms, good.

What I went through with my mother made me feel that I wanted to learn more about other people's experience of terminal illness and bereavement, to try to understand why we find it difficult to discuss death and to test the value of openness and intimacy more broadly. Whilst researching and writing this book, I was aware that such ideas are counter-intuitive. Death is eschewed in our society and, as many historians have noticed, it has become more private and individualized over the centuries. Death, as we practise it in the western world, tends to isolate more than it integrates us. Consequently, it is the experience of individuals which is likely to reveal most about the continuing existence, or not, of a taboo.

Yet I felt sure that my experience was not particularly unusual. What I found was a widespread acceptance, amongst the bereaved and those who look after the dying, that honesty and intimacy between the dying and those who have charge of their care can make the difference between dying in peace and dying in great distress; between a bereavement that is painful but reconciled and one that is disturbed and stuck. I hope to make clear in this book that staying close betters denial and makes for a better ending to the story. Those who suffer at the hand of sudden death have no chance to stay close; they see death in its most unforgiving form. Death from terminal illness can be ugly and exhausting, but it is unlikely to be made more attractive or tolerable by pretending that it is not happening. Staying close, when combined with effective symptom management, can not only enable the dying and their families to come to terms with the approaching death; it can transform the final stage of life into an achievement, for which everyone will be forever grateful.

I have described my mother's death in some detail, partly because it was the principal motivation for writing this book, but also because her experience, and mine, illustrate a number of the common experiences and worries of people dealing with terminal illness and grief. For the majority of us, whether we are the dying patients or the relatives who have gradually to accept their loss, terminal illness will entail living with uncertainty and struggling to acquire clear and reliable information. For those who are about to be bereaved, there will be the anxiety of watching a loved relative or friend decline and change, and of not knowing quite how much he or she knows, or wishes to know, of their condition. Finally, the bereaved will face the trial of a funeral and the awkwardness of grieving in a secular society. That these vitally important aspects of dying and bereavement are not more frankly discussed reflects a taboo which, in my view, remains firmly in place. This books aims to open up a discussion. I shall explore how care of the dying is changing and some of the new approaches there are to funerals and bereavement in a secular world in which we are all trying to cope with the inevitability of death.

1

Why We Think as We Do

There are two ways of not thinking about death: the way of our technological civilization, which denies death and refuses to talk about it; and the way of traditional civilizations, which is not denial but a recognition of the impossibility of thinking about it directly or for very long because death is too close and too much a part of daily life.

Philippe Ariès

Death, like flies or floodwater, is something we prefer to keep out of the house. As the guy in the TV soap said, 'Death is Death. It never comes in a fun kit.' After all, there appears to be no good reason for admitting it into our everyday thoughts. It will not improve our physical, emotional or moral well-being and, on the whole, it frightens us. By whatever means it strikes, it is emotionally exhausting and final. Relationships that may have endured argument, separation and the anxieties of social and financial crisis, even droughts and wars, will be terminated by death. Consequently, it has become a sustaining factor in our lives that we try to ignore the subject.

For a majority, death is a distant event, likely to occur

during old age. Most of us living in developed countries can expect to enjoy a long life, particularly given the medical services we have, which will more often than not cure our ills. Our children no longer die in infancy, and we can reasonably expect to see our grandchildren. In such happy circumstances, why should we bother with something that is depressing and spells ruin? Why burden earlier life with an unfruitful concern about its decline and end?

The drawback to this kind of thinking is that it leaves us wholly unprepared and because we are social, related animals who live in intimacy with others, death is therefore shocking and painful when it does happen. If we are lucky, we do not start to encounter death until mid-life. Many of us in the West reach forty or fifty before we have to face the death of a close relative or friend, or see a corpse on a slab. But when we do experience that first agony of bereavement, we are at a loss about what to do. We have not been brought up to expect death, nor have we learnt ways of dealing with it. We suddenly find ourselves wondering whether we really have been better off not knowing, not thinking or speaking, not preparing. Have we in fact lived more enjoyably, more profitably, in ignorance of what would undoubtedly happen, or have we made it much worse in the long run? Common sense would suggest that the answer to these questions is that the more prepared for difficulty we are, the more likely it is that we will able to cope with it. That was certainly the wisdom of earlier generations.

The literature of the past encourages us to believe that there have been at various times approaches to dying and grieving that were not only recommended but practised. There were rules for personal and social conduct, together with systems of belief that expressed a meaning for death. The important question for us now is whether, in a modern world that is uncertain and full of competing philosophies, we can learn anything from the past.

The hope that has sustained most of human history is

that death will be followed by an afterlife. In some form, something of our being will continue and although the character of that afterlife varies from culture to culture, the great civilizations of the past seem to have shared the same refusal to accept that anything as vibrant as life could ever be over. Some recent historians have argued that the idea of an afterlife has survived – indeed, may have originated – because of our need to resolve the problem of evil in the world. Why should the good be slaughtered and the evil prosper? Death is, in this way, just if it is the preliminary to an afterlife that will be blissful for those who have led good lives, excruciating for those who have been sinful. On reaching the Egyptian underworld, for instance, the heart of a departed soul was weighed in a balance against the feather of conscience. If the heart proved the lighter, the soul was rewarded with a life of eternal happiness in the company of the gods; if heavier, it was fed to the monstrous crocodile, Ammut. The Egyptians would recite prayers from the *Book of the Dead* in the belief that they could thereby lighten the heart on the scales and secure a good outcome for the soul.

Greek culture, in contrast, was slow to develop the idea of an afterlife that rewarded or punished the dead. In Homer's time, around 800 BC, the dead existed only as pale reflections of their former selves. They were ferried by Charon across the dark and poisonous River Styx to a realm of shadows (later known as Hades), where they lived out an eternity without happiness or development, as if asleep. The world of the dead was morally neutral, designed primarily to keep the dead at a safe distance from the living. In this version, the afterlife reflects the Greek belief that death was unnatural, the inferior of life. Funerals were statements of human achievement, and if it was considered preferable to die young, as many did, that was because it avoided the ignominy of old age and decay, and not because the afterlife held any promise of rebirth or spiritual fulfilment.

With Pythagoras, two centuries later, and still more under the influence of Socrates in the fifth century BC and Plato in the fourth, the image of the afterlife changed. Pythagoras believed that the soul would be cleansed by death and rewarded for good behaviour in life by a blissful existence with the gods in Elysium. Death, then, could be welcomed. It meant an end to care and, as Socrates put it, the ridding of the body allowed the soul to emerge. In this later Greek thinking, Hades became the seat of judgement, and Plato believed that the sinful, those with impure souls, would be dispatched to Tartarus, a place of perpetual punishment.

Many of these ideas are familiar to those of us who live in a Christian, or some would say post-Christian, culture. All people in all ages are exercised by the same desire to see beyond the finality of death. The prospect of a blissful eternity that has to be earned in the course of our lives has lent a significance to human existence which is consonant with our beliefs in purpose, achievement and reward. There is, with this view of life, a very powerful sense in which death has to be prepared for.

Rather less comforting has been the possibility of damnation if we fail to earn salvation. The concept of hell has, at certain times in Christian history, implanted a fear worse than the fear of death itself. Not only are we to lose our precious lives, but we are to enter upon an eternity of torment thereafter. The Dutch historian, Johan Huizinga, has argued that in the middle ages people were so obsessed with death and hell that they thought about them every day. This partly reflects the arbitrariness of death, as it appeared to the mediaeval mind. *Mors certa, hora incerta*: 'Death is certain, but the hour it will occur is not.' This succinct epigram summarized a world in which all the joys of life were snatched from the jaws of death. Life expectancy throughout the middle ages did not exceed thirty-three, though in London in the 1420s it was as low as twenty-nine. Diseases of the lung and intestines, together with typhus, measles and malnutrition, were endemic. In times of plague, the population could be decimated. When the Black Death hit England in the 1340s, it reduced the population from around 4 million in 1300 to between 2.25 and 2.75 million in 1349. Plague left the infected no time to prepare for death; 60–80 per cent were dead within eight days. It is easy to see why, in such circumstances, death was often depicted as God's punishment, as Chaucer has it in *The Pardoner's Tale*. The iconography at the beginning of the period saw death in terms of decay and decomposition, but by the later middle ages, death has become ironic, God's joke at the expense of the mortal. In the typical *danse macabre*, a man dances with his own skeleton throughout life until finally the skeleton sweeps the dying to the grave, thus harnessing an image of joy and the end of all joy for ever.

There developed a response to death that was elaborate and detailed, and every bit as codified as the Victorian etiquette that was to come later. The paramount aim was to avoid dying unshriven and going straight to hell. During a terminal illness, the dying were encouraged to pray alone and with their families, to confess and make a sincere repentance for their sins, to declare their faith in God and the resurrection, and to receive final absolution and the blessings of a priest. They were enjoined not to despair or lose faith, to be impatient, avaricious or excessively vain. Death, in short, was seen 'as both a physical and as a moral state.'[1] Towards the end of the fifteenth century, these principles began to appear in books of advice, which sought to comfort the dying and their families. *Arte and Crafte to know well to dye* (1490), for instance, argued that salvation was available even to the most wicked if they truly repented at the last.

The concept of Purgatory is interesting in this context. The doctrine, first promulgated in 1274, held that prayers for the dead could shorten their stay in Purgatory. The wealthy endowed chantries so that monks and priests could

sing rich souls to heaven. These intercessory masses provided a sense of practical intimacy between the living and
the dead, and served as a medium for the expression of
grief. The scale and grandeur of funerals, together with the
provisions that were made for these chantries, show how
carefully the rich and high-born prepared for death. Their
expensive effigies in churches, which were of course partly
there to assert their importance in life, were also seeking the
prayers of the faithful for the cure of their souls.

The Reformation changed much of that. Purgatory,
chantries and the paraphernalia of intercession were swept
away in Edward VI's reign, and with them went the chance
to influence the future of the departed soul. Any pleading
had now better be done before the final breath. For Protestant Britain, the individual was of the elect or he was
damned, and no amount of deathbed confessing and con-
trition was going to make a difference. Once the soul had
departed this life, the family were expected to be resigned.
However natural mourning might be, the bereaved should
not dwell on it. Death was God's wish and prolonged
mourning implied either a lack of belief or, worse, a
challenge to the divine will.

The key to the 'good death' was a progressive surrender
of that wish not to die, a gradual lessening of the ties with
life. Thus, three centuries ago, the poet and priest John
Donne spent his last days preparing to meet his maker.
According to his biographer and close friend, Izaac Walton,
Donne realized he was dying when he preached his last
sermon in St Paul's Cathedral during Lent 1631. Donne
commissioned an artist to paint him in his winding sheet,
his face turned to reveal its deathly pallor. Then he retired
to his chamber and invited his friends to visit him. After a
few admonitory words of moral comfort, he bade them
goodbye. He told his servants that if they needed to discuss
any outstanding business with him, they had until the
following Saturday to do so, 'for after that day he would
not mix his thoughts with any thing that concerned this

world'. He lay for fifteen days, anticipating death all the while, until on the last hour of his last day he complained 'I were miserable if I might not dye.' Short of breath, he prayed 'Thy Kingdom come, thy Will be done.' Those were his last words. Moments later, 'he closed his own eyes; and then disposed his hands and body into such a posture as required not the least alteration by those that came to shroud him . . . thus *variable*, thus *vertuous* was the Life; thus *excellent*, thus *exemplary* was the Death of this memorable man.'[2]

What occurred during the second half of the seventeenth century and into the eighteenth was that the importance of the deathbed demeanour, the reconciliation of the dying to God, was to some extent in competition with the physician's efforts to ease the discomforts of the dying. In the later 1600s, the church was still emphasizing the inescapability of death. As the 1662 Prayer Book says, 'in the midst of life we are in death'. The Anglican bishop, Jeremy Taylor, continued to maintain that the dying have need to confess and to receive their final absolution and communion to achieve salvation.[3] Death required the preparation of a lifetime. But at the same time, doctors were increasingly seen at the bedsides of the dying. Several new hospitals were built in London and elsewhere.

Attitudes to death were changing, and the tendency to see it as much as a medical problem as a spiritual had noticeable effects on the deathbed scene. The use of opium to alleviate pain was routine, which itself called into question the spiritual function of pain. To suffer at death had always been seen as a sign of God's love. To bear up was a virtue and, successfully done, an indication that the dying person was heading for heaven. Treatment with opium had, therefore, to be moderated for fear that the patient would become too sedated to demonstrate his faith, and there was often a conflict between the physician's desire to prolong his patient's life and the priest's duty to prepare his parishioner for death.[4] The seeds of the modern uncertainty about the physical and spiritual aspects of death were already planted by the eighteenth century.

Clare Gittings is probably right, therefore, to speak of the Victorian attitude to death as 'aberrant',[5] in the sense that it bucked the trend of secularization and restored a religious passion to death which had been on the wane. It was the Victorians who did most to create the ethos of death that later western society has both imitated and rebelled against. Life expectancy in 1850 was forty. One quarter of all babies died. A preoccupation, then, with both the manner and meaning of death was not merely understandable, but essential to the cohesion of what sought to be a civilized and religious society. Thus the familiar image we have of nineteenth-century mourners is one of prolonged and obsessive grief. Queen Victoria mourned the loss of Prince Albert for the better part of twenty years. After his sudden death from typhoid in December 1861, she withdrew from public life and declined to open Parliament. Albert's room and belongings were left untouched. Every day clothes were laid out for him, together with hot water and a fresh towel. 'It is the stay, support and comfort which is lost!' she wrote. 'To the Queen it is like *death* in life.'[6] From the families assembled around the deathbed to exchange farewells, to the funeral pomp of feathers, silks, hatbands and mutes on horseback, the Victorian way of death conveys to us an atmosphere that is cloying and morbid, opposed to the free expression of genuine feelings of bereavement we think we favour today.

That the Victorians re-created death as an event of solemnity and personal trial is undisputed. The documents we have from the middle and upper classes evince a clear belief that a 'good death' could be achieved through strict observance of rules of behaviour laid down for both the dying and the family alike. But these rituals, far from inhibiting grief, enabled the better-off Victorians to vent their sorrow in a well-defined etiquette of behaviour, designed to help them overcome their misery. They knew

what they were expected to do and what would be dis-
approved of, and they managed thereby to recover from the
deaths of loved ones. Frequent and rapid in succession
though the deaths might be, during an epidemic of, say,
scarlet fever, mourners tended to emerge from their grief
within a year or two. Chronic grief, lasting years, was
exceptional and the Queen was variously described as
mad or self-indulgent in consequence.

To the Victorians, a good death was an intelligible
ambition and it was widely proselytised by the Evangelical
Movement, which was at the height of its revival in the mid-
nineteenth century. In all too frequent cases of terminal
illness, middle-class families hoped that, in their declining
days and weeks, their loved ones would achieve a physical
and spiritual contentment that would ease the transition
from this life to the next. Good deaths occurred in the
home, usually from a lingering complaint like tuberculosis,
which was slow to kill and allowed time for the dying
person to resign himself to God's will. Medical prepara-
tions provided some pain relief and enabled the dying to
give thought to their spiritual comfort. The dying person
would atone for his sins, part affectionately from his family
and set about preparing himself spiritually for judgement
and the life ever after. When Edgar Allan Poe extolled the
virtues of consumption, wishing 'all I love to perish of that
disease', he would have us believe that death from TB was a
graceful fading away of the human spirit, permitting both
fruitful reflection on God and the anxieties of the soul.

The dying were going to a better place. Mourners con-
soled themselves with the certain knowledge of their reunion in heaven and brought in their children to witness a
cheerful piety, even in the face of the 'King of Terrors'. Such
deathbed scenes, with their 'last words' and the good soul's
'smile of death', were thought to have instructional value.
The family, including small children, was encouraged to
spend time in the company of the dying, partly to console
them but also to learn from them. The dying were, in this

idealized form, exemplars of the pious Christian reconciled to God. The good death was something slow, peaceful and full of love of God and love of family. It was imbued with the presence of God and a serenity of spirit, and is perfectly captured in Thackeray's deathbed scenes and, *par excellence*, in Dickens's account of the passing of Little Nell.

Such was the theory. No doubt, many fewer achieved the good death than the record of journals and letters would have us believe.[7] Victorian accounts of observed deaths were often motivated by a desire to idealize the dead and their writers' own feelings of loss. The 'good deaths' of the nineteenth century did at times produce extraordinary perversions of death's true nature. Poe's description of TB takes no account of the final blood-spitting distress or the emotional collapse of those left behind. For most people, death was harrowing and they struggled to maintain their faith and dignity. Despite their show of resilience, many journals suggest that the Victorians suffered the same agonies of bereavement that we experience today and sometimes worse. They went through more physical pain in dying than we generally do, and they faced up to the deaths of close loved ones more frequently and at a younger age. Particularly difficult were the deaths of children. Children in the Victorian era were taught that death was a constant threat, as indeed it was. A disease such as scarlet fever, until it was brought under control in the 1920s, could wipe out Victorian families of all classes.

Some modern commentators have argued that the Victorians simply did death better than we do and that the loss of the death and mourning rituals which sustained the Victorians has left western culture with a problem of anxiety it cannot easily resolve. The evidence is not straightforward, however. At its most commonplace, the good death, with its deathbed assembly of vulnerable children, frequently communicated deadly disease that could have been avoided by a more cautious approach. The Victorians were not entirely ignorant about communicable disease, but sometimes placed a higher priority on the spiritual value of witnessing death than its dangers. There is also a substantial literature of complainants about the Victorian way of death written by men and women who found prescriptive periods of mourning stifling and lonely. Indeed, it has been suggested that conventions of mourning dress for Victorian women were no more than a form of social control of their sexuality, which had little to do with respect for the dead or the sensibility of the bereaved. Moreover, the chance of future happiness for a widow was often destroyed by Victorian hostility to a widow's social inter-action and, particularly, to the idea that she might dilute a family fortune as a consequence of her remarriage.

As the Victorians saw it, the value of their approach was not that it solved all the problems of dying and bereave-ment, but that it acknowledged their profundity. Victorian etiquette insisted on the importance of death. It provided the dying and their mourners with beliefs and rules. They could look up in a book what they should do and when, and there was a good deal of comfort to be derived from the prolific literature of consolation produced by the many who had gone before them. They knew how they were supposed to die and how to mourn. Every detail of mourning dress, of funeral procedure, of letters of condolence and of social life following a death was prescribed. They were never at a loss what to say, never stranded – as has been said of the modern funeral-goer – like an actor without any lines.

Towards the end of the century, the grip of that etiquette and of the church on the public mind began to weaken. From the 1870s, church attendance no longer matched the birth rate and there was a marked decline in evangelical fervour. Condolence letters became less confident of re-demption, deathbed memoirs less vivid. With the loss of faith came funeral reforms and shorter mourning. This was a period of considerable change. The Victorians seem to have become exhausted by half a century of formal grief and the good death came to mean one that was peaceful and pain-free. Earlier Victorians had tried to interpret pain as a test of their faith, even as a sign of God's presence. The time for spiritual reflection now became of secondary importance to physical ease, or preferably unconsciousness. In the course of overturning the good death, Victorian and Edwardian doctors began to think that patients might be better off not knowing that they were dying, and thereby they established the precedent on which our contemporary crisis is based.

The Legacy of War

In 1915, Sigmund Freud was confident that the slaughter in the trenches would put paid to our European inhibitions about death. The scale on which death was occurring must lead, he argued, to a greater frankness: 'It is evident that war is bound to sweep away this conventional treatment of death. Death will no longer be denied; we are forced to believe in it.'[8] Freud was writing early on in the war, when the full horrors of the Somme and Passchendaele had still to be gone through. When trench warfare was at its height, an average of 7,000 men died daily. These losses were described by the army staff as 'wastage'. By the end, in November 1918, a total of 722,785 British soldiers had died, one eighth of the entire British Expeditionary Force. In all, 8 million people, of all nationalities, had lost their lives.

The record of those dead people is plain to see in the names etched on memorials all over Europe, America and the Commonwealth. In France and Belgium, there are 2,500 cemeteries of British war dead, and prominent in every parish church in England is a list of local men and boys who fell and did not return. A surname with initials and rank, the date of death, sometimes the evocative killing field itself, are all that relate the scything down of human life. When there are three inscriptions with the same surname, the devastation of a family is vividly apparent.

World War One is the world's most memorialized history of death. For the bereaved, the governing desire was to achieve what Alan Wilkinson has called 'a sense of completion' and many mourners travelled a long way to pay their respects at the graveside of their lost loved ones. It is an irony of the butchery that the travel industry – something we associate with holidays and pleasure – grew out of it. By 1931, 140,000 foreigners were visiting French cemeteries every year.[9]

This private need to perform an act of homage was mirrored nationally in the memorial to the Unknown Soldier. Its unveiling at Westminster Abbey in 1920 provided precisely the sense of completion experienced by those visiting the French graves for the first time. The Unknown Soldier stood for those known to have died somewhere, somehow, but who were never found. He was, as Pat Jalland puts it, 'every boy's father, every woman's lover, every mother's child'.[10] A collective sigh of relief went up. Those who were bereaved but had no memorial for their dead had been trapped in a grief that was haunted by uncertainty. The Unknown Soldier enabled them to put an end to their speculations about possible survival, traumatized wanderings in the wilderness, and if they could not forget, they could at least begin to move on.

The recognition of the dead might suggest a new kind of openness, but in fact the number of deaths and, in particular, the appalling circumstances in which soldiers died, produced a new reticence. During the war, funerals became less ostentatious and cheaper in consequence. It was thought insensitive to those who had no remains to bury to purchase a funeral that was lavish or conspicuous. The language in which death was spoken of also became more, rather than less, euphemistic. 'Passed away', for example, was scarcely found on gravestones before 1918, but it was to become from then on a staple term for those muted by grief.

Half a century on from two world wars, we can safely ask whether the quantity of death in war does anything to alter our responses to death and dying. There seems to be, contra Freud, a relationship between mass death and our unwillingness to speak openly about it. Although fewer servicemen died in World War Two – and their names were often added to existing war memorials – the unprecedented loss of both civilian and military lives in that war (56 million worldwide) did not result in the changes in attitude that Freud anticipated in 1915.

There is an important distinction to be made here between an awareness of, or guilt about, death and plain speaking in our personal lives. The Holocaust, Dresden, the Burma railway and Hiroshima have all generated candid discussion about the ethics of inflicted death and the conditions necessary to avoid the repetition of atrocities, and many moving and tragic stories are told of these events. But it is unclear that they, or indeed any of the many subsequent conflicts and massacres, have led to a readiness on the part of the majority to talk intimately about death or to prepare for its inevitability. Indeed, so horrific was the death toll of the twentieth century – in which World War One now strikes us as more of an intimation of things to come than an apogee – that it may start to explain our revulsion from the subject, our inability to speak about it and our intense reticence. The killing enacted in the genocide theatres of the last ten years alone is a violent affront to any idea we might cherish that life is sacred and worth preserving. As we duck the cigarette smoke and jog for eternity, we face up to brutal facts. One million killed in Rwanda during a few months in 1994; an estimated 500,000 children dead in Iraq since economic sanctions were imposed in August 1990; 80,000 civilians killed by Islamic extremists during one decade in Algeria; in July 1996, 100 people a day were dying in the civil war in Burundi; on average, the USA executes a prisoner a week. Does one figure sound any more disturbing than another? Few names emerge from the piles of bodies. Occasionally, we may remember someone like Baruch Goldstein and that he killed – how many was it?

– twenty-nine Palestinians when he swept into the West Bank city of Hebron one February day in 1994. Otherwise, it was a century of death that belonged to Hitler, Stalin, Mao Zedung, Pol Pot. Furthermore, the twenty-first century looks set to go through much the same routine of breathtaking slaughter followed by a popular disbelief that congeals into acceptance. The name on all our lips in 2001 was Osama bin Laden, vivid in our minds as the author of nearly 3,000 deaths in New York and Washington DC, but for how long will we remember the details of that atrocity on 11 September, still less be disturbed by them?

It might be inferred that the gory spectacle of death that is our daily news will perpetuate the public disquiet and our private fears. But there are signs that today's attitudes to death are undergoing a complicated process of change. Some of these signs point towards a greater openness; others towards a deepening inhibition, shame and neurosis. Alongside the private reticence of the many runs the unheralded interest of the few. Sociologists, historians, literary critics and some health-care professionals have, in the last twenty years or so, analysed the forms of death as openly as they would have discussed other cultural phenomena. So what is it about modern western life that produces such conflicting attitudes? This is a complex question, to which no one has easy answers, but three key developments of the twentieth century must have played their part. The significant improvement in life expectancy, the radical loss of religious belief and the growth of mass telecommunications have all generated their own illusions about what it is to live and what it is to die.

The Right to Live: Improvements in Life Expectancy

Six hundred and fifty thousand people die in Britain every year. That is more or less sixty an hour. Stark statistics like these might be expected to drive home the point: *We all die.*

But, as Spinoza observed in the seventeenth century, although we know we are going to die, we believe we are immortal.

Before the discovery of a means to determine life expectancy, this conviction was at odds with people's day-to-day encounters with death. Death's stroke appeared arbitrary. Human life, it seemed, could be snuffed out at any moment. But with the mortality tables devised in the sixteenth and early seventeenth centuries by Petty (1623–87) and Arbuthnot (1667–1735), the idea of determining life expectancy looked increasingly feasible. By the nineteenth century, it was possible to estimate the probable lengths of life for the average man and woman. From 1837 (the year Victoria came to the throne), the registration of deaths became a consistent practice and an average length of life could be calculated by taking the total number of years lived and dividing it by the total number of people who had died. Simple as the computation was, the absence of basic information had meant that it could not be undertaken before.

Life expectancy in the developed world has nearly doubled since Victoria's reign. In the Britain of the 1880s, half the population was dead by forty-five and to live longer you had successfully to elude respiratory complaints, typhoid, cholera, tuberculosis, influenza, scarlet fever, diphtheria, measles and whooping cough. TB has made something of a comeback in recent years, but in general not one of these diseases would be considered fatal in the modern developed world. Instead, we can look forward to living into our seventies. Men in Britain will reach the age of 74.2 years on average (72.2 in the USA); women will reach 79.4 years (78.8 in the USA). Longevity is best achieved in Japan, where the life expectancy for men is 76.6 years and 83 for women. Thomas Kirkwood, in a recent book on ageing, pointed out that if you really want to live a long life, you can hardly do better than move to the Japanese island of Okinawa, which has the highest proportion of centenarians (185 per million) in the world.[11]

We live longer and more of us survive. In 1900, there were 154 deaths for every 1,000 babies born in the United Kingdom. By the last decade of the twentieth century, that figure had plummeted to 8! Five out of 6 of us survive to the age of 65, and 55 per cent of all deaths occur amongst the 75+ age group. According to Kirkwood, the fastest growing section of the first world community is the over-85s. Soon there will be a billion of us on this globe who are over 60.[12]

It can be argued, as the late Roy Porter did, that the improvement in life expectancy, which steadily lengthened throughout the twentieth century, is more accurately attributed to improvements in diet, living conditions and preventative medicine than to the discovery of penicillin in 1928 or of other treatments developed to cure killer diseases.[13] In other words, a cure has often followed upon the natural or circumstantial decline of the disease. Nevertheless, it is to the medical profession that people have regularly turned, in ever-increasing numbers, to cure their ills. Long life is not merely the anticipated lot of the many, but a demand. On the principle that given an ell, people will take a mile, modern societies require their doctors to find remedies for each and every illness, be they mere inconveniences or a serious threat to life.

Doctors, to some extent, collude with the expectation that they can defy death, because it self-evidently enhances their status. But is the encouraged hope that with the right diet and the right measure of exercise, we can avoid ill health damaging? Has it instilled a belief – perhaps not conscious, but palpable all the same – in personal immortality? As Geoffrey Gorer observed as early as 1965, the medical profession's attack on cigarette smoking seems to imply that without cigarettes we could live forever.[14] Medicine, even as it becomes more sophisticated, constantly confounds this hope. That we can now purchase 'Death' cigarettes is a satirical fist in the faces of those who think they can circumvent it.

According to Thomas Kirkwood, our risk of death does, in fact, double every eight years.[15] We die now of the diseases of affluence, the diseases of old age. Cancer has recently overtaken heart disease as the biggest killer of people in the developed world. Over 25 per cent of us will die from it. This is how it will continue to be in the foreseeable future. The definition of death is now focused on the 'irreversible loss of function of the brainstem'. In law, we can no longer die of a broken heart or old age. The World Health Organization lists 999,999 forms of injury, disease and causes of death, each of which, it is claimed, is surmountable. In theory, then, death can be 'cured', and we harbour the thought that since all diseases are finally cured, the diseases that currently kill us could well be eradicated or made treatable in our lifetime. In December 1998, the London *Evening Standard* predicted that, in the new millennium, many more of us would live to over 100. Without cardiovascular illness, without cancer, what's to stop us? After all, only 4 per cent of us die in accidents.

The occasional simplification of medical science in the media encourages expectations that are bound to be disappointed. In the United States, the belief that we can live forever has been raised to the status of a secular cult. Sandra Ray, author of *How to be Chic, Fabulous and Live Forever* (1990), has persuaded some Americans that death can be overcome if we resolve emotional troubles that date back to birth. Her theory of 'immortalism' is that, through re-experiencing the traumas of our births, we are liberated into a new life that can last forever. A great deal of scientific journalism is highly responsible and accurate, but some is not, and readers will naturally take from articles what they want to hear. There are repeated invitations to imagine a longer, healthier life.

In July 1998, Canadian scientists were reported to have found a genetic treatment, *superoxide dismutase of SOD1*, that could add a further 40 per cent to our lives. The Canadians had been experimenting on fruit flies and succeeded in retarding their ageing with this modified gene. Don't hold your breath! By January 1999, another group of scientists had identified a string of genes – in particular, *daf-2* – which would similarly slow down the ageing process. And in 2000, scientists retarded the ageing of cells in calves. If the same can be achieved with human tissue, we could live to 200. As the leader writer in the *Observer* commented, 'Add to this the possibility of cryogenic storage for thawing out at a date in the future when technology is available and we could even do away with death.'

Historically, it was religious faith that many hoped would be the guarantor of eternal life. (The Christian Scientists still forbid the use of the word 'death' in their magazine *Christian Science Monitor*.) Today the comparable faith is that good health practice prevents death. It is not uncommon for hospice workers to be confronted with older patients who deny the very possibility that they could be dying. One old lady of ninety-four complained, on her admission to a hospice, that she couldn't understand why she had to 'go through all this fuss' since she'd never had a day's illness in her life!

The Loss of Religious Belief

The majority of people confronted by an article on 'immortalism' would dismiss it as wayward nonsense, of a piece with fanatical cults. Yet although Sandra Ray's invitation to eternity is marginal to mainstream opinion, the effect of extended life expectancy on contemporary attitudes to death has been to create a complicated illusion. The difficulty may be that we end up demanding more of life than life can give us.

In the past, that would have been the argument from religion. It is God's afterlife we should attend to, rather than the perpetuation of life on earth. The importance of the afterlife within a belief system varies from religion to religion but, in general, religions offer their adherents a

vision of peace and meaning which sublimates the depreda-
tions of death. The rituals devised to mark the transition
into afterlife, the crossing of the *limen* between life and
death, seek to dignify death as a prelude to new life, eternal
life, thus mitigating sorrow and pain with the hope of
serenity, of reunion or paradise, or a combination of these.
By the same token, if that is God's promise to the believer, a
stubborn pursuit of mortal life is either futile or sacrilegious.

For many societies, religion still provides a sustaining
ideology that helps people cope with dying and bereavement. But that shared conviction exists alongside an extraordinary diversity of beliefs and etiquettes, some subjective,
some tribal, some derived from several religious traditions.
Even within the relatively familiar behavioural framework
of the United States and Europe, there is no single concept
of death. Responses differ, not only because our cultures
are different and we as human beings are all different, but
because death has many faces and many forms. Moreover,
our views change as we get older and accrete new philosophies and painful experiences. In a secular age such as
ours, therefore, many people are actively looking for beliefs
and principles, stratagems and sources of succour which are
not grounded in a supernatural religion and which will
enable them to weather the undiminished storm that death
remains.

The afterlife, if it has not gone altogether, is threatened
with extinction. As recently as 1996, Tony Walter reported
that more people believed in an afterlife than go to church,
though the incidence of this belief varied from country to
country. In Eire it was as high as 77 per cent and in
Denmark only 26 per cent. Britain was 44 per cent, France
38 per cent and in the United States 71 per cent.[16] The
notable fact about this kind of attitudes survey is that each
new account demonstrates a slight, but measurable decline
in belief. It is hardly surprising, then, that a loss of faith in
God's afterlife should be accompanied by a determined

belief in the gifts of medicine. We put our new faith in doctors.

A huge problem arises, however, when death makes its inevitable presence felt. The church, particularly the Church of England, has hung on to its role as the focal point through which public grief is expressed at a time of national crisis or mourning. (One expression of this was the reported increase in the number attending services following the terrorist attacks in the United States on 11 September 2001.) At a private level, however, it is far less clear that the churches can any longer fulfil all the needs of the bereaved. People who do not recognize death as the doorway to another life lack the consolations of religion. The traditional funerary rituals are emptied of meaning for them. Where, then, does the unbeliever turn?

In fact, most people still cling to the exhausted formulae of the very religions they have not long ceased to believe in. This is frequently the case when, for example, grieving children need to be comforted. People still speak to their children of their dead grandmother having 'gone to Jesus' or 'gone to heaven'. They are perpetuating a way of dealing with a child's bereavement that might have made sense when they were children themselves, but which is incongruous and potentially confusing now. In the mid-sixties, Christian religious practice was in decline, but it had still a long way to fall before reaching the low levels of interest and belief of the early twenty-first century. These terms, when used by non-believers in the past, did at least have a wide currency that bolstered the parent unsure how to deal with a distressed child. Today, however, many of the religious euphemisms used to stand for death are not intelligible to the general public. Darwinism, as later evolutionary theory, has penetrated popular culture to the extent that religious thinking is not simply displaced, but fabulated.

When concepts like Jesus or heaven are known at all, they are often understood as comforting tales akin to

Father Christmas or the Tooth Fairy. In a March 1998 article in the magazine *Family Life*, a mother recalled her difficulties in telling her children about their grandfather's death. It may be that the author was a Christian, or held other religious beliefs, in which case her decision to describe her dead father as 'with God' makes sense, but on her mother's advice, she further considered reading them the closing passages of Richard Adams's *Watership Down*, in which a rabbit dies and its spirit lifts out of its body and lives on. She and her husband decided not to take the children to the funeral because they were 'too young'. What is interesting here is the disjunction between the parents' wish to convey an idea of death as natural and peaceful, the beginning of a new and better life with God, and their fear that the funeral would be too distressing for young minds. Their decision is the one taken by most parents today, but it runs against the advice of contemporary psychotherapy. In a supplementary note to the article, a psychotherapist makes clear that 'Young children benefit from opportunities to say their goodbyes and from joining in the funeral ritual unless they positively choose not to.' Here again, there is a mismatch between the secular approach of the professional and the need on the part of the parents to protect their child and make sense of death in a way that is spiritually comforting.

The struggle to qualify the finality of death, at a time when religion is declining and incoherent on the subject, has underlined the need for some kind of secular meaning for death, and also for rituals to go with it. Geoffrey Gorer, in the mid-sixties, claimed that there were only three groups living in Britain who knew, from their established etiquette, how to manage death, how to dress during bereavement and how to behave with mourners: Orthodox Jews, Church of Scotland followers and Irish Roman Catholics.[17] The orthodoxies of these faiths remain the same, but the number of their adherents has patently declined since Gorer's day. Almost invariably, we now call a doctor to the dying rather than a priest, and the rituals of mourning have been largely supplanted by bereavement counselling.

The problem we face is that, having abandoned religion, we are reluctant to adopt another code of behaviour that is similarly obligatory. Since we have no systematic belief in an afterlife and that has in turn discredited the collective rituals of burial and mourning we once availed ourselves of, new rites of mourning circumscribed by a rigid etiquette may not suit us any better. We are, after all, a society committed to individuality.

Nonetheless, the loss of ritual has, according to Tony Walter, left us 'thoroughly confused about the social rules for the display of grief.'[18] Should we show our grief or contain it? What do we say, do and write to console the bereaved or simply to recognize their loss? Should they be treated differently and for how long? Without an afterlife, what comfort is there to offer? Should we lie about the afterlife, or smother it with euphemisms? In short, where is the *ars moriendi* for the twenty-first century?

Death and the Media

No doubt death has always affected us in diverse and contradictory ways, attracting and repelling us, stimulating our minds to great thought or paralysing us into an embarrassed or agonized silence. It has always been an 'awfully big adventure' every bit as much as a 'dull, dreary affair', and that ambiguity co-exists with another: some deaths are deemed more significant than others. Whole countries have trembled at the death of kings, whilst the death of a peasant is scarcely noticed.

At some level of our collective consciousness, we know that death is too important to hush up. Our improved life expectancy, together with our doubts about the afterlife, make us cling to the idea of immortality, yet all societies feel the necessity to represent death in a public forum, to keep death, as it were, in the forefront of people's minds. Even if in private people find themselves unable to discuss the subject, they can in this way conduct a conversation, through a public medium, about what death is and how it should be viewed.

To a large extent, that conversation is constrained by our ignorance. Death is, after all, that 'undiscover'd country from whose bourne no traveller returns.' We can know nothing about it, or rather, as Ludwig Wittgenstein put it, it stands outside human experience. 'Death is not an event of life,' Wittgenstein observed in 1922. 'Death is not lived through.' Yet if death is not akin to other human experiences, is it necessarily beyond the scope of imaginative thought and language? If it is hidden and unrecoverable, should we, as Wittgenstein suggests, shut up about it? 'What we cannot talk about we must consign to silence.'[19]

We cannot, of course, remain silent. We want and need to see death publicly displayed, as part of our search for its meaning. Modern societies find exemplars in what they view and what they read, and one paradox of the modern era must be that we see less death than our ancestors did and, by means of television and the print media, much more of it. Deaths are the meat and drink of feature films, television fiction and the theatre. One way in which we sublimate our fear and confusion is to experience vicariously the death of others, and survive. Our very avoidance of private discussion of death attracts us to it in books, and on stage and screen. We crowd to *Hamlet* and *Pulp Fiction*, everything from tragedy to comedy, lapping up death. It is, as Cleopatra has it, 'the lover's pinch, which hurts, and is desir'd.' The critic Jonathan Dollimore maintains that the 'intensifying preoccupation' with death in literature stands in marked contrast to the denial of death argued by Philippe Ariès and other social historians.[20] His argument is derived from literature, but it could as easily find its evidence in films or television. Death has been the fodder of television news and as television documentary begins to turn its attention to the rituals of death, it challenges audiences to confront the real processes of dying as well as the summarized and distant deaths of news bulletins and drama.

We are exposed to death on a daily basis. Death, through our radios, televisions and newspapers, is a part of *our* technological routine. Whether it is the bombing of the Alfred P. Murrah Federal Building in Oklahoma (1995), the frequent suicide bombings in Israel, the Paddington rail crash (1999), the conviction of Dr Harold Shipman for murdering 215 of his patients, the drowning children in the floodwaters of Mozambique (2000) or the daily strafing of Afghanistan (2001), we are regularly asked to acknowledge and respond to tragic deaths, involving the wrecking of individual lives and sometimes of whole societies.

Two questions arise. Are these deaths 'real' to us? Do they, in any sense, inure us to death? Why is the death of a little girl in Michigan, shot dead by her six-year-old classmate, so much more moving and compelling than the deaths of countless refugees? Why did the death of a princess prompt millions of people across the world to switch on their televisions when they channel-hopped away from the last fatal shootings in Northern Ireland? What are the differences between these deaths? Is the viewer *bereaved* by any of them?

The death of Diana, Princess of Wales, is instructive in this context because it encapsulates much that is confused and contradictory about our contemporary attitudes to death and bereavement. According to Andrew Morton, Diana's funeral was 'the biggest event in history'. It exceeded, in his view, World War Two. After the Mercedes in which Diana was travelling crashed near the Place de l'Alma in Paris, she was taken to the Pitie-Salpetrière hospital and pronounced dead at 3.00a.m. on Sunday 31 August 1997. The following day the first of the visitors to Kensington Palace left their flowers. It was a day of mourning. Tony Blair cancelled two meetings at 10 Downing Street. Campaigning for the Scottish devolution referendum was suspended, even though the referendum was only a week away. Six hundred thousand people used the Buckingham Palace website to leave messages of condolence for the royal family. Suzanne Moore, writing in the *Independent*, told us 'things will never be the same again. For her family, for the people of this country, for the press.'

The funeral took place on Saturday 6 September and was watched on television by an estimated 31 million people in Britain and 2 billion all over the globe. The song that Elton John sang in Westminster Abbey, *Candle in the Wind*, went on to sell 250,000 copies in the first four hours it was on sale, and nearly 9 million copies were ordered worldwide. In a 'commemorative edition' of the *Observer*, Martin Jacques informed us that Diana had 'redefined the nation' and, in so doing, she had 'redefined each and every one of us'. The government gave its approval for the designing of a permanent memorial to 'the People's Princess'.

On 5 January the following year, Althorp Park issued the first 'day tickets' to visit Diana's grave. Two thousand people had called the hotline by the time it opened at 9.00 a.m. Later in the year, the London *Evening Standard* reported the launch of 'Diana Memorial Tours'. For £58.50, this company offered tourists a trip to places where Diana had stayed, places where she had worked and lived and, to round the day off, a drive along the funeral route. The company claimed the tours would provide a 'focus' for those who would not otherwise be able to satisfy their need for information about Diana's life and death.

It took about a year for sober reflection on 'the biggest event in history' to question whether it had been as significant as people had thought. Christopher Hitchins, again in the *Standard*, pointed out that the whole sequence of events, from the car accident to the funeral cortege, appeared 'slightly bogus' in retrospect, a thought that would certainly not have been voiced a year earlier. For some of us, it would have been hypocritical to pour scorn on what Brian Sewell termed the 'corporate hysteria, perhaps even corporate infantilism' that surrounded Diana's death.[21] I for one was very affected by it. I didn't go to Kensington Palace, but I did watch the television coverage of the funeral and was, again, affected by that. For whatever reason, there did seem to be an outpouring of grief amongst the British people during the week following that tragic car accident. Some commentators wanted to say that it was because Diana spoke for 'everyone's need for hugs and contact'.[22] Karen Armstrong went further. Noting that Diana had come to prominence during the Thatcher years, when Britain had become a harsher place, she claimed that Diana figured in our imaginations as virgin, mother and martyr. When Diana had talked about her feelings to the media, she'd touched the feelings of others who felt worthless in our society.[23]

In a shrewd essay in *Mortality*,[24] William Merrin has argued that Diana was so much a creature of the media that there was nothing of her to separate from the image provided by newspapers and television. 'All our experience of the life and death of Diana,' wrote Merrin, 'is irreversibly saturated with our media forms . . . We can find no un-mediated ground for our knowledge of Diana: for us her life was always imagic.' Merrin argued that none of the events surrounding her death and funeral could be regarded as 'real'. Television told us we *should* grieve (routine programming was disrupted) and showed us *how* to grieve (the mountain of flowers at Kensington Palace). Merrin's essay is persuasive and appeals directly to those of us who feel a mild embarrasment that they might have gone a bit too much with the herd, temporarily subscribing to an estimation of Diana which, on later reflection, appears exaggerated. It's comforting to believe that we were all, in some way, manipulated by the media. However, Merrin concluded that 'there is no difference for the mourning public between Diana in life and in death. Diana lives on: Diana, the commemorative stamps, the double CD tribute album; the tub of Flora margarine.'

This, it seems to me, is wrong. Diana lives on only in the sense that James Dean, Jimi Hendrix or Elvis Presley *live on*. There are the records, the books, the tee-shirts and posters, and looking through the archive footage and the movies, it is possible to recover a sense of what it was like to experience them alive. But there is a qualitative difference to our viewing. Much as replays of a football match have none of the energy and spirit of the original game, especially if you know the result, the 'merchandising' of Diana is lacklustre for being *all there is*. There is no possibility of renewal or addition or change, defining characteristics of life, and Diana's life was nothing if not changeable. There is nothing to look forward to. We've read the last chapter.

What does the death of Diana, and how it was communicated, tell us about our current attitudes to death? Were any of us *bereaved* and would our feelings have been very different had it been the death of our favourite character in *Eastenders* or *ER*? Doubtless, we can be moved to fear and pity by the death of such fictional characters. (Remember all the fuss when JR was shot in *Dallas*?) But to imagine that we do not differentiate between the cast of a television fiction and the figures in a news story or documentary is to underestimate the independence of the audience's thinking. Although audiences can be duped, their belief in the trust-worthiness of media reports is sustained by the knowledge that they could, hypothetically, verify what they are being told by other means. In most cases we don't bother; in others, it would be impractical, if it involved substantial travelling, for example, or access to a secure institution.

But the principle is sound. If I had flown to Mozambique early in 2000, I would have found people struggling to keep alive amid rising floodwater. We did not have to depend on the media to know that Diana Spencer married the Prince of Wales; we chose to. Throughout her life as a member of the

royal family, a few phone calls would have easily established that she had two sons, that she had divorced, that she
did work for a number of charities and, finally, that she was
killed in a road accident in Paris. These are meagre facts by
comparison with the impression we gained of her from the
media, but they are enough to suggest that it would have
been possible to begin to construct an idea of Diana
independently. This is not to underrate the impact of the
media so much as to assert that the attachment to Diana
which many people formed was rooted in aspects of our
culture that connect with, and in some cases pre-date, the
media. They include a respect for, or curiosity about, the
monarchy, a shared empathy with marital and maternal
experience, and – to return to an earlier theme – our
collective investment in the idea of an average life expectancy, to which the death of the young is a violent affront.
There was here a basis for affection and, therefore, for grief.
With hindsight, what was perhaps surprising was not so
much the 'herding' tendency of the public's mourning as the
profound bereavement that some individuals experienced.
In the month after Diana's death, suicide in England and
Wales amongst women aged 25–44 rose by 45 per cent.
Death seemed to be the answer to their loss.[25]

That said, people would not have developed such an
attachment to Diana but for the media, and it was the
coverage in newspapers and on television that mobilized
her mourners. Her death can be seen as the most recent in a
line of 'telly deaths' that have brought people onto the
streets or pinned them in their seats in front of the box.
Newspapers and television disseminate the initial story and
they then report how people are behaving in response.
What William Merrin alleged about Diana's death is true
of many others. 'To fail to mourn in that week was,
therefore, to fail to be part of the nation.' Could this suggest
that people use the death of a public figure as the opportunity to mourn all their own losses? In 1965, an estimated
20 million Britons and 350 million people worldwide

watched the funeral of Winston Churchill on television. Twelve years later, 100,000 people lined the streets of Memphis to see a white Cadillac carry the body of Elvis Presley to Forest Hills cemetery. Where were you the day Kennedy died?

Diana's death also raises questions about which deaths are remembered and which are not. How should we express our grief when disasters such as Aberfan, Lockerbie, Hillsborough, Dunblane occur, and for how long? It is clear from the evidence of two world wars, that western societies are reluctant to dwell on death, whatever the scale of loss experienced. Whilst we have retained Remembrance Day on 11 November and the Holocaust remains the *crise de mort* that persistently tests our moral equanimity, other historical events are under constant threat of losing their significance or of becoming muddied. The celebration of fifty years since D-Day in June 1994, and of VE Day in May 1995, straddled an unstable line between a victory carnival and a more sober reflection on the price paid for freedom. Neither, however, was preoccupied with death in its darker aspects. That Allied actions, such as Dresden or Hiroshima have come under ethical scrutiny goes some way towards explaining the uncertain status of these anniversaries, but it is hard to avoid a more general conclusion that, in François Mitterand's phrase, 'we panic at the idea of dying.'

Some of the deaths that we learn about from the media make very little impression. In Britain, reports of deaths in Northern Ireland, for example, have become routine and unsurprising. It was well known amongst broadcasters that programmes about Northern Ireland were a turn-off. There had been too many killings and, until the late 1990s, there seemed no prospect of a solution to the violence. Deaths in Israel, Algeria, Sri Lanka, Kashmir and other territories torn apart by civil strife, suffer from the same viewer familiarity and hopelessness. What perhaps distinguishes Bosnia, Kosovo, East Timor and natural disasters such as the flooding in Mozambique, is a recognition that something can and should be done to relieve suffering and prevent further deaths. The viewer colludes in a general sense of urgency.

In all these cases, the deaths are anonymous and cannot, by any stretch of our imaginative empathy, constitute bereavement. What, then, is the effect on us of so much reported and depicted death? It was estimated some years ago that a child growing up in the United States will have witnessed 18,000 deaths on television by the age of four-teen. More recently, a survey in 2000 revealed that the average American eighteen-year-old will have seen 40,000 murders on television or at the movies. If each was felt and suffered, it would be intolerable, but what are we to conclude? Are we to assume that their impact is negligible, that the American teenager – and, by extension, all deri-vative societies – are indifferent to these deaths? Illustrating T. S. Eliot's axiom that 'human kind cannot bear very much reality', there is perhaps a detachment which providentially underpins a culture that bombards itself with so many images of death. There are times when the depiction of utter deprivation and suffering in countries other than our own is rather like being put to sit in a classroom and made to watch instructive videos for our moral improvement. We know that the bell will ring soon and we can get away. It is akin to what Michael Ignatieff has called 'virtual war', a war in which military technology permits the prosecution of warfare with impunity, or without loss. What I am describing here is the witnessing of death with impunity; distance permits watching without loss.

We are left with the irony that a single 'telly death' can result in a whole viewing community simulating bereave-ment. The 'audience' wept at Princess Di's televised funeral service, imagining they were there. But we need not even know the victim or the bereaved to feel both fascinated and profoundly sorrowful. Take the little girl, Kayla Rowland, shot down in Michigan. Her six-year-old killer was deemed too young to be held criminally responsible. What happens to the demand for justice in such circumstances? Or take the murder of James Byrd. Black, forty-nine, living in a small town in Texas, he was grabbed by a man called John 'Bill' King, who chained him to the back of a pick-up truck and dragged him along a country road until his head was severed from his body. The anger evoked by such savagery, and the satisfaction derived from King's conviction, were Aristotelian in their depth. These deaths do not matter more, but they seem to. We care about them and we are hurt by them. Importantly, they occur on a scale we can comprehend. We can project our friends, our lovers, our children, into the circumstances in which they happened. We can also share in a sense of public shame that brutalized people of this kind exist. No doubt if they became routine, if the same events were reported over and over again, we would become too familiar with them and grow indifferent, as we grew indifferent to deaths in Northern Ireland.

There are occasions when the distinction between 'real' screen deaths and their simulacra in films seems to be particularly blurred. It is as if the fictional event were prophetic and, in some sense, prepared us for the thing itself. Alongside the shock we all felt as we watched the hijacked plane enter the second tower of the World Trade Center in New York, there was a palpable sense of a disaster movie having come to life. The two towers sank slowly in upon themselves and it was a shot we had seen on TV before, except that on the previous occasion the incident had been imaginary.

Ultimately, we cannot determine with any exactitude the degree of 'reality' we each attach to the deaths we encounter through the media. The credibility we give to television and newspapers is negotiated daily and it is a largely unconsidered calculation. That we should be fascinated and repelled by the deaths presented to us is inevitable. The intelligence and complexity of our technological civilization may have deluded us into thinking that we have outlived and outmoded the anthropological norms that regulate a society, but our continuing interest in birth, sexual relations and death should assure us that this is not so. Our rites of passage, the liminal stages of initiation or transition, are as necessary and as powerful as ever. They are eloquent of the human condition at its most intriguing and terrifying. This is what must lie at the heart of our contract with the media. Quite apart from the democratic value we may invest in the open propagation of information, stories about death are regularly told because we are enthralled by them. They are experiences that unite humankind because we know that death is our common lot.

The ubiquity of death in the media goes to the heart of the taboo debate. Is death taboo or isn't it? Professor Robert Winston announced in a 1998 television documentary that it was death, not sex, that was 'the last taboo'. In stark contrast, in January 2000, the broadcaster John Peel said he 'might just, well, die' if he heard death referred to again as one of the last great taboos. 'I don't know', he wrote, 'what the last great taboos are – sex with the dead is a possibility – but death isn't one of them.' Peel took as his evidence the open display of death that we see on our screens and in our theatres, and hear about from our news bulletins and newspapers. What is undeniable is that the evidence of death, that people are routinely dying, is publicly aired all the time. Whether we learn from that kind of openness, or are made easier in our minds by it, is far less clear.

The reactions to Robert Winston's 1998 programme on death encapsulated this ambivalence. Transmitted on BBC television in March, 'The End of Life' was the last episode in a series Winston presented called *The Human Body*. The programme attempted a serious discussion about the way in which we die and the attitudes we have to our deaths. The scope was ambitious. In just under one hour, Winston looked at historical views of death and dying, what occurs physically when we die, the principal causes of death and the possible causes of near-death experiences. But the whole episode pivoted around the filmed death of a man named Herbie. He was dying of stomach cancer and he had agreed to have his death recorded in order that 'everyone can see that there is a way to make the best of the end of your life.' He gradually declined over the course of the programme and when the end came, it was moving and peaceful.

'The End of Life' was promptly denounced by newspapers and lobby groups. The National Viewers and Listeners Association maintained that the BBC had cheapened death. The *Daily Mail* was sure it would 'distress recently bereaved families' and the *Sunday Times*, laying the blame on the unsuitability of television to handle such a moment, said the programme could only 'degrade the spectacle'.

Winston rounded on his critics in *The Times*. He accused them of hypocrisy. If we were happy to be served up 'violent death and other horrors' on television, why should we object to a sincere effort to depict death as it will occur for many of us? 'We live in a society which hides death,' he wrote, 'because it is beyond our control and, partly in consequence, we are terrified of it.' Dame Cicely Saunders, creator of the modern hospice, weighed in to support him. 'Death', she announced in the *Daily Mail*, 'is not the Great Unmentionable. It has to be talked about, it has to be thought about. We are not ostriches, and behaving as ostriches can only add to the inevitable pain.'[26]

The clash of opinions gives further evidence of the sensitivities that still surround the subject. There is a certain bullish attitude, which asserts that we are a mature society able to voice and confront our deepest anxieties. But subverting that confidence is a palpable neurosis. As Woody Allen observed, 'Personally, I don't have a problem with death, I just don't want to be around when it happens.' We try to push death out of our plan for the future, but never quite shed the fears and superstitions. We avoid discussing death because to mention it might be, in some way, to increase the risk of it.

The Possibility of a Good Death

Modern, developed societies have taken the view that death is not worth preparing for. Unlike the Victorians, we do not publish admonitory advice on how to achieve a good death, and the grim, hellfire sermons that reminded people that death was merely moments away have vanished from the parish pulpit and the public mind alike. They are an oddity of the past, found in dusty books with leather bindings. All the deaths on our televisions notwithstanding, death has withdrawn to the wings. Except perhaps in certain quarters where AIDS has decimated a community, the axiom *memento mori* has ceased to resonate in the western world. We don't think about death when we're in good health any more than the average eight-year-old boy thinks about marriage. Without consciously planning to, our minds silently resolve to face it when it comes.

That time, of course, never does come, or not in any way that we intended at least. The timing of death is always a surprise, either because it is sudden and we know no more of it, or because it is slow and unwelcome, and we scarcely could have imagined we could have that cancer or liver disease. We end up forced to confront death's imminence without having previously given it much thought. In other words, we are made to deal with it when we are least able to. People speak with a horrified surprise about the shocking and undermining effects of death, first of all upon the dying and, subsequently, on those left behind. Most of us are unprepared for the devastation of our confidence, the sense of lost or diminished identity death can effect in us, which is every bit as searing as the loss itself and which it is too late to try to rationalize once the death has occurred.

What alternatives do we have in a modern society? Is one strategy to dwell on death all our lives? Undoubtedly, that was the advice in centuries past. 'Practise dying,' said

St Paul. Jeremy Taylor, chaplain to Charles I and author of one of the most widely read works on death, argued that preparation was a daily obligation. His dissertation on the means to a good death, *Holy Dying* (1651) was still standard reading in middle-class homes well into the nineteenth century. As Keats lay dying in Venice in 1821, his friend, Joseph Severn, tried to help ready him for death by reading excerpts from Taylor's work late into the night. 'He that prepares not for death before his last sickness,' warns Taylor, 'is like him that begins to study philosophy when he is going to dispute publicly in the faculty.'[27]

Montaigne, too, advocated preparation as a means to defeat death's capricious advantage.

A man must looke to it, and in better times fore-see it . . . Let us learne to stand, and combat her with a resolute minde. And begin to take the greatest advantage she hath upon us from her, let us take a cleane contrary way from the common, let us remove her strangenesse from her, let us converse, frequent, and acquaint our selves with her, let us have nothing so much in minde as death, let us at all times and seasons, and in the ugliest manner that may be, yea, with all faces shapen and represent the same unto our imagination. At the stumbling of a horse, at the fall of a stone, at the least prick with a pinne, let us presently ruminate and say with our selves, what if it were death it selfe?[28]

Given the opportunity, most people would choose not to envisage their own deaths and, if pressed to consider what they would regard as a 'good death', they would say that it should be short and sweet, free from pain or anxiety. A survey in the USA a few years ago revealed that 80 per cent of Americans would like to die quickly and happily. Much of the evidence that a taboo remains powerfully in place is, of course, anecdotal, as anyone who has brought up the subject of death at a dinner party will confirm. That a greater frankness obtains amongst intellectuals and certain kinds of medical staff might indicate some erosion of the taboo. However, it is in how most people behave that the extent of change is measured, and the case for supposing a new and general openness at the private level is far less clear. In our personal, day-to-day dealings with each other, there is no reason to suppose that we are less inhibited than in the past. On the contrary, to many people grief is a love that dare not speak its name. Talk to the widow who cannot share her agony with her closest friends, or to the gay man excluded from his partner's funeral because the parents would not accept that he was their son's lover, and you get a very different story. At this level, we are undoubtedly the death-denying society which Philippe Ariès described. 'We act', Ariès wrote, 'as if it did not exist, and thus mercilessly force the bereaved to say nothing.'[29]

What troubles late modern society is the tantalizing anxiety that death might eventually be conquered or, failing that, substantially postponed. We are reminded again of Spinoza's dictum that we *feel* ourselves to be immortal. Might there indeed come a time when *mors* itself could be *incerta*? Battering the heart of this hope is the evidence of everyday life. People die. Yet we deny death its place *in life*. Medical diagnosis and prognosis have attained a sophistication that distances us from previous generations. We, unlike they, can be told in advance that we have a terminal condition. We can be told that it is *likely* to lead to death in six months, a year or some other finite period. Yet this is the very context in which denial of death most commonly occurs. There is a widespread conviction – call it a spiritual belief or a form of superstition – that the human will can sustain life even when the biological signs are irredeemably fatal.

So is there any possibility today of achieving a good

death? To describe something as good implies approval and the recognition of qualities that are beneficial and enhancing. 'Good' and 'death' are not words that sit alongside each other comfortably. The phrase tugs together opposing thoughts, much as in Dr Johnson's definition of metaphor: 'the most heterogeneous ideas are yoked by violence together.' There can be no good death, so the argument runs, because we regard the moment of death as intrinsically bad. It brings the end of achievement, the corruption of the body, suffering of an unforeseen depth and unpredictable duration. Death ruins everything. No one has a good word to say about it.

Undoubtedly, some deaths are bad. The accidental deaths of children and premature deaths arising from violence or suicide are intolerable. They will always seem brutal and wrong. Today's good death, if it exists, is not to be found amongst those who die suddenly; its application, if it has one, is to the terminally ill. As for a good bereavement, that will depend partly on what the individual personality brings from the past to the moment of crisis, and partly on the flexibility with which those in a position to help treat the bereaved. The term 'a good death' implies a formula.

We do not know what death is, or is like. Still less do we have an inkling of life beyond death. But the impact of death on others and the process of dying itself are things of which we now have a substantial knowledge, one that can form the basis of helpful advice. Much of a practical kind has been done to unveil the subject. The hospice movement has created a gold standard for care of the dying and there are now nearly 400 hospice or palliative care teams operating across the British Isles. In general medicine, too, there have been changes. It has for long been the belief within the medical establishment that, in order that they harden up, new student doctors should rummage around in a trough of body parts first thing on a Monday morning and dissect a corpse from foot to cortex by the end of their first term.

Medical training continues to take death as its starting point, but some efforts have been made to introduce new courses on how to inform patients and their relatives sensitively about a terminal condition. Largely as a result of the hospice movement, doctors have been encouraged – with some, limited success – to regard dying not as a failure but as the completion of life, the last phase of living for which treatment and care are every bit as necessary as at other times of life. These are developments which, if they do not amount to a good death yet, are heading in the right direction.

Professor Alison Kitson, giving the annual Abbeyfield lecture in June 1998, formulated her own idea of what I am choosing to call the 'staying close' approach. She argued that today's good death requires honesty and, alongside it, 'fidelity, connectedness and recognition of our inter-dependence'. In particular, she felt that life had become 'a series of unconnected episodes' and in the course of it, we lose a sense of 'complete identity'. There is the opportunity, at death, to restore completeness through truthful interaction. By telling to another human the story of one's life, the dying can recover a sense of the whole.

In the end, however, if there is a possibility of a good death in modernity, it must resolve, sublimate or attenuate a number of individual and important fears and anxieties that frequently accompany terminal illnesses:

(1) **The fear of the process of dying** entails not only the fear of pain and disintegration, but the fear of losing control. The dying person has, therefore, to be encouraged to express his needs and wants, and those in charge of his care must respond to those needs and inform the patient frankly and thoroughly, when he wishes it. If the patient is to retain some degree of control, he may also wish to stipulate where he dies – at home or in a hospice or hospital – and, in respect of all these demands, it is likely that they will change as dying progresses.

(2) **The fear of separation from family** (and from other people the patient has loved) will be acute, particularly when allied to the concomitant anxiety that those left behind may not be able to cope, either emotionally or practically, or both.

(3) **The fear of having failed**, of looking back and judging what has been done and finding that it doesn't amount to much. This is especially difficult for the young, for whom it is difficult to regard their lives as accomplishments. That said, many of us continue to have ambitions throughout our lives and, in old age, the dying may be prey to more profound doubts, about whether they have loved their children sufficiently or could have done more to improve or save their marriages, for example. The re-establishment in the mind of the dying of a sense of personal value is essential to a good death.

(4) **The fear of what lies beyond death** may not trouble all who are dying, but many people are exercised by it, even if they believe that death is no more than the extinction of the self. For the bereaved, the allaying of this fear is determined by a process of finding a place for the dead in their memories with which they can feel comfortable.

(5) **The fear of hopelessness** is intimately connected to other fears of dying. Perhaps of all of them it is the most fluid and subject to change. Hope for a miracle cure has, somehow, to give way to something else. A good death will ensure that, for the dying and for those left behind, it is not despair.

To these anxieties may be added the sheer anger and frustration that life has to be stopped at all. In a 1999 article for the *Spectator*, Peter (Lord) Chadlington suggested that the only effective way to subdue these feelings was to 'address mortality' earlier in life, before it is too late. 'The salve to that anger, the antidote to the railing against death,' he wrote, 'lies not in religious rediscovery (although I am sure that for many that would be a joyful remedy) but in preparing for death while we live fully in our mature, adult years.'[30] In so saying Chadlington's dictum joins the great *memento mori* tradition of Taylor, Montaigne and St Paul.

2

Terminal Illness

And things are both more trivial than they ever were
and more important than they ever were, and the
difference between the trivial and the important
doesn't seem to matter. But the nowness of everything
is absolutely wondrous.

Dennis Potter

Terminal illness can take many forms and develop over
widely differing periods of time. At the point of diagnosis, a
patient may have already undergone months or years of
treatment, or none at all. Patients therefore vary in their
responses to diagnosis, and their views may be at odds with
those of their families and those in charge of their medical
care. Creating relationships which are frank and intimate
can be especially difficult in such unpredictable circumstances.

The idea that there might be a perfect way to deal with
dying and bereavement is every bit as difficult to imagine as
an ideal approach to love or being a good parent. We bring
to the problem a complex of personality and experience,
which turns every death and bereavement into a unique
event, and we have all in a sense to muddle through as best

we can. There is, however, something instructive to be gained from looking at what other people have done, how they have faced up to the process and fears of dying and the anxieties of anger and separation.

What became very clear to me, over the course of several interviews, was that the issue of truth was of paramount importance. The 'truth' does, of course, have many languages. Problems can arise over the words that are used to describe the patient's condition. Should it be 'cancer' or 'growth'? The softer term may be more acceptable, but will it be as clearly understood? Moreover, each terminal illness has its own social status and preconceptions about a disease can get in the way of open communication. This seems to be particularly problematic in cases of cancer and AIDS, and so I have tried to convey a sense of the typical difficulties of terminal illness through the stories of a number of individuals who have struggled with one or other complaint. They are not intended to be read as paradigms of successful management. On the contrary, there are many instances within these stories of bad decision-making, negligence, self-delusion and, more particularly, of *not* staying close. But together they do illustrate much of what people go through when a terminal illness is discovered.

Living with Cancer

'Cancer' is not a neutral word. Unlike coronary heart disease or malaria, it has a dark side. When people are told that they have cancer, they know that however determined they might be to beat it and survive, there is something bad going on inside them, silently and secretly. Dennis Potter called his cancer of the pancreas 'Rupert', after Rupert Murdoch, whom he held personally responsible for the pollution of the British press and, in turn, British political life. People perceive cancer in this way, as an invasion or a pollutant, which needs to be repelled, but it is in reality much closer to the idea of death expressed by the Israeli novelist, Amos Oz. Oz argues that we all have death inside us, that we are 'pregnant' with death, and that is why we have premonitions about it, nightmares in which we are chased to our deaths or brought to the point of suffocation. The unconscious is only recognizing what is latent within us.[1]

At the same time, cancer can also invoke guilt, a sense that we are in some way to blame if it develops within us, because we have smoked too many cigarettes, or enjoyed too much sun or, simply, eaten the wrong diet. No doubt, lingering behind this anxiety is the Edenic idea that the pleasures of the garden were bought with Death, but there is, even in modernity, the tormenting thought that *if only* we had lived our lives differently, cancer would not have happened. If its mode of action were more conspicuous, we might have had the opportunity to reform our ways, but cancer is slow and unexpected, often hiding its deadliness until the eleventh hour. Against such an adversary, the individual's fight to survive is bound to be heroic and tormented. Is it no wonder, then, that for both the dying and the bereaved, cancer can be one of the most prolonged and complicated forms of death?

There is a vein of journalism running through our culture that disseminates the belief that cancer can be beaten, or that it will be beaten in the near future. Whether this serves the useful purpose of propping up the nation's hope it is hard to tell, but every week some branch of the print media will alert us to a new preventative measure which a recent study has proved to be effective in the avoidance of cancer. Over the last few years we have been advised that an olive oil rich diet helps protect against cancer of the colon, and that women with breast implants are less likely to develop breast cancer. Moreover, drinking green tea, taking a chocolate biscuit with your mug of tea and ingesting selenium (present in brazil nuts, bread, cereals, fish, poultry and meat) are all variously described as the 'key to avoiding cancer' or likely to 'reduce the risk' of cancer.

Perhaps more remarkably, given that in western society only 19 per cent of men and women survive lung cancer, we are told that mother's milk can 'cure' the disease and that there is an inhaler on the way that will 'repair' cancerous lungs. Mother's milk contains a protein called *alpha-lactal bumin* which scientists have found will destroy cancer cells in the lung, and according to the *Sunday Times*, an American firm called Introgen is altering the character of a virus in order to puff a human gene into diseased lungs and 'fix' the DNA.

In the meantime, a British scientist, Professor Sir David Lane of Dundee University, is planning to produce a gene-based anti-cancer pill, which would replace radiotherapy and chemotherapy as the conventional treatment. Professor Lane maintains that gene *p-53* generates a protein that blocks the growth of tumours. He expects his pill to be available by about 2005.

Furthermore, we are told, cancers will soon be detected as they begin to form. Too often, a cancer is found when the patient is presenting advanced symptoms and it is then too late to give effective treatment. But according to a Californian biotechnology firm, AMDL, their new DR-70 test can check for signs of any one of thirteen cancers. It claims to be 84 per cent accurate and can find in a small blood sample cancers of the lung, breast, stomach, ovaries and cervix. The test spots the antibodies generated by the immune system when a tumour starts to grow. It cannot differentiate between one cancer and another, which means that in the event of a positive result, further tests would be required. But the manufacturers maintain that what they have developed will save thousands of lives every year. The temptation is to think that with regular screening and a minor modification of our diets, the likelihood of us getting cancer will diminish and, in the unlucky event that we do, we need only petition our doctors for one of these 'miracle cure' inhalers or pills (or a good old-fashioned bottle of expressed breast milk) to recover full health.

It is easy to be cynical, and there is no doubt that it is in the nature of scientific progress that cancer will be tamed one day. The discovery of an immune cell that can seek out and destroy leukaemia cells is a first step, and a large number of gene therapy trials are also currently underway. Many of these make use of a genetically modified vaccine to implant a gene designed to recruit the patient's immune system into destroying tumour cells. The UK does, in fact, lead Europe in research into gene therapy treatments for cancer, and although the success rate is small so far, there are good reasons for supposing that this kind of science will lead to cures for cancer.

Some of the evidence in support of preventative measures is also persuasive. In particular, the *British Medical Journal* appears to accept that eating more fruit and vegetables, and less red meat, does reduce the incidence of breast and bowel cancers. 'What is remarkable about the diet–cancer story is the consistency with which certain foods emerge as important in reducing risk across a range of cancers,' wrote John Cummings, of the Dunn Clinical Nutrition Centre. 'Vegetables and fruit are almost invariably protective for the major cancers.'[2] It seems, however, that the expediency of other prophylactic or remedial therapies has yet to be as well demonstrated.

In the meantime, although some progress has been made in effective treatment, the incidence of cancer is increasing in both the developed and developing countries of the world. Cancers of the breast, colon and prostate are now turning up in places where they were unknown as little as twenty to thirty years ago. Overall, it is estimated that there will be an annual increase of about 0.5 per cent each year for the next 20 years. The majority of the change will occur in the developing world, while deaths in the developed world will remain constant, accounting for around 21 per cent of all mortality. In the year 2000, in both the UK and the USA, cancer knocked coronary heart disease off its pedestal to become the No. 1 killer. Over the last 30 years, cancer in Britain has increased by 20 per cent amongst men and 30 per cent amongst women, and it now kills 1 in 4 Britons. One-third of all Americans will also face a cancer of some type, and 2 out of 3 of those will die from it.[3]

The paradox of this crisis is, of course, that it derives from prosperity. We develop cancer because a reasonable standard of living, diet and public hygiene ensures that we do not die of anything else. As the *World Health Report 1998* put it: 'Most cancers arise at an advanced age, and the risk increases steeply with age. The cancer burden is therefore much more important in populations having long life expectancy.' By 2041, more than 50 per cent of British society will be over 75, which makes it all the more significant that one-third of cancers are preventable and another third can be cured if they are identified early on.

The most devastating cancer in the developed world attacks the lung. Historically, it has killed large numbers of men, but it now rivals breast cancer as the worst cancer-killer amongst women. In Britain the death rate used to be appalling. Between 1965 and 1970, there was an annual toll of 80,000 men dying from lung cancers caused by smoking. By the late 1990s that figure had halved. In the USA, too, lung cancer deaths have fallen overall, although the huge increase amongst women and cancers of the lung caused by car pollution have complicated the picture and had a countervailing influence on the statistics. Los Angeles, for example, has 30 per cent more cases of lung cancer than the whole of New York state. Whilst the general downward trend is encouraging, it should be put into perspective. According to Professor Richard Peto, of the Imperial Cancer Research Fund in the UK, amongst every 1,000 young adults who take up smoking, 1 will be murdered, 6 will die in road accidents and 500 will die from tobacco-related diseases, notably heart disease and lung cancer.

Amongst women, breast cancer remains a deadly and disturbing disease. Drugs such as tamoxifen have played a part in the improved ratio of diagnoses to deaths, but breast cancer sufferers in Britain still complain that they are denied some of the drugs that have proved to be effective in trials because they are deemed too expensive by the NHS. As Jacqui Thornton noted in the *Sunday Telegraph* in November 1999, 'Only 95p is spent on cancer drugs per head of the population in Britain, compared with £6.24 per person in Germany and £7.76 in the United States.'

That said, the incidence of death from breast cancer has declined. Figures released in the UK in September 2000, showed a 21 per cent fall in deaths between 1990 and 1998. Although 12,677 women died of it in 1999 in the UK, over a third of the 35,000 diagnosed, the results do tend to confirm the value of the current screening programme in Britain, under which women aged 50–64 receive a mammogram every 2 or 3 years. With an early diagnosis, 85 per cent of women sufferers survive 5 years.

We are, then, at a critical juncture. Cancer is booming, but there is news that the cavalry is on the way. At present only one-third of cancers can be cured by early detection and treatment. Medical science will improve detection by DNA testing and the identification of those genetically vulnerable to the disease. Surgical techniques will also be refined by the use of computers and robots.

Our response to cancer is consequently riven by ambivalence. The proliferation of cancers over the last century has meant that cancer today is commonplace, the curse of the modern world. The subject can hardly be concealed, one might think. But doctors continue to be reluctant to use the word, and patients continue to experience a feeling of self-loathing about cancer, and this is difficult to dislodge. Whilst more and more funding is put into the search for a cure, we live in a society which is not open about, or friendly to, the issues surrounding cancer and patients are made introspective in consequence.

In particular, patients, families and medical staff, if they are to remain close, will have to work with and resolve the issue of denial. Denial is not necessarily unproductive. When a patient is told he or she is going to die, it may afford valuable time in which to assimilate the basic clinical facts whilst avoiding the full impact of the emotional shock. Adapting to a new truth does not have to be a fully conscious process. As the conscious mind refuses to accept the finality of the illness, a subtle process of reconciliation may well have already begun. More controversially, there will be people with a terminal illness who will not acknowledge that they are dying to the very end. Denial becomes their 'coping mechanism', and no one experienced in terminal care would question their right to deny, provided that it is their profound wish and not the product of simple fear.

Patients can often become fixed upon their cancer and its extirpation. For some, to deny the possibility of death is a function of their hope and that can make it very awkward for a counsellor who is trying to help someone with cancer accept the reality of the condition and its consequences. Dr Sara Miller, Senior Holistic Doctor at the Cancer Help Centre in Bristol, believes the possibility of death is 'a difficult subject to introduce in this culture and most people choose to focus on hope, a positive outcome, rather than on dying.' The Centre estimates that they see about 1 per cent of people with cancer in Britain. Many of those who enter the courses they run are women, perhaps because women are more open to the ideas it promulgates of healing and forgiveness and personal nourishment. Dr Miller describes them as women 'of fighting spirit', and the Centre holds the view – and with good evidence – that the individual's quality of life can be positively influenced by self-help. The emphasis of its counselling is upon 'living richly and fully and having the death that you want whenever it happens.' When some people arrive, they are close to death and reconciled to it, but most are in much earlier stages.

Their emphasis is on beating the cancer and, if possible, recovering their full health. Nonetheless, they may well have underlying fears, and Sara Miller thinks it is regrettable when people in these circumstances are afraid of dying and feel unable to talk about it. 'If you're frightened of something and you run away from looking at it, it just gets bigger and bigger. And if you actually turn around and look at it, you get the measure of it and you actually feel it isn't anything like as big as you thought.'

As with so many anxieties, fear of death is often not what it first appears. Sara Miller's experience is that people with cancer often speak of death when they really mean the process of dying. Their emotional turmoil is so frantic that they aren't able to make the distinction. However, when the fear is properly uncovered, a flock of questions flies out. 'Am I going to be in pain? Will I be incontinent? Will I be alone? Will I smell? Will I look awful?' Their concerns are not generally about 'being dead' or indeed about what might happen to them after they are dead, but about how they will die and what kind of future their relatives face. In short, their fears are complicated. Thus, a patient can be determined to outwit the cancer and survive at the same time as, with help, she allows herself to think about the dread experience of dying and how fearful it might turn out to be. Is she a person who is living, or one who is dying? In which direction is she headed?

That women are left in this predicament is hardly surprising if we pause to consider how little we are prepared by life, by our education and by our parents, to face the prospect of death. 'No one ever tells us what it is like to die,' writes Dr Elisabeth Lee, ' it is a secret known only to the dying.'[4] There is a growing recognition that patients are better equipped to cope if they are well-informed about their condition, not only as a matter of ethical right, but because they are then able to identify the questions they need to have answered.

Unfortunately, frankness is by no means the rule in

cancer care, and it was to fill in the gaps that arise between patients and doctors that 'cancerBACUP' was founded in 1985. Dr Vicky Clement-Jones, who had experienced ovarian cancer herself, decided to create a service which would provide information and support to anyone affected by cancer, be it a patient, a relative or a health-care professional. It has grown into the largest provider of cancer information in Europe.[5]

Martin Ledwick, a Senior Cancer Information Nurse Specialist, joined cancerBACUP in 1995, after six years as an oncology nurse. Martin is convinced that people ring the helpline 'because they want to know something'. It may not be apparent at first. Callers vary a great deal in their willingness and ability to be truthful about what is troubling them, and they sometimes give the impression that they have just rung for a chat. But one advantage of the telephone is that it tends to reduce embarrassment, and Martin has learnt to differentiate between the voice of openness and the voice of denial. 'You pick up the subtext in different ways,' he says. Very often the call has been prompted by confusion. A doctor has said something, and the patient has failed to point out that he did not quite understand. 'Patients', Martin concedes, 'don't want to upset the professional through asking.'

Although most enquiries seem to require clear, factual replies, this does not mean that callers have accepted their diagnoses. They may still be in denial. They might ask about the side-effects of drugs, without mentioning that they are dying, or they might start to talk about their fear of illness, without admitting that that it is the process of dying that is worrying them. Martin can tell them, in an understanding and straightforward way, what will happen as their condition deteriorates. Sometimes their fears are worse than the reality. When they express particular anxieties about diarrhoea or vomiting, he can reassure them that palliative care is now very sophisticated and that these distressing symptoms can, by and large, be controlled or significantly mitigated. 'We are giving a lot of support by giving information in a sensitive way,' Martin says. 'That can help to empower them and to reduce their anxiety, to give them some control over the situation and help them both to communicate within the family and to access their local services. We're giving them the information they need to cope with what's happening to them.'

A serious question emerges from the cloud of unknowing. What should our response be to a diagnosis of cancer? Should we struggle to survive at all costs? Or are these costs so high sometimes that we would be better off not taking treatment and trying to enjoy the life remaining to us? Many factors will determine what we decide to do: our age at the time of diagnosis, the quality of information we are given, the prognosis of that particular cancer and its stage of development, our love of life, our ability to fight for what we want, and our perception of the greater good. Some cancers are more effectively treated than others. Some people will prize life above any debilitation. But is there a time when treatment should be discontinued, when enough is enough? How, if there is such a time, will we recognize it when it comes?

Holding on to Life

Janice Hunt is a fighter. She was a police officer for twenty years and it was in the police force that she met her husband, Alan. When Alan developed a brain tumour in July 1994, she was determined that he was going to get the best treatment available and that he was going to live for as long as possible. He was, after all, only forty-two, Janice just thirty-five: they needed more time together.

A biopsy was performed and a course of radiation therapy begun. Janice felt she could not accept that that was all that could be done. So she didn't. When I interviewed her in 1998, she smiled and said triumphantly: 'I changed the prognosis for my husband.' She was resolute.

The grit and good humour with which she had taken on Alan's illness were palpable:

> Having lost my parents early in life, they weren't going to take my boy without a fight. He wasn't going anywhere unless I could put my hand on my heart and say I could do no more.

It was not immediately clear to Janice what she should do. Every day she took Alan to the hospital for his radiotherapy, and she began to feel that they were going through the motions, that no one was really trying to cure Alan.

> I became quite hysterical in there one day, and I'm not an hysterical person. But I said 'What the hell are you doing? Everyone dies that comes in here. What the hell are you *really* doing?' And I just knew that this was just a waste of time, that he was going to go very quickly.

By chance, two or three days later, Janice found herself reading an old copy of *Reader's Digest*, in which there was an article about a New York surgeon called Fred Epstein, who 'did the impossible' with people suffering from brain tumours. Janice told Alan 'This man's the business!' Alan was sceptical, partly because he was afraid that Janice would be disappointed.

One of Epstein's patients was the son of a British policeman living in Gravesend in Kent. Janice rang them up and found that the boy, Ashley, had had an 'inoperable' brain tumour removed. It had proved benign and Ashley was now doing 'very well'. Janice telephoned Fred Epstein immediately. 'Can you come next Wednesday?' he asked. 'I'll buy you lunch.'

Janice and Alan arrived in New York in February 1995, for lunch, and stayed three months. Alan was operated on by Dr Epstein for nine and a half hours. At the end of it, he was 'a totally different man. His speech was clear. He could walk straight. Before he went he would have died in two or three months, weeks maybe.'

For the better part of the next two years Alan appeared to enjoy good health. His condition was from then on to be monitored jointly by the British hospital and the 'neuro-oncologists' in the States, and at the Americans' request, he was given regular MRI scans. The results were fed-exed to New York or, occasionally, Alan and Janice would travel to the States for the scan. In contrast to the fatalism of the year before, Alan got everything he needed.

Not everyone would agree with Janice when she describes Alan as having been 'completely well', but these measurements are relative. He was, by objective standards, *un*well. Janice summed it up in this way: 'Different sorts of chemo. Bit sick now and then. No big deal. Happy. Frightened at times, but happy. Tumour stable, but clearly there. My husband was never a downbeat man. He was going to beat this.'

Between the scans, Alan and Janice took holidays, cheap packages mainly, £99 for a week in the sun. During the winter of 1996–7, they visited Spain three times. It was a routine, not one that most people would envy, but the two of them were simply grateful for however many extra weeks and months Alan stayed alive. That went for the children too. At the time of the diagnosis, Alan's three children by his first marriage were twelve, fourteen and sixteen. As Janice remarked, not without a reasonable sense of pride, 'To watch children watch their father fail, that really does kill you inside. I gave them back their father for their formative years.'

Yet part of her knew this was only a postponement. Janice remained determined to keep up the struggle, to have her husband for as long as she possibly could, but she was aware that the children needed to ready themselves. 'I tried to prepare them for it over a long time, but I suppose they used to see me laughing and joking with Dad and sometimes maybe they wondered if it was for real.'

Early in the autumn of 1996, Alan developed epilepsy.

His first fit terrified Janice. 'Am I going to lose him? Am I losing him?' she screamed down the phone to one of the doctors in New York. She needed advice and reassurance about what had been a major seizure. The American doctor, Michael Gruber, gave her that.

Over the winter of 1996–7, Janice also got to know someone else she would depend heavily on during the coming months. Stephen Gill was a neurosurgeon at the Frenchay Hospital and Janice does not believe that Alan would have survived the following year but for Gill's intervention. Alan became very unwell in March 1997, only two days after one of his periodical visits to New York. He was admitted to Ward 5 of Frenchay. That was on a Sunday night, and Janice went home to get some rest. She told me that when she returned the next morning, she was horrified by what she found: 'Alan was unconscious. The nurses said he was sleeping soundly, so I swore very loudly and said, "He ain't sleeping, he's unconscious." He couldn't swallow his spit. They said "The doctor will be around soon." And I said "No, he won't! He'll be here now!" I was really bellowing then.'

Janice was desperate. She was convinced that Alan was dying and that no one was listening to her. She ran to Stephen Gill's office and pleaded with him to come and save her husband. As soon as he took charge, Alan was given a CT scan and a 'shunt' (plastic valve) was put in to relieve the pressure in his brain. Within four days, Alan was 'walking about in his shorts and a tee-shirt, and as fit as a flea.' He had stepped to the brink of the precipice and turned back yet again.

The year 1997 was characterized by further crises and rallyings. In June, Janice and Alan travelled to New York, where Alan was to have a long and difficult procedure to reduce the cancer mass. Although he made a good recovery from the surgery, by September Gruber was advising 'another protocol of chemotherapy to blast the tumour'. Janice recalls that the oncology department was reluctant to do it, on the grounds that it could destroy Alan's bone marrow and, therefore, the quality of whatever life he had left. Alan and Janice insisted and the treatment went ahead, but Alan proved allergic to one of the drugs used. Shortly after the treatment, he had a violently adverse reaction and for a while it was touch-and-go whether he would survive. His spasms were dramatic and required immediate and powerful drug treatment. Janice remembers 'holding Alan down while they were putting the needles in'.

Time seemed to be running short. Another operation was carried out in November to remove a clot, but it left him with partial paralysis on his right side and it became clear that he was going downhill. There was talk of sending him to a nursing home, but Janice refused, and with the help of a social worker and an occupational therapist, she kitted out the sitting room to look after him at home. The children did their bit as well. Even though Alan couldn't speak, he could make himself understood, and they managed to have a kind of family life in spite of it all. Alan ate toast and watched videos with the children; it was always he who decided what they would watch. If Janice went out, she took her pager with her. Occasionally, they managed short evenings together away from the house, but every time they went out to a pub or for a meal with friends, she wondered if it would be the last.

Every so often it all became too much: 'I'd holler and scream. If Alan wouldn't go to sleep, and I thought he was very tired, and sometimes he needed to sleep because he'd have seizures if he was very tired, I'd say "Oh sod you!" and I'd take the TV zapper off him and slam the door.'

Somehow they got through Christmas, but on 22 January 1998, Alan started vomiting. The pressure had built up in his head again. He was admitted, unconscious, to Frenchay, where a CT scan was done and everyone tacitly began to realize that the end was near. The hospital let them have a double room, and Janice sat down at his bedside for the long wait.

Alan had been pumped full of high-dose steroids and at one point he woke up.

> He said 'What are we all doing here?' I said 'You're in for your chest infection. You've got a bit of a cough. There's nothing to worry about. They're giving you antibiotics and fluids.' He talked to the kids. We talked about all the funny things we'd done, and he went to sleep. But he knew why we were there, and he squeezed my hand.

He remained like this for several days, until finally on 28 January:

> I walked in and I could see that one side of his face was discolouring and I knew that it was imminent. I put some teardrops in his eyes, and wiped them. The sun was shining down and I'd left the window open because I wanted him to fly away. And I just said 'Sail away, babe. I'm right here.' And he opened his eyes and looked up at me and died.

When Alan was first told he had a brain tumour, he was given six months. In fact, he lived for three and a half years. Janice maintains that they knew all along that, at best, their efforts would only delay the inevitable. That knowledge enabled her to grieve slowly; she began when Alan was given a finite time to live and from then on 'every day I was losing him'. Some people might observe what Alan and Janice went through – the scans, the endless surgery, the humiliation of physical decay, the hopes and disappointments – and conclude that the cost was too high, but for Janice and the children it was worth it. Over the three years they had together, and in the presence of death, they were still able to exercise some control over their lives. 'That doesn't mean going woe, woe, woe,' Janice says, 'it's about making the quality of life that you want and being able to make your own decisions.'

All Is Always Now

When I interviewed Janice, it was scarcely three months after Alan's death. She was resolutely cheerful and determined that I would take away with me an impression of a death well done. I've no doubt that it was, but no family can endure the anxiety of a prolonged fight against cancer without rupture. Tiredness, worry and anger make the burden of care unbearable at times. For the patient, too, it can be frustrating to have to make the effort to be friendly and reasonably contented. Whilst the patient is still able to take part in an active life, meetings in the work place or in a social context can test the limits of patience. The responsibility to be the first to mention the subject of cancer (which, in their uneducated kindness, is an obligation most people place upon the ill) can be wearing and risks damaging a friendship on which the patient may wish to rely in the coming months.

It seems that there are no simple answers. When the needs of patients can change dramatically from day to day, even hour to hour, it is hard for other people to know how best to behave towards them. In a postscript to the journalist Ruth Picardie's *Before I Say Goodbye*, her husband, Matt Seaton, recalls how unpredictable Ruth could be during the months before she died of breast cancer in 1997.

Sometimes Ruth would be furious with people for ignoring the C-word and just gossiping about the everyday; at other times, she'd declare herself sick of the subject and wish people wouldn't drone on and on about such-and-such a new treatment they'd read about in a magazine . . . There was no right way for any of us. If I learnt one thing over Ruth's last weeks, it was that the illusion one holds about a peaceful, dignified death and the family's perfect bedside farewell will almost certainly be tugged away. If one is left with any shreds of comfort, then they must be unlooked-for blessings. Dying is nasty, ugly and painful; it's so obvious, isn't it?[6]

These are very raw feelings, written within a matter of weeks of Ruth's death at the age of only thirty-three. What may surprise the reader of the book – a selection of the articles and e-mails Ruth Picardie wrote during her illness – is that her own account of her struggle with cancer sustains a kind of resignation which is funny and self-deprecating, and whilst it acknowledges her frustration and the pain of a lost future, it is never bitter. That contradiction in the writing was perhaps indicative of the experience she was going through. She was fighting to survive at the same time as she was adjusting to the idea of her own death.

It may be that it is the cancer sufferer alone who can inhabit such a paradox, and in this respect Ruth Picardie's death may have been better for her than it was for her husband. Matt Seaton repudiates the 'good death' as an illusion (it is unclear whether Ruth's pain and other symptoms were properly managed), but as Michael Young and Lesley Curren have pointed out, 'a good death can make for a bad bereavement'.[7] In the first months following a death, the carers can be so exhausted that they are unable to raise themselves out of their grief. It may take a long while for the bereaved to acknowledge that, final suffering notwithstanding, the time that the illness took to work its fatal course was precious and afforded opportunities that would have been denied by a sudden death. These opportunities, broadly summarized as 'saying goodbye', include the mutual adjustment by the dying and his or her family to the fact of death, the saying of things that have not been said and need to be said, the settlement of financial and other practical arrangements, and – slowly and subtly – a growing and deeper understanding of what it has been to be alive. No one could pretend that this final intimacy is without profound sadness and tears, but that does not mean that it is without profound value.

For the playwright Dennis Potter, the time of his illness was a time in which he saw life in more vivid colours. Potter was told that he had cancer of the pancreas on Valentine's Day 1994. Three weeks later he gave his last television interview to Melvyn Bragg for a Channel Four programme in the *Without Walls* series. He smoked throughout and sipped white wine from time to time. 'I can break any rule now,' he said. He also took occasional swigs from a hip flask of liquid morphine.

Potter appeared to be a man without illusions. He had, he guessed, a couple of months remaining to him. His only concern was that he should be able to finish his last television play, to be called *Cold Lazarus*, before the disease finally took over. In the meantime, he described how his sensibility had been refined by the knowledge of his coming death and how he seemed to be living within the quintessence of life itself. He was acutely aware of every detail, every sound and texture – James Joyce called it the 'quidditas' of the world around us – and what was so striking was that it was of the moment, the experience of that very second, isolated within all history.

The only thing you know for sure is the present tense and that 'nowness' becomes so vivid to me now that it's almost, in a perverse sort of way, I am almost serene. I can celebrate life. Below my window in Ross, when I'm working in Ross, now at this season, the blossom is out in full, there in the west – early. It's a plum tree. It looks like apple blossom, but it's white and looking at it, instead of saying 'oh, that's nice blossom,' now, the last week, looking at it through the window, when I'm writing, it is the whitest, frothiest, blossomist blossom that there ever could be, and I can see it. And things are both more trivial than they ever were and more important than they ever were, and the difference between the trivial and the important doesn't seem to matter. But the nowness of everything is absolutely wondrous.

Dennis Potter had, of course, a successful career of thirty years behind him. Ruth Picardie had scarcely begun her work as a journalist and she had a young family. She should have had a great deal to look forward to. Potter's cancer was deemed inoperable at the outset. He did not undergo the debilitating and, so often, futile suffering that goes with chemotherapy: the aching veins and the puking and the headaches that Ruth Picardie put up with, to no avail. These stark differences emphasize the choice between seeking therapy and accepting a shorter life of a better quality, but it is interesting to compare the accounts of these two writers. Ruth Picardie set out to be 'positive about maximizing length and quality of time I have left'.[8] Since that was to include orthodox and complementary treatment, the time of her illness was inevitably a struggle. She put up with it valiantly, but in addition to a physical misery, there was an emotional misery which she could not avoid. 'What hurts most is losing the future,' she wrote.[9] As far as we can tell from the interview he gave to Melvyn Bragg, Dennis Potter's experience was one of living life more intensely; his *enjoyment* of life was sharpened and, for as long as his symptoms were controlled by morphine and other drugs, the last stage of living looked like being as interesting and satisfying as what had gone before. Both writers had cancer, but dying came to them in very different ways.

Why Didn't They Find It Earlier?

Something that Dennis Potter and Ruth Picardie did share was misdiagnosis. The failure to diagnose cancers early on is an alarming and too common feature of modern medicine. Two years before the discovery of Ruth Picardie's breast cancer in October 1996, she had been told that the lump she had was harmless. Dennis Potter's pancreatic cancer had first been diagnosed as an ulcer or a spastic colon. By the time the true state of his disease was identified, a secondary cancer had developed in his liver.

If a cancer is missed by a doctor and then later identified when it is advanced and unlikely to respond to treatment, the patient's first reaction is often an understandable anger. Minnie Dibley was seventy-two when her cancer was eventually diagnosed, but that did not make her any the less angry that it had not been spotted earlier. When I talked to her, she had already been admitted to the Hospice in the Weald. Although she was quite weak, and her skin a vivid yellow, she was not in pain and she remained lucid. 'I was a bit annoyed,' she said, understating her feelings, but visibly still troubled, 'because he said it was something I was eating that was making me bad.' Minnie attended a consultant's clinic for thirteen months and even though she kept coming back, her cancer was not detected. She began to wonder whether the truth was being kept from her, so she made it clear that she wanted to know: 'I said I didn't want to be beaten about the bush and go home thinking I was in cloud-cuckoo land. I wanted to know what was going on and I wanted the truth.'

Minnie was unmarried and living on her own. She had no relatives or close friends, no one pressing to clear up her problem apart from her GP, the doctor who had identified the lump which the hospital denied was there. The lump started to get bigger and the GP wrote asking the consultant to bring forward Minnie's next appointment. Still, the hospital insisted that there was nothing to worry about. Then, during the Christmas break in 1999, Minnie fell seriously ill. The GP insisted that she be admitted to hospital and given a scan. Only then did it become clear that Minnie had cancer of the pancreas.

When I knew what I'd got, I was really angry because I felt that it's possible they might not have been able to do anything, but at the same time there might have been some treatment that would have suited me. I went home and thought about it for quite a few days. Somebody said, 'You ought to sue,' but I said, 'By the time I sue, I'll be dead and what good's the money anyway without making me better?'

Although the consultant told her it was impossible to predict how long she might have to live, Minnie pressed him. 'You must have hundreds like me,' she said. 'A rough idea will do.' He eventually guessed that it might be a matter of months.

Early in January 2000, the Hospice in the Weald contacted Minnie and suggested that she might like to attend their day hospice. Her cancer began to progress rapidly and she found herself falling about in the hospice corridors. After one fall, in April, she blacked out. The hospice admitted her to a bed immediately. She had internal bleeding, which they stopped, and she was given three blood transfusions. She refused chemotherapy when it was clear it would do nothing for her, but the effects of the cancer became so distressing that she began to long for her death.

Sometimes with all the symptoms I've got, occasionally now I'm fed up with it, so I wouldn't mind if it came tomorrow. People say about you missing good quality of life, blah, blah, blah, but to me I've got no quality of life. I've stopped being sick because they did something to my stomach to stop me. But when it's the pancreas, it affects the bowels as well, so you can't go anywhere, you can't do anything, you can't plan anything. You spend three-quarters of your life in the bathroom.

Minnie did, however, appreciate the kind of care she was receiving in the hospice. In hospital she had been unable to exercise any real control over what happened to her. She found that if she disagreed with a proposed treatment, she was regarded as 'niggly' and when she requested some-thing, the hospital staff were so rushed off their feet, it might take twenty-four hours for it to be done.

Minnie was not someone who was happy to leave decision-making to doctors and nurses. She wanted to be fully informed and to participate in a frank discussion about her care. She had made a 'living will' and expected the hospital to take notice of her wish not to be resuscitated should anything go wrong during the operation on her stomach. By the time she left the hospital for the hospice, she had lost any hope that her request would be respected.

The hospice, by contrast, she found 'lovely'. She valued the individual attention she got from nurses and their willingness to 'come and have a natter and try to lift you up'. Hospice life also provided contact with other people in a similar condition, although Minnie found that she was more willing than most to talk about the effects of cancer. ' "Oh, Minnie!" they say when I start on about death. But it comes to us all. What's the point of hiding it?'

It's probable that even though she was reluctant to admit it, hospice care did restore some of the quality of Minnie's former life, chiefly through the human kindness shown her. What the hospice could not altogether remove, however, was the sense of humiliation she felt as more and more of her personal autonomy was eroded by the disease. She objected strongly to her own need to be washed and helped to the bathroom. She felt embarrassed by her occasional falls, which would leave her prostrate until a member of staff found her and lifted her back into bed. For a woman who had lived on her own for fifty years, who had run her own home and looked after herself all her life, it was too much to bear.

It's very degrading to me. When I had an accident one night and rang the bell, a young student nurse (boy) came and then, of course, I started shedding a tear and he had to console me and he said 'Why are you crying?'

and I said 'Well, I'm a woman of seventy-two, and
you've got to clear up all the mess.' He was very kind
and put me at my ease and I wasn't so bad after that.

That student nurse provided the last intimacy of Minnie's
life. She found she could confide her most immediate
anxieties in him. She had no relatives or friends to visit
her, and by the end she felt God had deserted her. She could
find no place for God in a world in which her own life had
been ruined by a vicious cancer, and the lives of so many
thousands of children she had seen on television had been
destroyed by war and famine. Instead, Minnie's idea of the
afterlife was to imagine herself swept up by the elements
and absorbed by the seasons of the year. 'So when there's a
gale force wind blowing,' she said to me, 'you can say
' "That's Min up there".'

Dust in the Air Suspended

Cancer, it appears, is a condition which can often permit
patients to fight even as they begin to be reconciled to the
inevitable. Whether this combative stance finally improves
the patient's end of life is not always clear, but what is true
is that some are better placed to fight than others. Alan
Hunt was a man who had always been determined. His job
had been tough and physically demanding. When he faced
cancer, he also had the support of an extremely committed
and resourceful wife. Perhaps not surprisingly, they got
what they wanted. Minnie Dibley, on the other hand, was
on her own and much more vulnerable. As a society, we are
not usually aware of these differences because cancer is
largely invisible and we do not see one patient doing better
than another.

For those who have terminal cancer, the time of illness
often seems like a counterfeit version of life. They must wait
and see, and for as long as they do not feel ill, it may be hard
to take in that the disease is as active as their doctors

maintain. Ruth Picardie described this period as 'unreal' precisely because she continued to feel 'relatively well'.[10] These are conditions in which taboo thrives. The apparently good health of the person living with cancer becomes the pretext for avoiding the subject. After all, *why depress them when they are getting on so well?*

Difficult as it may be to judge when it is appropriate to broach the subject, however, those who care for people dying of cancer do need to talk openly with them. Most patients want to know the truth because it empowers them to plan their lives. The need for openness is urgent because many more of us will die before a cure is found. That will, of course, happen eventually. Cancer will be supplanted as a major killer in the same way that, early in the twentieth century, cholera, tuberculosis, smallpox and scarlet fever ceased to be the scourges of our towns and villages that they had been in Victorian times. But no one knows when or how the eradication will occur. Until then, it will increase.

But how quickly will attitudes change? Could there come a time when we are more comfortable with the idea of cancer and better able to discuss it? Will that happen only when scientific advances have been made?

Living with AIDS

Openness in the case of some terminal illnesses is made difficult by the prejudices which exist against them. People with AIDS are often isolated by their owns fears and embarrassment and by the hostility of the public. They are seen as dangerous and, in some way, morally deficient. In certain organizations, such as schools, they can even be regarded as a threat to the public good.

Acquired Immuno-Deficiency Syndrome, or AIDS, is not in fact a disease. In the 1980s, Susan Sontag was one of a small number of commentators who tried to insist on the recognition of this fact. She held up a flat hand of denial to the wave of prejudice and wild rumour that followed the discovery of a puzzling phenomenon that appeared to be killing off the male gay community in North American cities. 'It is the name of a medical condition,' Sontag wrote, 'whose consequences are a spectrum of illnesses.' In other words, AIDS was a predisposition, a vulnerability, an *immune deficiency*. Sontag went on to explain that the reason we conferred the status of 'disease' on AIDS was because we believed it to have one cause, whether in our panic we called that 'homosexuality', 'monkey glands' or 'God's punishment'.[11]

People were quick to latch on to the idea of a 'gay plague' and, despite the incontrovertible evidence worldwide that AIDS is communicated by heterosexual contact more than by any other single means, that association lingers. AIDS and the viral infection that can give rise to it, HIV (Human Immunodeficiency Virus), are popularly thought to have their provenance in wickedness, sexual deviancy and drug abuse. Occasionally, a voice is raised on behalf of another class of sufferer, the 'innocent victims', such as haemophiliacs; their AIDS, it appears, is the wages of others' sins. Furthermore, since AIDS is a form of punishment, the corollary is that there will be no recovery, no deliverance, no redemption. Physical decline and moral deficiency unite in a demonic death.

At the same time as there is no cure, there is no consensus about the cause of AIDS. It seems to have originated in sub-Saharan Africa and although AIDS did not come to the world's attention until 1981 – HIV not until 1983 – it must have been endemic there for decades. The millions of cases in that region testify to the depth and longevity of its grip on the African people, and the poverty of those countries largely explains the comparative tardiness with which they have responded to the crisis. Various epidemiologies have been adduced. Roy Porter, the medical historian, points out that in the 1970s the World Health Organization was vaccinating young Africans with live smallpox vaccine and 're-using needles forty to sixty times'. The potentially destructive impact of live vaccines is well documented; as Porter puts it, they can 'awaken sleeping giants such as viruses'. More recently, a book called *The River* advanced a similarly controversial theory that AIDS was started as far back as the 1950s. The author, Edward Hooper, shares Porter's belief that scientists were agents of its dispersal. Hooper claims that an experimental oral polio vaccine, contaminated with chimpanzee tissue, was administered to one million African people living in former Belgian colonies and that there is a correspondence between the demography of those vaccinated and the first known outbreaks of HIV 1m variant. Speaking on BBC Radio 4's *Today* programme in March 2000, Hooper argued that 64 per cent of the earliest AIDS cases and 82 per cent of the earliest HIV infections took place in the very same towns and villages where the vaccinations had been given over forty years ago.[12]

Hooper's critics maintain that the HIV virus is too unstable to have been transmitted in this way and that the presence of chimpanzee cellular material – which most do not dispute – is more easily explained. For those living around the African rainforests, chimpanzees have long been an important source of food and it is likely that hunters, over a period of years, were repeatedly bitten and infected. The virus was slow to spread, it is argued, until the late twentieth century when the medical use of blood transfusions and the escalation in drug-taking led to a rapid multiplication of cases.

To die from AIDS entails a more or less humiliating and painful degeneration of most vital systems. Common dysfunctions include shingles, diarrhoea, thrush in the mouth and genitals and blindness. To this can be added the neurosis that results from not being able to speak openly about it, a silence enforced by the fear of opprobrium. The writer Bruce Chatwin, for instance, invented a rare Chinese fungal illness to conceal his AIDS. Others have masqueraded as tubercular or as victims of cancer or multiple sclerosis; anything is better than AIDS.

'He died of a tropical disease in foreign parts'

In the 1980s and early 1990s, the ignorance about AIDS and the social pressure on its victims to conceal their condition were boundless. Dina McCullough's stepson, Stuart, died of AIDS in 1994. He was twenty-five. Not only had he been unable to reveal his HIV status to his family, he had also felt compelled to conceal his homo-sexuality, at least until his father died. Stuart had good reason to hide his feelings. Had his father known, he would have, according to Dina, 'thrown him out of the house and never supported him again.'

Stuart's mother had died when he was eight. When Dina subsequently married Stuart's father, Robert, she took on his two children, Stuart and his elder sister. Then Dina and Robert had two children, twin boys, of their own. They were a well-off Jewish family living in London's Hampstead Garden Suburb and from the moment Dina first saw Stuart, she adored him and took him everywhere she went. Stuart, even at that early age, had a very poor relationship with his father and he readily attached himself to his new step-mother. They became very close.

When Stuart was in his teens, around the age of fourteen, Dina became convinced that he was suffering from a deep-seated unhappiness. She attributed it to chronic grief, because he appeared not to have got over his mother's death even after six years. Dina pleaded with his father to let her take Stuart to a specialist, but Robert refused. It was probably the most serious error of judgement he ever made.

Four years went by. Stuart reached eighteen and in that year his father developed cancer of the liver and died within three months of discovering it. The shock of such a loss was difficult for the whole family, but on Stuart it seemed to have the effect of making him uncomfortable with the fundamental dishonesty at the centre of his life. He felt he had to come clean to Dina. During his confession, Stuart revealed that he had begun to realize he was gay at about fourteen, at precisely the time Dina had thought he was still struggling with his bereavement. In retrospect, Dina believes that at some level she probably suspected what was going on, but was not prepared to face up to it.

That autumn Stuart took up a place at Bristol University and became heavily involved in student politics. Whilst he was away, an audio tape turned up at Dina's house, addressed to Stuart. Dina assumed that it was something to do with his political activities, but something made her curious.

> As chance would have it, the package was open and it almost fell out, and it had a name on the label which I didn't know, and beside it was 'HIV', and I must have known because I thought, 'I'm going to keep this and I'm going to listen to it.' So I played it in the car and it was about how he felt about having HIV and I was deeply shocked by this, shocked because he hadn't told me.

The tape was an interview that Stuart had given, under a false name, to a radio station. He was clearly anxious to speak out about his illness and Dina is convinced that he kept it a secret from her because he was afraid that she would not allow him to come to the house and mix with the younger children.

To some extent, he may have been right. Dina did not lack sympathy, but like the majority of people in 1990, she lacked information. Stuart's condition deteriorated rapidly. By the time he'd got his First in finals, he had developed full-blown AIDS. Living in England, particularly in his stepmother's house, did not seem like an option to him, so he moved to San Francisco, where there was a gay community that could understand what he was going through. A number of his gay friends from home had also drifted over there.

Stuart's final trip home, shortly before his death, sums up the desperateness of his physical condition and the poignant ignorance of everyone around him. When he arrived at the family home in London, Dina was shocked by the state he was in. He was nearly blind and heavily dependent on various medicines for his day-to-day survival: 'He could barely see the salt on the table, and he had a huge bag of drugs with him. No one knew about AIDS then. When he passed his champagne glass to one of the twins, his sister took it away. Or we wiped the toilet seat. We really didn't know how to deal with it.'

Stuart understood that he could not stay, so he soon returned to California, where he died a few weeks later. None of his family was there at the final moment, and he was buried in San Francisco.

Dina and her children all felt that a stigma attached to Stuart's death. They could discuss what had happened amongst close friends, but they concealed the truth, as Stuart had done previously, from many of the other people they had to tell: 'For my mother's friends, we all said that Stuart had died in a car crash in America, because everyone was embarrassed. And the boys said, "I had a brother who died in San Francisco. He was a businessman out there."'

Dina is reconciled to the apparent necessity for secrecy at the time. In the climate of antipathy that obtained in 1994, when there was little chance of living with AIDS for very long, pretending that Stuart had died of something else seemed like the only way to avoid social disapproval and save his reputation. By saying that he had had a car accident, Dina elicited sympathy for her loss, and Stuart's death went down in history as a tragedy. Their fear was that if the truth were known, his death would be seen as just desserts, and much as we might like to think that we are more enlightened in the new millennium, the important difference is not that we are now more tolerant, but that people with AIDS are surviving longer.

It's not over yet . . .

There has been a tendency in recent times to think that medical science has contained AIDS, even got it on the run, at least in developed countries. Writing in the *Sunday Times* in November 1998, Andrew Sullivan, HIV positive himself, declaimed 'It's over', and the subtitle of his article referred to the new world of hope Sullivan had entered 'since drugs turned back the Aids plague'.

It is true that there has been, and with good reason, a paradigmatic shift in medical thinking and practice, from regarding AIDS as a death sentence to dealing with it as a treatable condition. That is not to say that a cure is just around the corner, but that palliative care of AIDS and HIV patients can both alleviate symptoms and prolong life. The evidence is persuasive. The triple cocktails of drugs and protease inhibitors – perhaps a combination of Ritonavir, Saquinavir and AZT – have meant that life expectancy has increased and it is now difficult to predict when a PWA (Person With AIDS) will die. The patient will have to take as many as two dozen pills a day and put up with a variety of unpleasant side-effects, but he or she may be able to sustain a life of some sort for years beyond the kind of predictions made in the early 1990s. Much depends on the individual's physiology and personality, still more on the avoidance of opportunistic infections and the continuing availability of effective drugs at affordable prices.

Furthermore, a number of indicative factors are emerging with sufficient clarity that scientists are now able to develop some experimental vaccines. Bacterial infections are, on the whole, swiftly treated with antibiotics because the bacteria are easily found; they occur outside cells. But in the case of a viral infection, the virus amalgamates with cells and is not so readily distinguished from them. The usual medical approach is preventative; a vaccine is given to stimulate the patient's immune system. The HIV virus is particularly elusive because it mutates rapidly. Development of an effective vaccine has, therefore, been made more difficult and protracted by HIV's restless nature.

There are clues, however. Some West Africans, for example, have a single gene mutation which makes it more likely that they will catch HIV, but after infection, it develops more slowly in these individuals than in other people. If the genetic constituent that retards development can be isolated, it could form the basis of a treatment. Moreover, at Oxford University, they think they are already close to producing an effective vaccine. A tiny minority of Kenyan prostitutes, though vulnerable to HIV infection, are immune to AIDS, and the aim of the Oxford vaccine is, according to Professor Andrew McMichael, to reproduce that immunity artificially by combining 'a DNA vaccine to stimulate an immune response, and a modified vaccinia Ankara (MVA) which amplifies the immune response.' This is all to the good, but it's a moving target. Drugs that hold the virus at bay today may not do so tomorrow, and whereas it was believed until recently that the drug cocktails would wipe the virus from the body, it is now apparent that it remains in the system. The drugs simply cause it to migrate from the blood into the brain and bone marrow.

Hope must lie in medical progress, however, and not in statistical evidence. Andrew Sullivan's article noted that the death rate from AIDS in the United States fell by 67 per cent in 1997. This was a remarkable step forward and, for the first time since 1992, AIDS took second place that year to 'Injury' as the principal cause of death amongst young American adults. In Britain, too, the rate was falling during the 1990s – 1,684 deaths in 1994, 364 in 1998, 369 in 1999; so too was the number of new HIV infections – down from 2,825 in 1998 to 2,457 in 1999. Whilst these statistics are encouraging, in that they demonstrate the capacity of advanced societies to meet the challenge of AIDS and begin to contain it, there are signs that the downward trend is not likely to be sustainable, let alone permanent. The problem turns on the protean character of the HIV virus and the careless behaviour that results from complacency.

The demographic profile of AIDS and HIV is changing, but it is no less dangerous. During 1998–9, 30 per cent of those newly infected with HIV in the USA were found to have strains of the virus that were resistant to the drug-combo therapies. The US death rate from AIDS is set to rise in the next few years, as is the rate of first-time infection. The incidence of HIV is rising most steeply in rural areas of America and the vast majority of these cases result from heterosexual contact. The same is true in Britain, which lags behind US developments by about three years. The government has predicted a 40 per cent increase in cases of HIV in England and Wales by 2003. 1999 had been the first year to show more people being infected through heterosexual than homosexual contact. Of the 2,457 new infections reported in Britain that year, 1,096 were amongst heterosexuals. The same trend continued in 2000, with an overall increase in new infections of 7 per cent, and in 2001 the number of reported new infections rose to 4,000, the majority again heterosexual. This suggests that many heterosexuals continue to feel that they are not at risk. Particularly worrying is the widespread ignorance amongst children. An article in the *Observer* in November 2001, reported that 40 per cent of British eleven-year-olds had never heard of AIDS.

AIDS has stood alone because of the public perception, which remains widespread, that its victims are in some way to blame for their condition. Sheila Cassidy summed it up in her foreword to *Why Me? Interviews with Seven People with AIDS*:

Nice people don't get AIDS, (though of course even we forget those poor innocent haemophiliacs). But everyone knows that you get AIDS by having the wrong sort of sex: perverted sex, or sex with the wrong sort of people. It's not the sort of thing you'd catch from your wife or your fiancée, you get it from prostitutes, from promiscuous men and women, people who've led dirty lives. The other way you get it is from needles, dirty needles shared at horrible, debauched parties or in dirty squats in decaying houses. AIDS people are simply not respectable.[13]

We are as a society dependent on the media to keep a public health concern in the forefront of our minds. No amount of parental admonition or NHS advertising will persuade people that they are in danger unless television and newspapers say so too. The combined effect of declining statistics, which render AIDS instantly less newsworthy, and a general ignorance about the sections of the community in which infections are growing, has made for complacency and an impression that, as Andrew Sullivan said, 'it's over'.

The truth is more sobering:

Even if current increases in new infections seen in many parts of the world could be stopped or reversed, morbidity and mortality will continue to increase for another decade as a result of the long latency period between infection and the development of the disease. Gains in survival achieved over the past few decades will, in some places, be cancelled out by the effects of HIV infection.[14]

AIDS is, in fact, the fourth biggest killer in the world. By 2000, a record-breaking year, 36 million people were living with HIV or AIDS. A report presented by the United Nations to mark World AIDS Day in December forecast further growth in infection worldwide and detected alarming upward trends in south-east Asia and the former Soviet

Union. It notes that in Latin America and the Caribbean, AIDS has already taken over from road traffic accidents as a primary cause of death.

Perhaps the most alarming projection is that 13 million women will be infected and that as many as 10 million children may become orphans as a result of their mothers' deaths from AIDS. When Sarah Rowland-Jones, a professor of immunology in Oxford, visited South Africa recently, she found that in the Durban area 40 per cent of the women attending antenatal clinics were infected, and in South Africa as a whole, 24.5 per cent of pregnant women are HIV positive. Women, it seems, are vulnerable, and they are likely to pass on their positive status to any child *in utero*. In Professor Rowland-Jones's opinion, it will take a whole generation to effect lasting change.

More than she bargained for . . .

One woman who passed on her HIV infection to her child was Anita Binns. I first met Anita in 1992, when I was directing a film for *Heart of the Matter*. The subject of the film was whether there were exceptional circumstances in which a man or woman could be morally justified in breaking his or her marriage vows. One example we gave was that of serious road accidents which result in severe head injuries and a tragic descent into a permanent vegetative condition. Such was the case with Anita's husband. When she was seventeen, Anita had married Glenn Binns, then a soldier, and had gone to live with him in Germany, where he was stationed in Munster with the King's (now Royal) Hussars. The accident occurred during the afternoon of 5 April 1989. Glenn was in charge of an army Land Rover, which went out of control. The injuries to his head and spine were extensive and beyond treatment, and Anita's life was changed for ever. She was three weeks pregnant and her husband was unlikely to survive more than a few months.

When we made the *Heart of the Matter* three years later, Anita was living in London. Each weekend she took their son, Glenn Junior, then two, on a five-and-a-half-hour coach journey to Lancashire in order to visit Glenn in the Leonard Cheshire Home at Stockport. Anita had fought with the doctors who would have allowed Glenn to die. She'd been set on his full recovery and still believed in the possibility of a miracle. With Anita's permission, and what she assured us was a sign Glenn had given her that he had agreed to it too, we filmed the two of them in the garden of the home. He was shockingly thin by comparison with the thickset soldier we'd seen in photographs. He'd become a paraplegic, moving very little and when he did with difficulty. He appeared to recognize Anita and she took this to indicate that they continued to have a special and intimate relationship. To an outsider like me, this was wishful thinking. His speech was virtually non-existent and it was impossible to distinguish his response to Anita from his behaviour with any of the numerous friendly nurses in the home. That said, Anita made a point of staying overnight with Glenn on occasion and, although there was no possibility of making love, that closeness of contact may have made a lasting impression on Glenn's shattered mind.

This was the man to whom Anita, in her own fashion, was faithful. Had it not been for her little boy, Glenn Junior, she believes she might never have come through after Glenn's accident. She didn't refer to suicide by name, but that was the clear implication.

By March 1995 all that had changed. We had decided to make a *Heart of the Matter Revisited* programme to mark the end of the series. I had always wondered what had happened to Anita and so we approached her a second time. She had moved with Glenn Junior to Garstang in Lancashire, to be near Glenn Senior. Glenn Senior's health had deteriorated and he had had to be transferred to another Leonard Cheshire Home, where they were better able to care for him. He could no longer swallow and he'd stopped even the non-descript, incoherent talking he'd managed three years before.

Anita was twenty-three at this point, Glenn Junior five. They dutifully went to see Glenn every day and Anita continued to sleep with him overnight, as she had always done. Her resolution to keep Glenn alive was now qualified by a tormenting thought that perhaps he wouldn't have wished to have survived this long. But still she maintained that she couldn't in good conscience let him die, even if objectively it might have been better for him.

Anita was much more in control of her life in 1995. She had her own home and was hoping to start training to be a social worker. Glenn Junior had started school and he too seemed to be settling into his new life. The two of them were very close indeed, and very open with one another. The proximity to Glenn Senior eased Anita's mind. She had a sense of its rightness. She tried hard to hold back the tears when she said to me:

> God brought us together for the right reasons. You can't change fate. I wish He could have made it a lot easier for us and I'll never understand why our time together was so short. But no, God has done as much as He could and I think we were very lucky we had Glenn Junior, very lucky. I'll always have a part of Glenn with me, whether Glenn is alive or not, I will always have part of us with us.

These were the closing words of the interview with Anita in the 1995 *Heart of the Matter*. They gave simple testimony to the love felt by a very brave woman for her tragically damaged husband. They were also a poignant valediction to her life as it was then. Only a matter of weeks later Anita's life was to change again, as dramatically and radically as it had the first time, after Glenn's accident.

In July 1995, Anita telephoned me and told me that both she and Glenn Junior were HIV positive. She believed that she could only have contracted it from Glenn Senior and she estimated that she had probably been infected at the time of their marriage or shortly before.

When I first went to interview Anita for this book in 1996, she had overcome the initial shock. Over most of the last seven or eight years she had given herself almost entirely to the cause of helping her husband, ensuring that he was properly taken care of and dedicating time to being with him that few men in his condition could have hoped for. In return, he appeared to have given her and their son death sentences. The discovery that she was HIV positive seemed like the most cruel betrayal. That Glenn Junior was too amounted to a crime. But Anita managed to overcome her anger and resumed her visits to the home. Interestingly, though, she'd come to believe that Glenn Senior should be allowed to die.

The story of how Anita and her son came to learn about 'their illness', as Anita calls it when she's talking to Glenn Junior, is heartbreaking. In retrospect, Anita thinks Glenn Senior knew that there was a danger their son would be born with HIV. She recalls him being extremely moody the day after she discovered she was pregnant. The new and alarming thought that Anita has had is that Glenn's crash might not have been an accident at all. She can only speculate, but she wonders whether Glenn was simply overwhelmed by his own sense of guilt.

Glenn Junior had never been well. From the age of eighteen months, he'd had a series of bad headaches, diarrhoea and glandular infections. His face would swell up and he developed a couple of lumps, which at first were thought to be mumps. That was the beginning of a long haul for little Glenn. No one could satisfactorily explain the weakness of his immune system. At Guy's Hospital in London, he was given whole body and brain scans. There was talk of cancer and a fungal infection in his jaw. By the age of three, it was clear his immune system was in decline and Anita was told that she could not expect him to live beyond twelve.

These were the circumstances when on 31 March 1995, after Anita had donated blood at a local donor centre, she received a letter from a doctor in Lancaster: 'It just said they had found major discrepancies in my blood, and to contact him as soon as possible and that I wasn't to discuss the letter or show it to anybody.'

She went to see the doctor. He explained that he had yet to complete his tests, but when pressed by Anita, he revealed his concern that she might be HIV positive. As Anita started to voice her worries about Glenn Junior, he tried to reassure her that if Glenn had been HIV positive from birth, they would have known by now. Guy's, Anita remembers him saying, is one of the four best hospitals in the country. If they think he's got cancer, then that's what he's got.

In the course of the next few days, Anita's HIV status was confirmed and Glenn Junior was tested at the GUM (Genito-Urinary Medicine) clinic in Garstang. When the results came through, the verdict was obvious to Anita from the clinician's face. She remembers kicking over the table in his office, before a friend persuaded her to take Glenn Junior home.

At the house, Anita could not find words to tell him: 'I just kept staring at him and he kept saying what's the matter, and I said nothing, nothing, I will tell you tomorrow.' Glenn went to bed, and it was then that Anita vented her anger in full.

Upstairs, in the back bedroom, I used to keep Glenn Senior's clothes and all his army memorabilia and bits and bobs. I remember opening the window and chucking them all out into the garden, and I threw my wedding ring out. I got all his photographs and all the letters he'd sent to me and I made a bonfire outside. One of my girlfriends came round and she said what's the matter, I've been trying to ring you all day. And I said if I tell you, you can walk away that's fine, but if you ever tell anybody else, I will kill you. I said me and Glenn are HIV positive and she just looked at me and she went thank fuck for that, and I went what, and she said at least we know you're not going to die *now* don't we? You've got a few years.

Glenn Senior was tested two weeks later and, as expected, he too was positive. But how did Anita know that it was Glenn who was responsible for passing on the HIV virus? 'I knew it because we had the test done before we got married and mine was negative at the time and the boyfriend I had previously was a virgin when I met him and for Glenn Junior to be infected, I was quite sure about it.'

Initially, this had provoked anger, but then, remarkably, she began to look at it from his point of view.

I didn't think I could ever face him again, but then once the anger had gone, and not understanding why or how he could have done what he did, I went to see him. It was hard seeing him face to face and then I thought what would I have done if it had been me. No one can really say and I could kick his head in and shout at him all day, but it wouldn't even register . . . And if you found out a few weeks before your marriage that you were HIV positive, would you honestly and truthfully say you would have told her?

This question was challenging enough in the days when AIDS was frequently reported in newspapers and on television. But the confessions of famous AIDS sufferers reconciled to their fates – Kenny Everett, Arthur Ash, Rock Hudson, Oscar Moore in his columns in the *Guardian* – have been succeeded by a new optimism and, paradoxically, a concomitant silence. The belief that 'it's all over' has had the perverse effect of turning the clock back, of reinforcing the hush that surrounds forbidden subjects. The last thing we discuss is the possibility of dying from AIDS.

Screaming in Silence

The problem with optimism of this kind is that it denies a hearing and a community of understanding to both those who are dying and those who wish to prevent the spread of the infection. In the 1950s, the same was true of cancer. People were expected to deal with their own more or less imminent deaths discreetly, without fuss, not burdening others with their suffering. This approach to terminal illness is now generally held to be destructive and cruel. Patients need time and willing listeners to explore their fears about their illness and the inevitable deaths that will follow. Many HIV/AIDS patients find themselves in the intolerable position of wanting to discuss what is happening to them and feeling unable to voice anything for fear of recrimination. This inhibits the possibility of reconciliation. As Margje Koster observed in her introduction to *Why Me?*, 'To go through the process of dying, whispering mysteriously about the cause of the illness until death, is unbelievably painful and makes it virtually impossible for the patient to accept their situation.'[15]

For Anita, in her private life, this has meant confiding in a handful of understanding friends and putting on a brave face to the rest of the world. 'If I turned round to 90 per cent of people and told them I was HIV positive, I would not see them again. Or me and Glenn Junior would have bricks thrown through the windows or paint rubbed all over your house.'

The expulsion of AIDS from our midst, the casting out of both the illness and those who fall prey to it, has led to what Kenneth Doka has described as 'disenfranchised grief'. Doka coined the phrase in 1989 to identify those who are excluded from the public process of grieving, including funerals, because society does not recognize their loss. He mentions the mistress who cannot call herself the 'widow' and the friends who are outside the immediate ring of family mourners. What Doka deplores are, in effect, vestiges of a code of conduct that has largely vanished, a code that made rules about who grieved for whom, and for how long and in what circumstances. In a more recent book, *Living with Grief after Sudden Loss* (1996), Doka reformulated his idea to extend its application from the accepted circle of mourning to the accepted circle of dying.

> Grief can be disenfranchised for a number of reasons. The relationship is not acknowledged (a friend or lover), or the griever is not perceived as capable of grief (a person with a developmental disability or a growing child). But there are also disenfranchising deaths, such as suicide or victim-precipitated homicide, where the very circumstances of the loss can complicate the survivor's ability or willingness to attract support. In certain losses, such as suicide, survivors may be ashamed to share their loss with others.[16]

AIDS is one such 'disenfranchising death' and the silence around it is manifested in all sorts of ways. Some funeral directors, for example, are unwilling to provide their services if they know the deceased has died of AIDS. For this reason, funerals are sometimes conducted as if the deceased had died of something else. No mention is made of it and, by implication, a fundamental part of the life that has ended is wiped from the family's memory. Many obituaries similarly fail to state the truth.

The impact of denial on the living is a brutal victimization. Not only is a PWA a pariah, but in some countries he or she may be barred from precisely the help they need. In France, there is a shortage of suitable palliative care units because, according to Marie de Hennezel,[17] the French have always opposed segregated care. 'No sanAID toriums' was a slogan of Le Pen's and its appeal is to precisely the kind of xenophobic constituency that tried to find the cause of AIDS in swine fever or a disease amongst green monkeys.

Children who have HIV from their mothers can also find themselves the targets of discrimination and bullying. A Channel Four documentary in 1998, *Playing Nintendo with God*, depicted a number of HIV kids in the western United States. Nearly all had become positive *in utero*. Despite their appearance on television, all were fearful of new people knowing their HIV status. They were afraid of teasing and isolation. One teenage girl thought death would be easier than the unending teasing she had experienced. Those children that didn't tease, it seemed, simply stayed away, afraid of 'contamination', which left many of the smaller children uncomprehending, lonely and in tears. They had been encouraged by their parents to believe that they were not a danger to others and yet encountered daily ostracism in the playground.

Perhaps the most poignant moments in Anita's story relate to the conversations she has had with Glenn Junior. The assumption that our children will grow up into adulthood and outlive us is deep-seated, even though it only came to be widely true in the twentieth century. Glenn Junior seems to have had an intuitive understanding of the inequality of good health and life expectancy. The fatalism he has displayed, in frank conversations with his mother, is doubtless informed by his own history of illness and what happened to his father. But one can also hear in his plans for death a kind of resignation that suggests a little boy who has never entertained very high hopes of life. It's possible that, after all his suffering, death holds a certain attraction.

There's something I have to tell you . . .

When Anita came to tell her child about his HIV positive condition, it was a Saturday morning. Generally, on a Saturday, she would take Glenn to a cinema and then on to a dancing class that he loved. On the Saturday following the diagnosis, however, Anita said she didn't want to go because she didn't feel well. Glenn wanted to know why. Anita then embarked on what was undoubtedly the most difficult conversation of her life.

> I said well you know them times you were ill and the doctors didn't know what to do and things like that. I said that's because we have got an illness that not many people and children get. But it only affects the people themselves and it's very hard to catch so don't worry, you can't give it to anybody . . . And he just looked at me and he said are we really ill. I said yes Glenn and I said I am not going to lie to you. I said the thing I can tell you is there is nothing anybody can do and we will die, and he said it's alright mummy, I'll get to see my cats again, won't I?
>
> He said will I die first or will you, and I said nobody knows. I said we are both as ill as each other, but if I die before you, don't worry, we will find you a new mummy and daddy and they will look after you and he said oh right. And he said well if I get to heaven first, I will build us a nice house and if you get to heaven first, you can get the house ready. He said I'm sure Jesus will help us anyway. That's just the way he has been about it all along. I just sat there. I just wanted to cry and I thought I daren't cry in front of him again today. So I went upstairs and I cried in the bath for an hour.

After his initial acceptance of their condition, 'our illness', Glenn became curious and later fearful in ways that Anita could never have anticipated.

> He kept asking questions about why his blood was bad and then he asked how do you get it, so I told him you get it from sex. And he said but I haven't had sex. That's why I explained to him he got it because he was in my womb. When you are a baby and you are in your

mummy's womb, you have all your mum's blood going into you. So if I've got an illness, the chances are the baby gets it . . . Then he looked at me and said so who did you have sex with then. I said with your daddy Glenn. He said oh right.

A child's acceptance that he or she must die is bound to be gradual and it will be marked by contradiction and reversal. Glenn Junior has often appeared to grasp what has happened to him only to forget a few days later what he had previously understood. Progress can be haphazard at times and Anita has had to show great patience with him. The finality of death sinks in very slowly and, in the case of a child, can be complicated by all sorts of eccentric fantasies that add to the child's already considerable torment.

When he has a bad night or whatever, I give him a massage, because I'm into that sort of thing. So he came downstairs and he asked me to massage him and he laid on the floor and put a towel around him and he just started crying, and I said what are you crying for, and he said when I die, will you tell them to make sure I am really dead before they put me on the cross. Because he thought you got put on a cross and I said Glenn they don't put little boys on crosses. I said they only did that to Jesus years ago because they didn't understand him and they didn't understand the things he talked about.

Although Glenn Junior's fears centre on the process of dying, some of his anxieties relate to what will happen after his death. Anita had arranged that they would be cremated and she was a bit taken aback to find that Glenn was strongly opposed. It may be that by focusing on ideas like crucifixion and cremation, Glenn Junior was trying to articulate a complicated intuition that his death might be preceded by considerable pain. Anita has never employed the terms HIV positive or AIDS in conversations with him – she believes he would only be confused by them – and she has chosen not to be explicit about what the last phase of the illness will be like.

For Anita, there is also the guilt of a parent who has passed on a terminal infection:

> I couldn't believe he'd never grow up or laugh at his first fumble in the bike sheds, his first girlfriend, his first job. I had taken all that away from him. It's a strange feeling being told you're going to die, but being told your child has the same illness is hard to explain. It takes all your confidence in yourself and self-respect. You feel so cold and alone because our illness is unacceptable to most people. I felt I couldn't tell or discuss it with anyone. I was ashamed. If it had only been me, I maybe would have ended it all, but I had to be there for my son, so I had to smile . . .

Sitting opposite Anita on a sunny morning in July 1996, it occurred to me that I hadn't asked about her current state of health and that of Glenn Junior, then aged six. I hadn't asked because she seemed to be a picture of health. She replied:

> Your CD4 T-cell count, which is what tells you what your immune system is, it should be up above 800 and mine is down below 50. They say the average age for living is 10 to 15 years, but at end of the day I have been infected for 8, so it doesn't leave that long really, and with Glenn Junior it's the same. On a child the count should be between 400 and 600 and Glenn is 18. So he is quite susceptible to infections.
>
> All I have really got is thrush that's in the mouth. It works its way down your throat, but when you are HIV positive, because your immune system is really low, it can infect your stomach, and they have to do

like a stomach washout with like an acid thing to get rid of it.

Glenn Junior suffers from thrush, in his mouth and he also has severe shingles on his bum and his penis. Shingles comes where he had chickenpox and that's the only place where he had chickenpox, on his bum. I don't think it will ever go away.

I asked Anita how Glenn copes.

Do you know it really doesn't bother him? I mean last night he got up about three because he had an accident and he was sat on the toilet for about half an hour with the runs, and he just cleaned himself up. I didn't get out of bed – he only calls if he needs me – I was listening, mind. I bought him bunk beds so if he has an accident he gets out of the top bunk, and he puts his sheets in the washing machine . . .

That will never go away, the incontinence. But he has huggies now, the pull-up and pull-down nappies. So there is less mess and he can control them. He doesn't moan or whinge. He knows his own limits, like Sundays he'll sit and eat chocolate all day, if he knows we are not going out at night time. If we have a 'doss day', he will eat anything he wants. But if we are going out, he won't. He will only have toast in the morning.

Anita has tried to ensure that Glenn Junior's remaining months or years are lived to the full. Later that year she spent £2,000 taking him on a special Christmas excursion to see 'the real Santa' in Lapland.

In March 1997, Glenn Junior took a dip and his weight went down from 3.5 stone to 2 stone. It looked as though he might not make it through, but he did, which was yet another indication of how peculiar and unpredictable this condition has become. Anita, too, had a crisis that year. In June, she became very ill and lost a lot of weight, which it took her several months to regain. She was prescribed combo-drugs – AZT, ddI, Zovirax and one or two others. In order to be given these, patients have first to undergo a 'viral load test'. This measures the amount of free virus in the blood. If it shows a reading of 10,000 or more it's worrying, because that means there are 10,000 copies of the virus in every millilitre of blood. Ideally, the viral load should be around 500. Anita's was 500,000. As of Christmas 1997, her immunity was rated at zero and she was classed as having full-blown AIDS.

Death itself seems to hold no horror for Anita, at least on her own account. She is sure of her place in heaven. What concerns her is Glenn Junior. If he dies first – as seems likely – Anita is 'scared of being without him'. They have had such a close relationship that she can't imagine a life in which he doesn't feature. Equally, she doesn't want to be the one to die first because although she has made detailed arrangements for Glenn Junior's fostering, she dreads the trauma he might go through at a time when he would be physically least able to cope with it. What you hear between the lines is that she is working through the process of final acceptance that she must separate from Glenn, at least for a while. This, in the opinion of people who work with AIDS and others terminally ill patients, is essential if death is to be accompanied by any degree of peace.

For those who are not morally outraged by it, AIDS appears to be an affront to the values we attach to human affection. The form of its mortality undermines the self-confidence not only of those who fall victim to it, but of everyone else too. When large numbers of young people die, as they did during the First World War, public self-esteem is sapped. AIDS similarly drains something from our collective vitality. It appears not so much as retribution as a reminder that we all have to die.

HIV and AIDS need to be placed more firmly within our circle of compassion. If immuno-deficiency is to remain with us as a terminal condition, it should be understood passively, as something that happens to the individual rather than as the punitive effect of an active and culpable cause. This is not to underrate the need for preventative caution. Just as we inoculate and wash our hands, safe sex and needle exchanges diminish the risk of infection. But we do not altogether ostracize the drinker, the obese or the smoker, with their much condemned habits and fatty diets, who now lie in hospital gasping with heart failure. They command our sympathy and our pity by virtue of their suffering.

This is a point Marie de Hennezel stresses in her account of those dying from AIDS in a French palliative care unit. In place of ugly and meaningless pain, she puts a view of death as enriching, the completion of the personality. It is hard to imagine the poignancy and pleasure of a warm bath administered affectionately by people unafraid to touch your broken body, when for months no one would even shake your hand. 'Anyone who is no longer touched by someone else,' de Hennezel writes, 'as is all too often the case with our AIDS patients, experiences this bath as the ultimate restitution of themselves, an ultimate recognition.' De Hennezel's account of her work in Paris is at its most moving when she describes her efforts to stay close to her patients, to give physical comfort to the emaciated body of a man weakened by AIDS, or hold another patient in a long embrace while his pustulous legs are dressed by a nurse. She emphasizes the need for 'haptonomy', the use of emotional and physical contact in the treatment of the dying, and she makes something touching and affectionate out of scenes that most of us would find repugnant to witness.[18]

Inclusion of those with HIV and AIDS within our circle of compassion is one test of a civilized community. Its results will be felt at all levels of action, from the provision of funds to research into treatments and an eventual cure, to an adequate network of care units in which people can die with dignity, to nurses giving warm baths, to acknowledging that a PWA is a PLU, a person like us.

Anita is not within that circle of compassion, and her display of resilience is misleading. She has 'black days', when she can be watching a comedy on television and suddenly find herself crying her heart out. For much of her life she has been busy caring for Glenn Junior, visiting Glenn Senior, working at her various jobs, or planning and giving talks for the Health Promotion Units of various hospitals. She hasn't really paused to think about her own condition. 'To outsiders,' she says, 'you're still Anita and you're still happy-go-lucky. But you're not inside. You're rotting away from the inside out.'

Glenn Senior died on 12 November 1998. Although the death certificate recorded that he had died of a chest infection, his HIV status was mentioned as a contributory factor. Anita has been unwavering in her loyalty to him. Twice since 1989 she has had the chance to establish herself and her son in a new family and each time she has decided against it, even though it has meant loneliness and the loss of emotional support.

When I spoke to Anita at the end of 2000, she was as cheerful and optimistic as ever. She made light of her poor immune system and the fact that her viral load score had continued to be 'disastrously high'. Since our last conversation, the combo-drugs, which on the face of it had sustained her in apparent good health for over two years, had started to give her dramatic and unpleasant side-effects. Her diarrhoea had become so debilitating that she'd lost two and a half stones and was forced to eat while seated on the loo. In March of 1999, she took the decision to discontinue them and, inevitably, Glenn Junior spotted what she'd done. He asked her permission to do the same and, having spelled out the risk to him and made sure that he fully understood what it might lead to, Anita agreed. The diarrhoea stopped and both of them gained weight and they went without drugs for a year and a half before their health began to deteriorate again.

By December 2000, they had both resumed courses of combo-drugs and felt better for them. Throughout the time that they have been ill, they have had to cope with the chicanes and reversals of HIV and AIDS, endeavouring to make their own sensible decisions in the context of what has been, at best, insecure medical knowledge. Glenn Junior's progress has been especially peculiar. His immune system, in September 2000, had returned to what his doctor termed 'normal'.

At that time, Anita had yet to place Glenn Junior in a secondary school. When it came to his primary education, Anita had found that the views taken by local head teachers were mixed. Some were liberal and informed, others bigoted. Interestingly, of the eight schools she considered for Glenn, none said that his AIDS was an obstacle to him having a place. But that does not mean that he had an easy ride. On the contrary, he was bullied, at times severely. On one occasion, two kids kicked Glenn in his testicles, and called him a poofter because he went to ballet classes. Glenn's penis was already swollen from his illness and so he had to be taken to hospital. Anita then moved him to a private school, where he was much happier.

Anita and Glenn Junior have relied heavily on each other to get through the discomforts and anxieties of AIDS. It is in their relationship that they have discovered the benefits of staying close, and of openness and honesty. They, like Alan and Janice Hunt, have managed to exercise some control over what has happened to them. Indeed, most of the people that I have talked to, who work with the dying in hospitals and hospices, argue that patients and their families do on the whole want to know about the nature of their illness and the course it is likely to take, and benefit from that knowledge in the long run. Discontinuing their drug treatment has very probably shortened Anita's and Glenn's lives, but it gave them a period of respite and happiness, which made it the right decision for them.

In their relations with the world outside their home, they

have had to be more guarded, and they suffer as a result. Anita has been prepared to speak in public to audiences she perceives to be at risk, but in general she is circumspect about the people she confides in. She can never know whether she will meet with sympathy or opprobrium. Glenn, too, keeps it from his friends and tends to avoid playing rough games that might lead to a cut or a graze. Their caution seems to be prudent. Three secondary schools refused Glenn a place on the grounds of his HIV condition and the head teachers' fears about 'snogging behind the bike sheds'. Whether this represents a decline in enlightened awareness, or the greater paranoia of secondary heads, is hard to determine. It added unnecessarily to the burden of worry under which Anita has struggled every day of her life. But then, as she says, she is lucky and surprised to have Glenn Junior alive at all. Choosing a secondary school was not a decision she imagined she would ever have to make.

Having failed to secure a place for her son, Anita decided not to inform schools of his condition when she applied. Not surprisingly, Glenn Junior was immediately admitted. In the autumn term of 2001, he signed up for a school trip, and Anita realized she would have to tell the school about his HIV status, if she was to let him go and not worry about him. The school seemed to take the news quite well, with the result that, in May 2002, Glenn Junior, a child not expected to live beyond the age of ten, set off on a hiking and mountaineering trip in northern France. Aged thirteen now, Glenn continues to defy all medical expectations.

3

The Gift of Hospice

The aim [for the patient] is no longer cure but the chance of living to his fullest potential in physical ease and activity and with the assurance of personal relationships until he dies . . . The achievement we will be looking for will be the patient's own.

Dame Cicely Saunders

The prospect of dying is inevitably suffused with sadness, for those who are about to die and for those who are about to be bereaved. None of us can know much in advance when it will happen, but if it should fall out that we are to die over a number of weeks or months, it is not hard to imagine that death will be made easier if we are confident that we were receiving the best care available. If we feel that our pain has been alleviated and that people still value us at this critical moment, we are likely to die with a greater acceptance and understanding. We may also, in these circumstances, be able to stay close to the people we love and benefit from their affection.

But what is the best kind of care for the terminally ill? Is it better for all those involved to accept the inevitability of death, or is there value in the hope of recovery? Should patients be sedated to subdue their suffering and their anxiety? Should they be fully informed of all there is to know? Or should they be cajoled into thinking things are not as bad as they seem? These questions are not easily resolved, but we do at least have a substantial body of professional advice to draw on these days. In the past, patients had to confront the pain and loneliness of dying with whatever fortitude and faith they could muster. To-day, they can benefit from the highly sophisticated techniques of palliative care, a method of ministering to the dying pioneered by the hospice movement.

Palliative care, understood simply as medical and nursing care that seeks to alleviate the symptoms of a disease without expecting to cure it, has a long history. It was, for example, the mainstay of nineteenth-century medicine. However, many of the skills of Victorian palliative care were displaced by the advances made in medical science during the middle years of the twentieth century. In its contemporary form, it is a specialization of relatively recent origin, not recognized formally until 1987, and at present there are only seven professors of palliative medicine in Britain. It has not been easy to introduce palliative care onto hospital wards, because the assumptions on which it is based conflict with the aims of cure and recovery proselytized by many consultants. As Dr Richard Hillier, Chair of the Association of Palliative Medicine, points out, the decision to recommend palliative care requires doctors to state with confidence that the patient is dying, and *that*, Hillier says, they are 'terrified of saying'.

Palliative care is, however, in the ascendancy. The number of units is growing all the time and, in principle, we should all be able to benefit from one. It is worth remembering, however, that these developments are the culmination of a long struggle between the advocates of modern life-saving medicine and the radical alternatives proposed by the hospice movement. To grasp what palliative care is about, we need only look at the work of today's hospices.

What Is a Hospice?

Hospice care attempts to palliate the experience of dying by means of a well-defined strategy of symptom control and a philosophy of care that attends as much to the emotional welfare of patients as their physical needs. It also seeks to develop a sensitive and intimate relationship between dying patients and their nurses and doctors. Cicely Saunders, the founder of the modern hospice movement, begins her book *Living with Dying* (1983) with a quote from Francis Bacon: 'I conceive it the office of the physician not only to restore the health but to mitigate pains and dolours; and not only when such mitigation may conduce to recovery but when it may serve to make a fair and easy passage.'[1]

It is an interesting injunction, not least because it demonstrates Saunders's wish to place the hospice approach to dying within a wider tradition of care, one which saw death as a transition to the next world and dying as a process to be managed collaboratively by patient and physician. Much of what Saunders has introduced into care of the dying is not new but the restitution of older practices, and in this quotation she hints strongly at the loss of skills and attitudes that she perceives in the modern practice of medicine. Her succinct summary of what is required of the hospice will strike a strange note in the ear of anyone who has observed the hour-to-hour business of an overstretched hospital ward. 'In our care for the individual in pain,' she writes, 'we try to be attentive to the body, to the family and to our patient's inner life.'[2]

The quality of peace that can be enjoyed by patients who are dying in a hospice, or receiving hospice care at home, is striking and very much in contrast to society's general expectations of death. Most of us anticipate that death will be a grim event. It lies out there waiting for us, and happiness is best maintained by ignoring it, not thinking about it. We expect that in our last moments, death will rush at us, 'a catastrophic, destructive force' bearing down on our fragile lives.[3] In a hospice, that fear is not so apparent. Walking around, you would not imagine that death had any place there, at least not death of the violent, destructive kind.

There are two distinct aspects to a hospice unit. One conveys the image of order, reassurance and homeliness that all hospices seek to project. The other reflects the grim truths about helping people die. Hospice buildings do not conform to a single design. They vary in style and quality and many are not purpose-built, but housed in whatever accommodation is available. Nonetheless, in Britain and in the United States, most in-patient units share essential features. They are light, clean, dry and warm. Flowers seem to be everywhere, or are judiciously arranged to give that impression. The single rooms or small four-bed wards are generally comfortable and well-equipped. There are rooms where patients can talk among themselves, meet their families or watch television. Above all, there is no sense of imminent tragedy, nor of it being a place where the sick and dying are kept out of sight of the rest of us. On the contrary, from the examples I visited, I gained an impression of the hospice as a place of good humour, of laughter and kindness.

To some extent, of course, this is a sentimental impression. Hospices are about managing, and sometimes ameliorating, the most difficult event in life. They seek to create a comforting atmosphere, without trying to mask death or pretend that it can be assuaged. As Dame Cicely Saunders says, 'Anyone who thinks that hospice is all sweet and nice, and nothing but hearts and flowers, just doesn't know what hard work dying is.' The trial of death must inevitably be exhausting and no amount of care will entirely overcome that. 'Hospices are actually very physical sorts of places,' says Andrew Knight, a director of hospice nursing. 'People are in extremis. People are dirty, people are dying. They aren't in control of their bodily fluids. You have to see beyond that to get a proper appreciation of the whole picture, of what we're doing.'

Whilst some people working in hospices are determined that we should not romanticize the methods and environment of an in-patient unit, it is self-evident that this care of the dying is, by and large, enriching for patients and staff alike. Far from being a charnel house, the hospice is a place where life is lived in its most vivid colours. Marie de Hennezel writes:

> I didn't know, that a place dedicated to receiving the dying can be the diametrical opposite of a house of death – that is, a place where life is manifested in all its force. I didn't know that it was the place where I would discover my own humanity, or that I would in some fashion plunge into the very heart of human life.[4]

The results are persuasive. Eileen, a cancer patient at the Marie Curie Hospice in Liverpool, was reminiscing about the deaths of her mother and a great friend when I met her. She'd fought cancer for thirteen years, but it had finally entered her lymph glands and her bones and she expected to die soon. This appeared not to worry her. She said she was entirely content with her environment and the people looking after her, so much so that she could muse on death without evident anxiety about her own. Part of Eileen's contentment came from having sorted out what dying meant to her. She'd decided on a cremation and she was looking forward to meeting the spirits of her mother and her brother in the 'afterlife'. She'd emphasized to her daughter that after her death, her hair was to be made 'nice' and her nails 'done'. Her daughter laughed at this and said, 'No one will see you, Mum.' But Eileen was adamant.

These might seem trivial considerations, but another way of describing Eileen's plans would be to say that she had resolved her spiritual beliefs, planned her funeral and given thought to those who were going to be left behind and who would see her when she was dead. Would she have been as well prepared for dying without the benefit of a hospice? What is beyond doubt is that a proper regime of drugs ensured that she was not in pain and that her other symptoms were under control. She could very easily have been in agony or, had the drugs been irregularly administered, alternating between pain and extreme disorientation. As it was, she was not suffering and the attention of the staff and her relatives did much to alleviate loneliness. She was – if this is a credible notion – happy to die.

The Origins of 'Hospice'

Cicely Saunders recalls that 'there was no provision for the acute and difficult dying in the health service until hospice came along.' In its twenty-first-century form, it is no exaggeration to say that the hospice has been Saunders's creation. In applying the word 'hospice' to her modern institution of caring, she was invoking a tradition dating back to the fourth century, when Christians offered food, shelter and a degree of healing to their *hospes*, guests who were strangers or, often, pilgrims. 'Hospice', with its connotations of 'hospital' and 'hospitality', is beautifully judged. We have tended to separate these meanings, but historically they belong together. Hospitality, the friendly entertainment and looking after of visitors, was always a function of the 'hospital', a place of healing. The famous hospital of Jerusalem, founded by the Knights Hospitallers of St John in AD 1100, combined cordiality with ministration to the sick and dying. As Margaret Manning has noted in *The Hospice Alternative*, these 'hospice-type units' flourished in the middle ages. During the Crusades, there were thirty of them in Florence and forty in Paris. Manning believes there may have been as many as 750 in Britain, but most were fatefully dependent on monastic orders for their funding and therefore went into decline after the Dissolution under Henry VIII.[5]

These early hospices were as interested in the diseased as the dying, and it was not until 1879, when Our Lady's Hospice for the Dying opened in Dublin, that the hospice – at least in the British Isles – came to be understood as a place specifically dedicated to the care of the dying. Our Lady's Hospice was, in fact, the first of a number of institutions created by Victorian or Edwardian philanthropists to look after the dying. In part, they were a response to the widespread practice of discharging incurables from hospitals. Whilst the prosperous and the upper classes might be nursed at home, there was little or no provision for those who were dying and poor, apart from the much-hated workhouses and Poor Law infirmaries. In London, St Luke's House, opened in 1893, set out to provide a comfortable shelter for 'the respectable poor of London', men and women of the middle class who had lost whatever wealth they had and faced death in poverty. The age of these terminal patients was shockingly young. In 1896, the average for male residents was thirty-four and, amongst women, it was forty-three. Most were dying from TB or cancer.[6]

Another London home which used the term hospice was St Joseph's Hospice, opened in the East End in 1905. It was run by Catholic nuns belonging to the Irish Sisters of Charity and it was the Mother Rectress that decided who was to be admitted. St Joseph's was concerned to relieve the patients' physical distress, but it had as its primary objective to save their souls. The sisters spoke of 'soul cures', bringing patients back to God. Pain was seen to be not only the will of God, but a contributory factor in advancing the patients' spiritual readiness.

These were early attempts, in recent history – what Clare Humphreys terms 'stepping stones' – to revive concepts of a wider care than was conventionally available in hospitals. In the 1950s, certain hospice ideas were incorporated into the care provided by the Marie Curie Homes, but it was not until 1967, when Dame Cicely Saunders founded St Christopher's, that the hospice as we know it today was created. Although it has now become a teaching hospice, as well as an internationally renowned research centre, St Christopher's continues to give care to the terminally ill of Sydenham and nearby areas in south London. It has fifty beds and admits over 1,000 people a year into residential care. In addition, the nursing staff make over 10,000 domiciliary visits as part of a twenty-four-hour, seven days a week home service. Overall, the hospice looks after about 1,600 patients through its various schemes.

St Christopher's was the culmination of years of writing, lobbying, organizing and fundraising. Saunders wrote her first article on the care of the dying in 1957, when she was a medical student, and much of what she wrote about came out of an earlier experience of caring for a dying Polish emigré, David Tasma, whom she'd nursed in 1948. When he died, he left her a legacy and the thought: 'I will be a window in your home.'

The growth of the hospice movement over the last thirty years has been remarkable. In 1969, there were only seventeen in-patient units. By 2000, this number had grown to 220. In 1969, there was one home care team operating in England and Wales, and that was based at St Christopher's. By 2000, there were 367.

In the United States, the development of hospices since they first opened in 1973 has been equally rapid. There are now a staggering 3,139 hospice programmes nationwide, most of them funded by non-profit-making private companies. But the approach in the USA is slightly different as 97 per cent of hospice care takes place in patients' homes. Across the country, there are fewer than 200 in-patient units, one-third of which (according to the National Hospice Organization) offer only acute services. The day hospice, a concept which is highly developed in the UK and which allows the patient to receive care for a few hours at a time, is scarcely known in the USA. Furthermore, American medical insurance schemes have very tight regulations regarding whose hospice care they will and will not pay for. To gain entry to a hospice programme, an insured patient must have six months or less to live. This condition tends to discriminate against patients with diseases that are difficult to predict. The advent, for example, of effective combo-drug therapy in the treatment of HIV and AIDS patients has led to longer life, but it has also meant that fewer hospice beds are now available to such patients.

Clearly, the hospice approach was an idea whose time had come. Nonetheless, awareness and use of hospices is not necessarily routine, either in Britain or the United States. Hospices in Britain tend to serve the white middle class, who make up 90 per cent of all hospice patients. At present, only 4 per cent of all deaths in Britain occur in a hospice, and of those dying from cancer, less than 20 per cent die in hospice care.

The situation in the USA is better, although the improvements made there have been recent, and the take-up today is largely a result of outreach work done by nurses and social workers in the nineties. When I visited the Hospice of Washington in November 1997, only seven of the nine in-patient places were taken and the monthly average was around five or six. The hospice also had the capacity to care for fifty in the Home Programme, but that autumn there were twenty-five on the books. By 2000, all that had changed. Local physicians had begun to lose some of their hostility to the hospice movement and to recommend hospice care to their patients. The monthly average had risen to eight and a half, which was full capacity in practice, according to director Matthew Kestenbaum. The upper limit for the number that could be cared for in the Home Programme had been scrapped, and in December 2000 they were looking after thirty to forty patients. Nationwide, it is now estimated that between 25 and 30 per cent of people are served by a hospice.

The Hospice Approach

The medicine Cicely Saunders has consistently objected to is macho and quasi-heroic. It regards doctors as life-savers. They present themselves as skilled professionals, possessed of an expertise that cannot be shared. They know the biology of their patients better than the patients themselves, and consultation is therefore a matter of courtesy, not necessity. They will continue treatment even when they know that patients are dying and they will re-admit the dying to acute wards when it is clear that they can do no good. It is an autocratic approach, which demeans the patient and marginalizes the family. The consequence is that when death does occur and the hero has not saved the patient's life, it is seen as a failure. 'Our patients don't die,' said one doctor. 'They just fail treatment.'

Dr Sara Miller, at the Cancer Help Centre in Bristol, thinks doctors have also lost a bit of the 'heart' they used to have and replaced it with clinical procedure: 'The doctor used to go and sit by the bedside and hold people's hands and be much more aware that that was part of a life process. That's been lost. Very often the doctor says "There's nothing more that can be done," and that's the end of the doctor's role.' The implication is not merely a death sentence, but that the patient's life is already over.

The doctor's sense of defeat, possibly of embarrassment, affects the regime of the hospital. When a patient is told he is dying, a silence falls on the ward. Eyes are averted. People hurry past the patient's bed more swiftly than they did. The patient may then be neglected or given inadequate pain relief. 'We often fail the people who die in hospital,' says Dr Miller. 'People have to die on a busy ward. Nobody has time and they have to die in a corner somewhere. It's noisy and busy and they're tucked away and nobody's being with them.' And when death is imminent, a discreet curtain is drawn around the bed and the body has vanished by morning.

This, according to Julia Wootton, Medical Director of St Nicholas's Hospice in Suffolk, is the terrible indictment of a profession that long ago ceased to see the care of the dying as part of its function. Wootton says:

> The modern day hospice movement developed in response to a medical profession which, because of such developments as antiobiotics and anaesthetics, leading up to your transplants and what have you, no longer peceived death as being its remit. You literally had doctors who, as soon as they had finished their acute treatment, washed their hands of the patients . . . They'd completely forgotten that everything a doctor did in the nineteenth century was palliative.

The hospice movement rails against these practices, and insists that patients who are in the final stages of dying are nonetheless alive. Instead of death being regarded as a taboo, a tragic denial of life, the hospice tries to naturalize it and integrate it into life. Doctors and nurses go out of their way to spend time with their dying and often apprehensive patients, and to discuss with them any anxieties they may have concerning their illnesses and the approach of death. The hospice clearly empowers many who would otherwise feel helpless and without worth, and through careful attention to their needs, develops their confidence. De Hennezel quotes Lacan's memorable statement: 'It is someone else's gaze that brings me into being.' Time taken by a nurse to pause and smile can restore life to the dying.

One of the important fears of dying is of losing control, particularly physical control. The reality of death from cancer is ugly and involves symptoms which can be acutely distressing. Anorexia, vomiting, constipation or diarrhoea, incontinence, urinary infections, fungating growths, dehydration, breathlessness: any or all can occur. But with hospice care most of these can be brought under control and nearly all patients can be made significantly more comfortable. If a dying patient can be assured that most symptoms can be treated and that it is not a humiliation to smell or weep or have a catheter fitted, the spectre of death begins to shrink.

Cicely Saunders was convinced that the greatest fear amongst the dying was the fear of pain. She conceived of a 'total pain', which was continuous and sapped the patient of all his strength. This kind of pain is without value: it has no function within a healing process. Saunders observed that patients at St Christopher's spoke of 'the implacable heaviness of pain' and of feeling no better than 'some kind of scrap heap'.[7] It was also noticeable that the fear of pain and its intensity were directly related to previous experiences of uncontrolled pain. Fear of that happening again would intensify the new pain and larger doses of drugs were therefore required to subdue it. The cycle of pain became a trap.

The subversion of pain must be an ingredient of any good death. Although historically pain has been regarded as redemptive, its prolonged erosion of patients' energy and spirit makes it impossible for them to manage their suffering or accomplish any degree of peace. The hospice approach rightly sees pain as an interference, something that gets in the way of the patient fulfilling his last days and finishing the business of life. 'With pain controlled, they can think,' says Molly Sherwood, a staff nurse at the Hospice of Washington (DC). 'They can think about other things, like wills, funerals, tapes for the grandchildren, saying goodbye, and especially the afterlife.'

As late as 1983, Saunders's anger at hospitals which failed to understand the use and effectiveness of pain-killing drugs in the treatment of cancer trembled through her writing. She remembered being outraged by a medical student who proudly announced: 'In our hospital patients *earn* their morphine,'[8] a concept apparently based on the concern that terminally ill patients might become addicted! Saunders has always maintained that if morphine is 'given regularly and with a slightly relaxed schedule so that no one is obsessively clock-watching and at a dose that covers the extra period of relief that may be required should a dose be delayed, then pain can be forgotten and the self-perpetuating spiral of misery and dependence is not initiated.'[9] There is no ambiguity here. Pain can be *forgotten*. If the hospice movement had achieved nothing else, the effective management of pain would have gained it an honoured place in medical history.

Patients are admitted to a hospice on the recommendation of a GP or a consultant, and it continues to be a sensitive subject. It is vital that the proposed referral is broached in the right way, because the first mention of a hospice can be alarming. Joan Patterson, a cancer patient in Bury St Edmunds, told me that she was extremely loth to accept a place at St Nicholas's Hospice when it was offered. She had a history of cancer stretching back ten years to a lumpectomy in 1991. She was reasonably well after that until the late nineties, when she developed a second lump. A further lumpectomy was done, then a mastectomy and radiotherapy. In November 2000, she was getting back trouble, which proved to be caused by a tumour on her spine. As far as Joan was concerned, it had all occurred very quickly, one event rushing upon another. When in December it was suggested that she go to a hospice, it came as a shock. 'I was absolutely petrified. They came to talk to me, the people from the hospice, on Day Two, just after the diagnosis, and that was far too quick. I mean, I hadn't accepted the fact that I had a tumour in the bone anyway, and they were too fast.' Joan was convinced that they were telling her that she would be put into St Nicholas's and only allowed out in a box.

Although much has been done to publicize the work of hospices, there are still lingering beliefs that these are places where you are taken to die and that, once in a hospice, you never emerge again. That was, of course, true at one time, but it is more and more common now for the dying first to spend a few days in hospice care to receive treatment that will stabilize their condition. In this way, they can be introduced gently to the environment in which they may well subsequently spend their last hours.

In fact, Joan Patterson settled in at St Nicholas's very quickly. When she talked to me in February 2001, she couldn't praise the hospice and its staff highly enough.

It's wonderful. The care is wonderful. It's luxurious. At Addenbrooke's you had about three nurses to I don't know how many patients. You've got three nurses to five patients here. The food they serve up on a tray with a cloth. It's all the little extra bits that make it pleasant. You've only got to move and they're at your side. In Addenbrooke's you might have to wait five or ten minutes.

When patients are dying, they will on average, stay for thirteen days (eight days in the USA) and in that time the staff are expected to try and 'get alongside' them. They meet at a moment that is quite different from the rest of life, and they may come to know each other more thoroughly than would be possible in almost any other circumstance. For Marie de Hennezel, the secret of people who are dying is that they experience 'eternal time within everyday time'. They have become more attentive to the world and to people, which makes them savour every moment. They are able to stand still and listen to 'the soft rustling of existence'.[10] The phrase is inflated with gallic charm, but its value lies in the recognition that the quality of relationship between staff and patients in a hospice is not easily measured by conventional criteria.

In the few days available, the hospice staff will be asked to sustain the patient's hope and to gain his or her trust, to be sensitive to the family's distress, and to have the self-possession to know when all that can be done has been done and that it is time to stand back and take a break.

Hospice care is unlike much of the rest of medicine in this commitment to the individual's emotional welfare. It is not about professional detachment, but about professional engagement and the staff of any hospice expect to be distressed from time to time.

A Fair and Easy Passage

Is the hospice trying to blur the division between life and death? The idea of death as a rite of passage is commonly applied to funerals and disposal of the body, to the experience of bereavement as well, but less often to the process of dying. Yet it is a pertinent phrase. Patients do seem to benefit from seeing dying as a transition. It implies that the patient need not see life and death in a permanent opposition. There is a congruence; the two are interrelated.

Elisabeth Kübler-Ross, the Swiss-born psychiatrist who (in the footsteps of Cicely Saunders) pioneered hospice care in America in the early 1960s and 1970s, famously devised a five-stage description of how the individual moves through that transition and comes to an eventual acceptance of death. She emphasizes that the theory is a groundplan of common experience. Patients may go through all the stages or none, may begin and not finish. They may find one or two more important than others, and some they may repeat.

The five stages are:

(1) **Shock and denial** This is what Elisabeth Kübler-Ross paraphrases as the 'No, not me' stage, when the overwhelming shock of grief at losing life is too acute to be rationalized, and the patient will react with horror and denial. This stage is sometimes compounded by a doctor's denial. He may decline to discuss dying with his patient and their shared denial becomes inhibiting. Nevertheless, for most, it is a significant and unavoidable phase, during

which the patient adapts. For others, it can last until death itself, and the hospice philosophy is that this should be respected too.

(2) **Rage and anger** Kübler-Ross calls this the 'Why me?' stage. It's also the 'Why now?' stage. During this phase, patients will often rail against doctors and nurses. But Kübler-Ross believes these outbursts are based on envy. The conspicuous good health of doctors and nurses will 'rub in what the patients are losing'.

(3) **Bargaining** This stage marks out some progress towards acceptance. It is a time when patients put their houses in order. They will make financial arrangements and may be able to resolve old problems with relationships. They write their wills and make plans for care of their children. All this is constructive, but alongside it will often run the need to bargain with God for a little extra time. This might be 'until my daughter has graduated' or 'until my grandson is born'. All too commonly patients will hang on until a particular event is past but, then, they quite naturally want to rene-gotiate terms. 'The promises these patients make, they hardly ever keep,' writes Kübler-Ross. 'Mothers are most difficult when it comes to bargaining; they rarely keep their promises. They ask God to allow them to live until their children are out of school. The moment the children are out of school, they add the prayer to stay alive until the children get married.'

(4) **Depression** Following, as often happens, so closely on a phase in which acceptance seemed likely, depression can only appear as a set-back. Kübler-Ross observes two kinds of depression. The first is focused on tangible losses – home, job, children, spouse – but the second is, in a sense, more personal. It is about future loss, what it will be like to lose life itself. Men have a harder time of it during this phase of preparatory grief, notably because they are less accustomed

to crying and not comfortable about it when they do. Above all, this phase requires supportive care. You can't simply buck up.

(5) **Acceptance** Acceptance is fundamentally different from resignation. Resignation represents a surrender of interest and effort. Acceptance, on the other hand, is the active achievement of a full contentment, inner and outer peace.[11]

Hope and the Centrality of Relationship

Although Elisabeth Kübler-Ross does not insist that these are necessary stages through which the dying must pass, it seems to me that the third stage represents a turning point on which the whole process pivots. Kübler-Ross calls it 'bargaining', when the patient is pleading with God to be allowed a little more time in return for accepting that death is imminent. It is a *quid pro quo*. More straightforwardly, this idea might be understood as the need for hope.

None of us can live without hope and no definition of a good death would exclude it. But the confusion between hope and recovery is widespread and it exacerbates the neurosis of death. Many patients who intuit that they might be dying cling to any hope of recovery. It is a kind of hope that is rooted in denial. But that hope can be transformed into another, a hope that can sustain and uplift the terminally ill after it is clear that recovery is impossible. When the treatments have not worked and the prognosis is that the patient will die, hope needs to be re-thought and applied to new objectives that are realistic. Hope is not, after all, grounded in wild fantasy; it is a form of optimism about a future which is possible and may be realized. It is the 'expectation of something desired', or 'desire combined with expectation'. In other words, real hope inhabits the realm of reason, and not of fantasy and miracle, and whilst it plays an important role in the good death, it has to change as we die. What begins at the moment of diagnosis as the hope of a new medical discovery, can become a hope that a teenage grandson will succeed in his ambition to be a doctor, though the dying patient may not live to see it.

Hope becomes a function, paradoxical as it might seem, of acceptance. It prospers when pain is controlled and the patient can enjoy a relationship with others, when there is occasional laughter and when others engender in the patient a sense of being valued. Research done by Rod MacLeod and Helen Carter shows that 'Caring behaviours such as thoughtful gestures, being friendly, smiling and addressing people by their names were the extra small "touches" that personalized care and enhanced hope.'[12] Essentially, hope is a dynamic of relationship.

Telling the Truth

Finding meaning in life, realizing that one's life has been of significance, can produce a profound peace and a sense of acceptance. But acceptance can only really occur in the context of a general commitment to truth. Whether patients should be frankly appraised of their condition is a vexed issue in professional medicine. The current debate focuses on what is said, when it is said and to whom. The reluctance to give patients distressing news reflects a paternalistic attitude rooted in the widespread misconception that openness with patients demoralizes and discourages them; the truth, it is argued, will take away their sense of the future.

Pat Jalland's study of the Victorians suggests that, in the nineteenth century, frankness between doctors and patients was much more common. The advice of *The Lancet* in the 1880s was to place the best possible construction on unfavourable symptoms for as long as there was hope of the patient's survival. In the event that death was inevitable, however, a plain statement of the truth was required.[13] This practice seems to have declined as the century came to its close and by the 1960s, when Cicely Saunders was developing her theories about how to care for the dying in a hospice, it was by no means usual for doctors to make a full disclosure to patients. One GP, who was sent a discussion paper by Saunders on how a hospice should be run, objected to the idea of telling patients about their condition; he had found 'the very reverse to be effective'.[14]

The problem that this lack of candour poses for those involved in palliative care is that it engenders denial. Doctors, from kindly but misguided motives, have considered it better to keep the patient's hope alive by encouraging the belief that they will recover. When it is evident that the condition is irreversible, the patient may be shipped off to a hospice, where the hospice staff have to pick up the pieces. Patients will often quarrel then with the gentle truths put to them. If the consultant in the hospital said they would get better, what right has the hospice doctor to say otherwise?

Averil Stedeford adds to the ethical and compassionate reasons for disclosure a number of specific circumstances in which it is essential for the patient to know he is dying. The patient and his partner might be planning a family, or treatment may be urgently required, which the patient might reject if he hasn't grasped the absolute necessity for it.[15] The consequences of patients and families not being informed can be tragic. However painful the knowledge of imminent death might appear, it can, as has been noted, generate a sense of freedom and afford irreplaceable time in which patients and their families can adapt and rehearse their eventual parting. False hope can be devastating, as Dr Caroline Anson found when she admitted to the Hospice in the Weald a man with a cancer he thought he could beat. She was unable to be entirely frank with him because he was, strictly speaking, in the care of another doctor, who had taken the decision not to reveal the truth to his patient.

We have this young man, who died last night and who had had chemotherapy for a tumour that isn't sensitive to chemotherapy. He'd been sick for ten days after each treatment and I said that he should ask his oncologist what benefit he was supposed to get and whether feeling ill for ten days out of every three weeks was reasonable. It was not well received. Our social worker went to see the wife and children and they'd clearly been very upset about my message, because chemotherapy was 'his only chance'. But he had no chance. He died last night and that was the first his wife knew that he was dying, and I think that is disgraceful. You know they could have had two months and they could have used that time, used it better than dreaming on. Even last night his wife was saying to the nurse that she hoped he would be well enough for his chemotherapy later in the week and the nurse felt all she could say was that she thought he wouldn't be.

That man's wife and children were shocked by the apparent suddenness of his death and, in consequence, unprepared for the grief that was to follow. For this reason, amongst others, it has become axiomatic that hospices will not now withhold the truth if they are asked for it. Ellie Bennett, ward coordinator at St Nicholas's, is often confronted by people who insist that the patient should not be told the whole truth. Ellie is gentle, but firm:

We always carefully explain that while we won't go out of our way to tell him he's dying, if he asks us questions, we must answer them honestly, and we have found through experience that it usually eases the situation between patient and family if there is open and honest communication about what is going on. Some are quite angry about that, but it's sort of misplaced anger. People are angry that their loved one is dying. It comes out in all kinds of different ways, projected into other situations, but we'll usually find after a few days, once we've got alongside them and

they can see how we work, that they will come round
to our way of thinking.

Some doctors protest that their patients cannot cope with
the knowledge of their own imminent death, but the
experience of Cicely Saunders and others is that patience
and time spent with a patient will clearly reveal the extent to
which he or she understands how things are and wishes to
know more. 'Clues are given,' Saunders says, 'as we listen
to questions and to silences and observe a patient's choice
of time and listener for his comments and queries.'[16] The
patient, by various signs and gestures, can increase or
restrict the flow of information if he wants to. It may be
that a patient who is tentatively admitting to himself that he
might be dying, will seek reassurance that he will live. *I'll be
all right, won't I, doctor?* can be a cue for the beginning of a
series of progressive discussions, at the end of which the
patient will have grasped that recovery is impossible. In
other words, it is not that full disclosure should be offered
at once in all cases, but rather that each case has to be
assessed and a careful judgement made about how quickly
the patient can be brought to an understanding of his
situation.

There will be a minority of patients who prefer to remain
in ignorance of their condition and who benefit from their
'unknowing' or denial. Doctors and families alike fear, quite
naturally, that disclosure will be demoralizing. If a patient
does not avail himself of opportunities to ask questions,
there may be good reason for supposing he does not wish to
know more. On the other hand, the decision to withhold
information tends to ignore the nature of terminal illness. A
patient's decline will be more or less slow. There will be
ample time for deliberation on the illness. More importantly,
relationships will continue with relatives, who may betray
what they know or, by the frequency and quality of their
visits, arouse suspicion. The overwhelming weight of evidence from surveys is that both the patients and their

relatives want to know that the patient is dying if that is the irrefutable case. What Elisabeth Kübler-Ross calls the 'all is well' approach, when 'we visit terminally ill patients only with a smile on our face and cheerful, superficial conversation or silence,'[17] is inappropriate and out of date.

The onus of disclosure falls, inevitably, on the patient's doctor, but the acceptance of that responsibility is only slowly being acknowledged. From a survey reported in 1981, it was clear that most patients gained their information from the hospital staff, fewer from GPs. A larger proportion 'knew' intuitively, but had not been told by anyone. Far exceeding all these groups who knew something about their condition was the majority, who knew nothing. Of course, most of these results are garnered from interviews with patients and denial is such a potent weapon in the patient's defences that it is possible patients are told things that they later deny they have been told. Saunders examined admissions to St Christopher's Hospice during 1977 and found that 22 per cent of patients admitted to the hospice, and who had ostensibly been fully appraised of their prognoses whilst in hospital, had no knowledge of their condition when interviewed by hospice doctors. Had they been told? Or were they rejecting the truth because it was too awful to accept?

Clive Seale and Ann Cartwright conducted surveys of a similar kind in 1969 and 1987. By 1987, a very high percentage (81–3 per cent) of GPs, community nurses and doctors in hospitals said they preferred patients with a terminal cancer to be aware that they were dying. But the willingness to inform was largely lacking. Although Seale and Cartwright concluded that there had been a trend towards a greater openness, they noted that 57 per cent of doctors in 1987 were more likely to discuss prognoses with relatives as opposed to 17 per cent who consulted patients. Almost half of the GPs they interviewed found it 'difficult', or 'rather difficult', to handle the distress of patients and their relatives. Britain compared unfavourably in this respect with the United States, where 98 per cent of cancer patients were then being told of their conditions by their doctors.[18]

Seale and Cartwright made a distinction between diagnoses and prognoses. There was an improved willingness amongst doctors in 1987 to tell the patient what was wrong, but it did not follow that doctors were prepared to say that patients would die. Perhaps their most surprising finding was that most of the people they interviewed said that what had happened, irrespective of who had told what to whom, was *for the best*. 'It may be,' Seale and Cartwright commented, 'that responses are influenced by a desire to perceive events in a favourable light.'[19]

More recent research, conducted by Dr Fellowfield at the Royal London Hospital and reported in *The Lancet* in 1994, showed that 95 per cent of patients with cancer want to be given all the information there is about their condition and prognosis, for good or bad. Yet some doctors are still not persuaded that patients should be given the full picture. They remain willing to provide a diagnosis, but chary about forecasting death. Time and again, people working in hospices have told me of doctors who have asked them in desperation: 'What do I say?' The answer that comes back from patients is simple. By and large, they wish to know what is wrong with them, what the future is likely to hold and what medicine can do for them. But the absence of agreed practice has meant that patients have often been told too much too early or too little too late. One common observation about doctors' reluctance to speak plainly to the dying is that they are hardened to death themselves and in consequence find it difficult to discuss it with those who do not share their views. Another is that prediction of death is notoriously uncertain, and as Richard Hillier, Chairman of the Association of Palliative Medicine, says, 'Uncertainty is something that doctors don't handle well.'

Furthermore, since dying patients represent failure within conventional medicine, many doctors and nurses prefer to chivvy up patients, sustaining their desperate need to believe that a cure is round the corner or that death can be postponed if this or that therapy is adopted. Such relationships may be motivated by kindness but they are rooted in misunderstanding and can have an adverse bearing on the care that the patient receives. As one American palliative care provider has observed:

> Doctors' prognostic estimates are important to both patients and clinicians in making good decisions about appropriate terminal care. Recent studies indicate not only that doctors seem reluctant to speak to patients about death, but also that they are inaccurate and systematically optimistic about the future, thus delaying timely sharing of information and referral to appropriate palliative care services.[20]

Sometimes the absence of a clear and openly expressed appraisal of the patient's condition is the result of a collusion between the doctor and patient to avoid the subject when it becomes distressing. Whilst it is generally acknowledged that patients wish to have their diagnosis and their treatment options made explicit, they may take away from the meeting a firm belief that they can be cured. Anne-Mei Thé, a university researcher working in Amsterdam, observed a number of lung cancer patients over a period of four years. Her findings, published in December 2000, show that patients' interpretations of a diagnosis are frequently more optimistic than those of the doctor.

Patients found it hard to believe that any treatment would be undertaken that was not likely to produce a full recovery. Thus, if patients produced 'clean' X-ray pictures after chemotherapy, they tended not to ask for a prognosis because they were convinced they were cured. In most cases, when bad news was presented to them, regarding the aggressive character of the tumour or the failure of recent therapy, patients would hurry to discuss the possibility of further treatment rather than consider the eventual outcome. Doctors, according to Anne-Mei Thé's research, happily cooperated in helping these patients 'forget' the future. But the overall effect of avoiding the truth and perpetuating a myth of recovery was to damage the patients' capacity to cope. Anne-Mei Thé concludes:

> Recovery stories and the optimism sustained by them helped patients and relatives to endure the treatment phase, but, on the other hand, it was extremely painful when later it became clear that this optimism was based on illusions. Moreover, it made it more difficult to accept imminent death and it obstructed 'saying farewell' in time and making necessary arrangements.[21]

This is the evidence of one researcher, and it has to be said again that denial, if it is informed denial, may help certain individuals adapt to dying. Anne-Mei Thé's concern arises out of the number of cases she discovered in which denial was not so much the muscle of a resolution to stay alive, as the thin fibres of an illusion based on ignorance.

Patients can also find themselves excluded from information as a result of the succession of doctors they are examined by. If the buck is routinely passed, no one doctor takes the overall responsibility for patient care and keeping the patient properly informed. When there is a change of doctor, an inadequate record may be passed on of what the patient and the family know, and the uncertainty about what is known can lead to argument and the loss of trust.

These issues have gained in moment and urgency in the United States as a result of the system of medical insurance and the increase in lawsuits for malpractice. Doctors are increasingly obliged to provide an exact diagnosis and prognosis if they wish to be protected from dissatisfied patients or their relatives. The trend in Britain must be towards a similar openness, and although Britain lags behind, it has begun to be recognized that it is not the sole prerogative of doctors to control information. It is, after all, the patient's right to know about his or her own life.

Communicating Care in the Future

Central to the general crisis surrounding disclosure is the paucity of training in communication skills which has characterized the medical curriculum in Britain. Whilst nurses have been taught how to communicate and been examined on what they have learnt, doctors generally have not. According to Richard Cowie, Director of Nursing at the Hospice in the Weald, communication skills have been an 'optional extra' for most trainee doctors. Many people are, as a result, understandably sceptical about the likelihood of doctors changing their behaviour. In an article for the *Observer* in October 1999, Kate Kellaway described the insensitive treatment she had received and she very much doubted that training would have made a difference. 'The new curriculum of medical schools', she wrote, 'includes the teaching of "communication skills". No one has qualified yet so there are no new doctors to judge, but I fear communication skills cannot be taught.'

Dr John Ellershaw is the Medical Director of the Marie Curie Hospice in Liverpool and Consultant in Palliative Medicine at the Royal Liverpool University Hospitals. As long ago as 1996, he was emphasizing the necessity for doctors to learn how to relate to patients. For him, it was a cornerstone of medical training.

In Liverpool, he said, there is a big element of palliative medicine in the curriculum and the idea of communicating with people is very important, and truthtelling is also very important. From Day One they are learning communication skills so that they understand the basis of communication. You *can* alter the way people communicate and give them strategies for breaking bad news.

Those trainees are now entering the health service and beginning to disseminate their new ideas.

Ellershaw is adamant that, with proper training, doctors should be able to evaluate what it is necessary and valuable to say.

You should be able to elicit from the patient how much they want to know about what is wrong with them. There are very few who want to know on a cellular level, but the vast majority want to know what perhaps is making them lose weight or feel unwell or what is causing them to become increasingly breathless over the past six months. And if the answer to that is that they have a cancer of the lung, the majority will want to find that out. Even though the answer is a painful one, they want to understand what is happening and, given the right kind of questions and the right lead-in, a dialogue can be opened.

Inclusive Care

Palliative care has always argued for the treatment of the whole person, and treating the whole person must include family and friends. They, together with the doctors and nursing staff, share a responsibility for ensuring that the patient dies not only in physical comfort but also mental ease. They help the patient, to use Bacon's phrase, 'make a fair and easy passage'.

Working with the family is a process that begins with making judgements about what each member of the family knows, and needs to know, about the condition of the patient and ends with bereavement counselling if that is requested. Hospice nurses are encouraged to treat all the family members as if they were their own family, giving them time, sharing their grief, crying with them sometimes. The hospice becomes an extension of the immediate family.

A good death would entail the patient's full reconciliation with his or her family and a degree of preparation by all. From her work with AIDS patients, Marie de Hennezel has come to recognize that, beyond the ordering of one's affairs, preparing for death means 'excavating the bedrock of one's relations with other people, teaching oneself to let go.'[22] Michael Young and Lesley Curren similarly discovered, from their conversations with east Londoners, that a separation which is resigned and harmonious is not only better for the patient, but equips those left behind to tackle their grief with equanimity. 'The person who dies in peace, with acceptance rather than bitterness,' they contend, 'bestows a gift upon the survivors which lasts for them, and can quieten their own fears.'[23]

Anxiety about how a surviving partner will cope will never be resolved whilst it remains a silent and private worry. It seems curious at first glance that the closing weeks of a couple's relationship might be the time when they choose to receive marriage guidance counselling, but this is not uncommon and usually indicates a deep need to separate without rancour, to finish on a good note. Indeed, they may have well-founded concerns, which need to be talked through. The surviving partner may want to express anger about his or her inability to cope with loss. Kübler-Ross speaks of men, particularly, who can't accept 'the loss of normal life'. These men are not ready to take care of the children, or to pay the bills, to face an empty house and deal with friends and neighbours on their own.[24] The recognition that they probably will survive and manage can be slow to emerge and the hospice can play a crucial facilitating role, urging both partners to discuss their problems and thereby reduce their magnitude.

The benefits of staying close, discussing what will happen after the death, will be felt by both survivor and patient. Without that openness, patients can feel tormented by a worry that they cannot leave their partners to fend for themselves. Cicely Saunders is convinced that a couple's fears of parting and of what will happen to the survivor can not only inhibit patients, but also intensify their resistance to death. If one partner is in a state of being dumbfounded and horrified, it can further enhance the isolation of the dying. 'Those who distance themselves,' says Saunders, 'feeling they can bring nothing but a lack of comprehension, do not realize that it is often their attempt to understand and not success in doing so that eases the patient's loneliness.'[25] There is nothing worse than saying nothing.

At the Cancer Help Centre in Bristol, Dr Sara Miller is equally aware that terminal illness can expose problems of honesty within a couple's relationship and that these may have a direct bearing on the quality of care that the partner can offer. Commonly, patients attending the centre are accompanied by a close family member, or other primary supporter. Very often supporters are unsupported themselves, and the centre offers them the same programme that it offers residents, which includes counselling and healing sessions, art therapy and nutritional advice. But for Dr Miller, however, the key to improving the relationship lies in a more open dialogue between the person with cancer and her supporter. The two may have very different views of the future. If one believes that the cancer can be beaten, whilst the other is preparing to face up to the likelihood of death, a distance can creep between them. The problem can seem intractable at first, but much can be done to encourage openness by non-linguistic means. There is huge scope, Sara Miller believes, for helping relatives to 'do something' while their loved ones are dying. Massage, for instance, is a gentle and affectionate gift of love and comfort, which can create the conditions of intimacy and trust in which new disclosures are made.

Although the inability to confess worries or doubts may appear to be motivated by concern for a relative's wellbeing, it is frequently complicated by factors in a shared past. Differences of opinion which have never been reconciled, guilt about incidents (revealed or not), the long-term absence of candour: these can all inform the quality of contact between the dying and close family and friends. Cicely Saunders sees the final stage of life as potentially a 'fruitful time', when such lingering tensions can be discharged. 'People in crisis can often show an astonishing ability to resolve long-standing problems and even to handle new ones.'[26]

If the evidence of those who have been helped by hospices is reliable, the strategy of including the family can be a salvation, but in recent years, some doubts have emerged. One criticism now voiced is that the hospice idealizes the family. Another is that the hospice has a tendency to infantilize family members. The staff become implicit 'parents' to them. If this is true, perhaps it is a relic of mainstream medical practice as it is conducted in hospitals. The parent–child model, the autocratic assumption that the doctor knows best, is endemic in most western hospital systems. Hospices have struggled to give equality of status to patients and staff, but old habits die hard and as the hospice approach becomes more established, it becomes progressively harder to hang on to the original ideal of responding to individual need and not imposing a regime simply because it has been proved to work in the past.

Some hospices have also been slow to adapt to the changing character of the family. Families today do not conform to the model of thirty years ago, when hospices began. There may not be a father and a mother living together with their children. A man's partner may be another man. A man's mistress may expect to be at her lover's deathbed as often as his wife. In short, families are more complicated in structure than they used to be, but the whole thrust of the hospice's treatment is based on the idea of the family and the dying as one domestic unit. It presupposes a complex of historical relationships that have occurred, at one time and in some way, under one roof.

This means that when it comes to solving problems within relationships, the emphasis is upon the unreconciled mother and daughter, brother and brother, father and son, rather than upon the looser, but no less intimate, relationships for which we have no name.

Death Unites, Death Divides

The hope is that disagreements will be resolved before death, making death easier, and indeed there is a great deal of evidence to suggest that death exerts a unifying influence on 'warring clans'. But some successes are only partial. Loris Thurston was visiting her sister Doris when I met her at the Hospice of Washington. Her sister's cancer had been diagnosed only ten weeks before. Doris had had pains in her joints and had lost quite a lot of weight, but no one had suspected that her condition was serious. The cancer had already reached her liver by the time she was examined, and the professional view was that she was beyond treatment.

The responses of the family to Doris's terminal illness were diverse. Loris had always been close to her sister. They were brought up in southern Virginia and ended up living together in DC after graduating. They shared a strong Baptist faith and that, along with the support they received from the hospice, had helped Doris to find peace and Loris to come to terms with the finality of her sister's cancer. For the first five weeks following the diagnosis, Doris appeared to accept that she would die. She arranged her will and settled a number of business matters. Then, in the sixth week, her liver stopped functioning and it became clear to the family that any hopes of a miraculous cure were going to be disappointed. Loris believes that, in general, this experience pulled the family together. 'We kiss and hug when we meet,' she said, 'which we didn't used to.' This gave each of them a great deal of strength, particularly when Doris became confused in the ninth week and began to think, in her delirium, that she was getting better.

The reunion of the family didn't work for everyone, though. Doris had a fifteen-year-old son, Derek. He was told, but he didn't accept that his mother was going to die. Her death would be shocking and painful for him. Similarly, her father denied the possibility of Doris dying. He was a disabled army vet, living in a veterans' hospital, and one of Loris's brothers had the task of telling him about Doris. His father immediately said, 'It's not true' and slammed the phone down. When Doris died on 7 December 1997, her father and son both faced difficult bereavements.

The hospice can only do so much to rebuild relationships and, generally, when a relationship was good before, it will be made more profound and mutually supportive in the face of death. Whether the denial that set Doris's son and father apart from the rest of the family reflected anxieties and divisions that existed beforehand, Loris did not disclose. The counselling services at the Hospice of Washington were available to all members of the family, but both son and father would have had to be open to help before it could be given. It is never imposed.

Spiritual Pain

The origins of the hospice movement are in Cicely Saunders's religious convictions and not in any tradition of humanism, but Saunders was quick to realize that if hospice staff were to gain the confidence of troubled patients, there should be no pressure put upon people who are patently vulnerable to accept a staff member's private belief. That said, the preoccupations of patients with religious belief, and with the fear that to die is to enter the unknown, should leave us in no doubt that the existential anxieties of dying are every bit as important as the symptoms of physical distress and the problems of relationship within families. The task of the hospice is to treat the patient and help him

towards as good a death as is possible for that individual.

A significant anxiety that affects the terminally ill arises
from a sense of guilt, which may in turn be allied to a sense
of worthlessness. Saunders's belief is that by staying close to
patients, we can create the conditions of trust in which
some kind of resolution of guilt, or absolution, can take
place:

> There is a progression from trust in the acceptance by
> others of all the things in ourselves that we regret into
> a faith in forgiveness, where we at last believe that they
> have no more power to hurt us or anyone else. We
> cannot change what has happened or what we have
> done, but we can come to believe that the meaning of
> the past can be changed. From this comes the ability to
> forgive ourselves.[27]

Saunders's somewhat involuted statement touches on the
same central anxiety of dying that Kübler-Ross identifies as
'unfinished business'. These two architects of the hospice
approach share a view that dying is complicated by guilt, a
sense that the past is not sufficiently atoned for or ac-
quitted. This is for many the essence of their spiritual life as
it expresses itself at death and it is, perhaps surprisingly,
much more common than a concern with ideas of the soul
or an afterlife. The patient, riven by uncertainty about the
value of his or her existence and undermined by evidence of
past shortcomings, may find no meaning in the life he or she
has led and, consequently, none in the universe. It seems a
tall order, then, for the hospice nurse on night duty – and so
many of these conversations begin after midnight – to
reassure the patient that his or her life had a purpose,
which makes sense within a larger universal plan. But
hospice staff are routinely faced with precisely this kind
of philosophical or theological crisis.

Cicely Saunders sets a great deal of store by the value

of recalling patients' life histories. She recommends that patients be encouraged to look back over the story of their lives in order to make sense of them. She further suggests that patients will in this way begin to grasp the idea of something greater than themselves, 'a truth to which they can be committed'.[28] Indeed, since stories survive their narrators, the patient's biography can in itself amount to a sense of life continuing beyond physical death.

This strategy of biographical recovery goes to the heart of what Norbert Elias has observed about the loneliness of dying. The value found in a life story can become a bulwark against that loneliness.

> The way a person dies depends not least on whether and how far he or she has been able to set goals and to reach them, to set tasks and perform them. It depends on how far the dying person feels that life has been fulfilled and meaningful – or unfulfilled and meaningless. The reasons for this feeling are by no means always clear . . . But whatever the reasons, we can perhaps assume that dying becomes easier for people who feel they have done their bit, and harder for people who feel they have missed their life's goal, and especially hard for those who, however fulfilled their life may have been, feel that the manner of their dying is itself meaningless.[29]

The hospice approach strives to reassure patients that whatever their life story has been, it has integrity and value.

gooddeath@hospice.com

Reading accounts of life in a hospice, one might be forgiven for thinking that death had been overcome, or at least harmonized. So is the hospice death as good as any modern death can be? Much has been argued against it. The hospice cannot turn the profoundly self-deceiving into frank and open patients. It cannot bring those hostile to religion to a belief in God. A recent book by Julia Lawton has gone much further in suggesting that the act of placing a patient in a hospice is tantamount to sequestration, keeping the dying away from the living. Lawton is critical both of the claim that personal dignity can be preserved when the body has ceased to function autonomously and of the practice of allowing patients to die in front of others.[30]

It is hard to criticize a methodology that appears to meet Bacon's requirement of the physician. If the patient achieves 'a fair and easy passage' into death, isn't that the sole objective? There is, however, a risk that the approach will become formulaic and fail to discriminate between the patient who cooperates by reason of firm belief and one who goes along with it for fear of making a fuss. If the patient dies in peace, it is a gift to all those associated with the death, but the residual concern is whether that peace is, in all cases, authentic. As Tony Walter has pointed out, the atmosphere of a hospice is conducive to tranquil behaviour. Patients may decide not to call out, or may say they are not in pain when they are, because they do not wish to disturb the governing ambience or pester busy staff.[31] Is it not possible that some incidents of patients' spiritual ease arise out of similar acts of complicity?

What residential care in a hospice does not obviously cater to is the patient for whom a 'good death' entails anger and resistance. Cicely Saunders has acknowledged that this might be a problem: 'Only as a team becomes more experienced and confident,' she writes, 'do its members find it easy to allow or even encourage the expression of anger and other negative feelings . . . We have to learn to listen in a way that will help the complainer to find the route to the real trouble and the way to face and handle it.' It might seem paradoxical, but if we suppose that a good death must maintain the patient's integrity to the end and that, above all, it must be an individual achievement born of individual character and individual need, a frail raging denial of everything in the final moments might make the perfect conclusion. If indeed that patient's life story is a log of angry incidents and arguments and protest, why should his death be any different? Tranquillity is not for all.

The ready answer will be that he could not have been happy in his anger. But is that necessarily true? It might have been his life force, the expression of his inner being. A noisy, defiant, anti-social bursting-out of life might be the fulfilment of that individual, his final assertion, and who is to say that would have been a 'bad death'? 'Do not go gently into that good night,' Dylan Thomas warned, and perhaps some of us shouldn't. Ellie Bennett is in no doubt that an angry exit is right for some: 'I think we should give them plenty of time to talk about their feelings about how they're dying, but for myself I have a recognition – and I'm not the only person – that if people choose to go out fighting, fighting is the way they'll go, and that is their right.'

The modern hospice movement affirms the right of the patient to control as much of his or her dying as possible. The hospice has now to confront the fact that a peaceful and friendly environment is, in some respects, unnatural and may inhibit the patient. 'Niceness can be a horrible way to treat people,' says Richard Cowie. 'It can be horribly patronising.' His staff at the Hospice in the Weald are now, somewhat reluctantly, beginning to tackle the issue of anger and how nurses can allow their patients to express it without feeling abused.

Why Is It Not Available to All?

The constituency that makes use of the hospice remains lamentably small. If the hospice does offer a good death, it is not yet to all. Richard Cowie says that his hospice does not attempt to provide care for everyone dying in the local community because the emphasis is, as it has always been, upon cancer sufferers. Those with multiple sclerosis or motor neurone disease (MND) account for less than 1 per cent of the hospice's patients. People with other fatal conditions, such as end-stage renal failure or a cardiac disease, don't get much of a look in.

Unquestionably, the hospice movement now faces a challenge to help the wider community, both in terms of the number of conditions they treat and the ethnic diversity of the patients admitted. Some hospices have begun to address these issues and perhaps it was inevitable that the first signs of change would be observable in large cities. At St Christopher's, in south London, up to 10 per cent of patients may have MND or HIV/AIDS, and at the Hospice of Washington DC, 10 per cent of those in care have HIV/AIDS, MND (ALS) or heart and lung diseases. These are slow but significant improvements on the admissions profile of only five years ago, and it can only be hoped that changes of this kind are not made at the expense of deserving cancer sufferers.

It has already been remarked that hospices tend to serve the middle class, but there is also a concern about the failure of hospices, by and large, to cross ethnic boundaries. Whilst St Christopher's in south London has a very mixed community of patients, that cannot be said of hospices around the country. There may be a prevailing view, amongst some communities, that the facilities are inappropriate. A Muslim woman, for instance, would require private washing facilities, even when she was unable to wash herself. It is equally possible that, irrespective of ethnic background, it is the educated middle class who are most likely to get something out of a hospice because it is congruent with their own experience. Ellie Bennett is worried that people from other backgrounds could be put off by the 'middle class atmosphere. I think it's a mixture of the better educated you are, the better you know what facilities there are and the better you are able to get what you want . . . But even if other people do come in, it's a bit five star hotel-ish, and not everybody's comfortable with that.'

That said, the hospice movement has done a huge amount to ameliorate the experience of dying and the circumstances in which dying occurs. Allan Kellehear has identified five criteria that a modern death has to meet to be 'good'. The patient must be: a) aware he is dying; b) adjusted to the certainty of dying; c) prepared for dying; d) relieved of all his roles and duties and responsibilities; e) able to make his farewells.[32] These are elusive categories, but they describe an ambition which broadly resembles the aims and tactics of the hospice movement. What the hospice can do is provide effective symptom control and the possibility of honest relationships. In the end, it is the patient who has to understand the process of dying and the need to prepare for it, but the hospice staff can do much to relieve the patient's anxiety and loneliness simply by staying close to them. They can also try to bring family and friends into a better relationship with the dying. The good death will depend on a successful collaboration between all those involved so that the dying do not have to die alone.

Hospice practice developed in what David Clark called 'the interstices of the health service', plugging the gaps that existed in the care of the dying. The important question for the future is whether these principles of care can survive the exigencies of new financial constraints and the integration of hospice methods within the public health service. In particular, much more care of the dying is likely to take place in patients' homes. Will visiting doctors and nurses, together with family carers, have the time and the resources to preserve the closeness that the institutional hospice has demonstrated works so well?

4

Dying at Home –
the Future of Palliative Care

Death is not an action, but a whole state and
condition.

Jeremy Taylor

What has been well observed by Cicely Saunders and, in the
USA, by Elisabeth Kübler-Ross, is the value of seeing dying
as a part of life. Dying is, *pace* Wittgenstein, experienced by
the living and the greater the preparation for, or at least
awareness of, dying during life, the more comfortable that
transition from life to death is likely to be. Saunders's
invocation of Francis Bacon, and his expectations of the
physician, hints at a deeper intuition, which she must have
had early on, that death can be 'befriended'. There is no
hint of the ghoulish in such a friendship; it has none of the
macabre and yet cynical terror of a mediaeval Dance with
Death. Friendship with death is the sublimation of fears in
the real peace that comes from acceptance of the inevitable.
Bacon knew that death could be a 'fair and easy passage', so
does Saunders. Perhaps we all know such deaths are
possible, but we resist the idea because we don't wish to die.

Acceptance, in this philosophy, is an active stance. It is built upon a relationship between patient and carer which recognizes that the last phase of life has its own dignity and that the best way to respect that is to accord to the dying the rights of any other human individual. Acceptance should secure for patients a degree of independence and control over what is happening to them. If the dying can continue to live in that trust, they can begin, through their relationships with others, to examine what they feel about the threshold they are imminently to cross. The families of the dying can also be accommodated to death in a way that they could never have anticipated, and for them, too, there is an opportunity for personal growth and enrichment. As Cicely Saunders says, with characteristic humility:

> From the dying themselves we learn not only to understand something of the ending of life but also a great deal to make us optimistic about all life and about the potential of those ordinary human beings who work their way through it . . . we will come continually to know people at their most mature, their most courageous.[1]

The crucial question we now face is where that mature and courageous death will best be achieved.

Most people with a terminal illness want to die in their own homes. Whilst there is considerable evidence to support this contention, it is not the practice in western countries. In Britain, 73 per cent of us end our lives in hospitals or hospices; only 26–7 per cent at home. As Liz Lloyd has recognized, this means that something is going wrong with our treatment of the dying. 'The modern way of death,' Lloyd writes, 'is generally not good for most, since it does not meet people's hopes and desires.'[2]

The reason people wish to remain at home is that they hope to sustain a greater degree of control than would generally be possible in hospital. They wish to remain with their families, and to exercise some choice over their remaining lives and they do not want to be dependent on strangers. The common view of hospitals, by contrast, is that they have become associated with many of the features of a 'bad death'. Liz Lloyd quotes a summary of them provided by Clarke and Seymour: 'a loss of individual choice; fear; isolation from family, friends and professional carers; lack of knowledge about the dying state; and . . . prolongation of the dying career.'[3]

A well-run hospice may not be the answer either because, as Matthew Kestenbaum is all too aware, the hospice environment does not suit everybody. His hospice in Washington DC tries to evaluate the suitability of applicants so that they won't be disappointed. 'We don't do heroic measures, hi-tec medicine or rescue,' Kestenbaum informs them, 'and if that's what someone is after, hospice isn't right.' That the hospice is also not very good at dealing with patients' anger has persuaded Elisabeth Kübler-Ross that the home is the only place for expressing those 'negative feelings and fears'. Is the home perhaps the ideal place to die?

There's No Place Like Home

The view taken by many hospitals and hospices is that they are happy to support home care if it is a practical proposition, and this more often than not turns on the quantity and quality of care that families can provide. Clive Seale and Ann Cartwright point out that whereas in 1969 an average of three relatives or friends looked after the dying at home, by 1987 that figure had declined to two.[4] The consequent increase in demand for formal services, both to facilitate the comfort of the dying in their homes and to relieve their carers, has been predictably huge.

There is clearly a balance to be struck. Where there are no family members or friends to support someone who is dying and dependent, the cost of home care to the NHS is prohibitive and it is therefore likely to be ruled out, irre-spective of the wishes of the patient. At the same time, as the need for hospice and other palliative care grows, there are fewer resources to create and run new residential units. This shortage has arisen at a time when the hospice movement is, in any case, considering the related issue of whether effec-tive care is better delivered in a hospice or at home. We can only hope that the answer to this question will be deter-mined by the best interests of patients and not simply by a lack of funding.

The tendency for people to die in institutions, which steadily increased in the course of the twentieth century, is no accident. It directly reflects on the one hand, our progressive detachment from the physical act of dying and on the other, our growing dependence on hospitals for the expertise and technology we deem necessary at the end of life. There has, additionally, been a natural and quite understandable apprehension about caring for the dying without nursing skills and in an often ill-adapted home setting. Looking after the dying at home *without* the sup-port of a hospice or similar service has always been, for the carer, a seemingly interminable endurance of misery and exhaustion. When there is no prospect of recovery, objec-tives can become blurred and the claustrophobia of daily nursing produces resentment and counter-productive care. The dying are not always improved by their condition and it may be a shock to carers to discover that they have, alone, to deal with a curmudgeonly ingrate, whom they scarcely recognize.

Death in such circumstances is not good for anyone. Liz Lloyd cites evidence that 'becoming "over-burdensome" is associated with a bad death in old age'. If it does not tangibly quicken the event, it suffuses death with a feeling of lost dignity. 'The extent to which someone *feels* that they are a burden,' Lloyd observes, 'will be strongly influenced by the context in which they are helped to cope with changes in their physical condition and ability to function.'[5]

Implicitly, this comment calls for a kind of restorative care which deals not only with the routine disturbances to patients' physical well-being, but with their whole emotional response to their predicament. The dying require care which renews their self-esteem and values their continuing existence, which honours their right to speak and their right to choose, and which finally asserts the individuality of that person even as he or she is on the brink of personal extinction.

That's a tall order for perhaps an elderly wife, none too fit herself, who is faced with providing round-the-clock care for a difficult husband. Many relatives, whilst feeling unequal to the burden of physical care, or simply unable to watch the slow process of dying day by day, are ridden with guilt when they ask for help from a hospice or hospital. But their guilt is misplaced. The help available to carers is substantial and intrinsic to any successful strategem of home care. Those who know that they can draw on the resources of a hospice, or a good NHS palliative care unit, generally fare much better than carers who struggle to cope unaided.

The hospice movement has once again set a gold standard for care of the dying in their homes. The home care provided by a hospice team differs from any other in the breadth of its service. At the outset, the dying and their families will be encouraged to talk about their needs and anxieties and the hospice will do its best to resolve them. For carers, this can be a huge relief. They have the security of knowing that the hospice nurses, who will make domiciliary visits every day if necessary, will try to ensure that the patient does not suffer pain, and that the carer is able to manage pain and other symptoms in the nurses' absence. Carers can also make use of shopping and patient-sitting services, together with the back-up of twenty-four-hour emergency nursing and the opportunity of short respites when the patient is admitted to the hospice for a few days at a time. These services can make the difference between the kind of caring that becomes intolerable for the carer and a source of bitter division, and care which is characterized by dedication, affection and, ultimately, a sense of achievement. It will none of it be easy, but hard work and emotional strain can take on a different aspect when conducted in this kind of supportive environment. Ninety-eight per cent of Elisabeth Kübler-Ross's patients (a figure in line with hospice practice in the USA as a whole) are cared for in this way.

Given the rising costs of residential institutions, it seems increasingly likely that care of the dying at home will become the dominant method of nursing the dying in Britain and Europe as well. The key advantage of home care is that it allows the patient to die with his or her family close by. This can have a significant effect on how well children in particular adapt to the loss of a parent. Parents may be reluctant to impose their deaths on their children, and this can make parting especially difficult. Elisabeth Lee argues that the pain of leaving children can be felt so greatly by a dying parent that he or she is unable to discuss what is going on, with the result that the sorrow of leaving is never shared and the children are never reassured by the knowledge that they are dearly loved.[6] For as long as the dying patient is resident in a hospital or hospice, the opportunity to overcome inhibition, to regain the intimacy that usually goes with mutual honesty, is confined to the children's visits. Regular as these may be, that restriction tends to induce more anxiety, not less. In the home, however, the time to meet and talk is unregulated.

Kübler-Ross's experience has shown that after the initial trauma of learning that a parent is dying and will never recover, American children settle into a pattern of care that is often uplifting for the whole family. Playing their favourite games or their favourite music might be irritating on occasion, but more routinely it insists on the continuity of life, which is reassuring for a parent anxious about the children's welfare after his or her death. Sharing in watching television programmes can gain a new significance and the displacement of power, away from the parent, can lead to a new intimacy. Children become protective of the dying parent and will be uninhibited about making sure guests do not tire their parent and leave when they should. There will, of course, be moments of friction, when a child is scolded for banging doors or staying out too late, and moments of real anger or distress when the loss is scarcely to be borne. However, the tasks of caring, together with the venting of anger and the development of intimacy – which is at the same time the unravelling of intimacy – can begin to prepare the children for their loss. 'The feedback of the grief resolution of these children,' Kübler-Ross tells us, 'has been far better even than those who were allowed to visit without restriction in a hospice. It is a form of preventive psychiatry that cannot be overestimated.'[7]

The knowledge that the best that could be done has been done to help the children accept their loss is of enormous comfort to a dying parent. To the last, the dying father or mother has been able to act in a sense *as a parent*, having remained in the family home and made sensible preparation for the time when he or she will die. A number of techniques have been developed to accommodate children to their loss, and it is clear that these are most easily achieved in the home and with the parents help and participation. Dr Barnardo's, for example, has come up with the idea of a 'memory store', in which children place sentimental items for later use. Elisabeth Lee says that it usually takes the form of 'a brightly coloured box the size of an attaché case. It includes drawers for small keepsakes, space for a video of family events and recordings of the parent's voice. There is a memory book for parents to record essential information, with space for addresses, photos, maps and a family tree.'[8] Some of these may be painful to re-examine in the short term, but mementos do assist the grieving child to reconstruct a sense of the lost parent's identity and their own story of the parent's life. Indeed, reaching the point at which the child can sit and watch a video of the dead parent will be a high-water mark.

Commonly, children are excluded from the dying process. The assumption is made that they are too vulnerable to hear the full story and too 'unaware' to need to tell their own. Both generalizations are unlikely to be true. Whilst it may be that very young children have difficulty in grasping the finality of death, most modern therapists agree that children do grieve and that they benefit from inclusion within the rituals of grief. Although children under the age of eight tend to see death as a temporary event, even they can be helped to develop their own narrative understanding of what has happened. Elisabeth Kübler-Ross describes how she used natural imagery to create a metaphor of transition in the child's mind: 'We pictured a cocoon together,' she writes, 'and I was just explaining that at the right time, every cocoon opens up and out of it comes . . . when she hollered, "A butterfly".'[9] At some level, the child may well have made the connection, at least enough to seed the idea that becoming a butterfly is an irreversible change in form. The butterfly will never be a caterpillar again.

Preserving Identity

Dignity is of critical importance to the dying and the more that they can retain a sense of the autonomous self, the less they will feel death – to use Kübler-Ross's phrase again – as 'a catastrophic, destructive force' rushing up at them. John Stroud, the chaplain at St Nicholas's Hospice in Suffolk, thinks that the individual's identity is made up of many factors and experiences, but what unites them is the control that, as an adult, the individual is accustomed to having over the identity he or she presents to the world. So much of that disintegrates in the face of death, as experience becomes 'frighteningly uncontrolled and chaotic'. If the dying person is to achieve of equilibrium, any kind of reconciliation, it is, Stroud says, 'a question of trying to perceive whether there is any trustworthiness in some sense within the experience.'

That trust is easily lost during the crisis of death, because so much of a dying patient's autonomy can be snatched away. If trust is to be kept with the dying and their families in their homes (and, equally, the dying in nursing homes or cottage hospitals) home care, whether it is provided by a hospice or palliative care unit, must seek to resolve their anxieties. In other words, death in the home can only become the ideal practice once the gold standard of care, so ably defined by the hospice movement, is made available everywhere.

The evidence that this can happen in the foreseeable future is patchy and confusing. Effective home care of the dying relies on a thorough integration of the health and social services provided, so that omissions and duplications are avoided. No doubt in some areas this has been achieved, but because we as a society lack a uniform strategy, it is inevitable that other areas are less well served. Very often this comes down to the absence of a coordinating figure. When a patient decides, usually in conjunction with his family, that he wishes to die at home, the help he is most likely to seek is that of his GP. Yet GPs are not always best placed to provide the right kind of supervision. They are generally oversubscribed and complain themselves that hospital consultants do not routinely provide them with sufficient information for them to tell the truth to their patients and decide on appropriate action. Further, there continue to be complaints about the failure of doctors to make home visits to the old and dying, and this to a great extent reflects the poor ratio of GPs to older people in Britain. In short, although home care of the dying has to include GPs 'in the loop', it may be better organized by other service providers.

The absence of others has often prompted local hospices to plug the gaps. St Nicholas's in Bury is on the verge of starting home care for that very reason. As Julia Wootton, the Medical Director, explains: 'In this area virtually no GPs do on-call at night. Basically, the service for these patients [the dying] out of hours is appalling, and we are thinking about setting up hospice-at-home in order to allow people the choice of dying at home with decent cover.'

St Nicholas's has increasingly become, in the words of the Clinical Services Manager, Jennifer Field, 'an oasis of care', as nursing homes in the region have closed and the number of beds for the terminally ill has dwindled. Home care seems to be the answer, but in west Suffolk, it is only the hospice that is likely to offer such a service.

Forty per cent of home care nursing services are now provided by voluntary hospices all over Britain. But the hospice movement, which relies on charitable donations for 70 per cent of its funding, cannot be expected to supply the country's principal method of caring for the dying. That it has set the standard and provided an excellent service until now does not mean that it can be ubiquitous or comprehensive in the future.

Other Service Providers

Although palliative care began in hospices, it is to an extent now provided by NHS hospitals and it can go by a number of names. Care may be offered by the Hospital Palliative Care Team, the Macmillan Support Service or the Symptom Control Team. In an ideal health service environment, those dying at home would be in the care of a highly coordinated and multi-disciplinary NHS team. The family doctor, hospital consultant and a variety of nurses and other health-care professionals would provide treatment and support that allowed the dying patient to feel that he or she was not only in good hands, but valued.

If the patient is dying of cancer, the local care apparatus is likely to be more helpful than if he or she has another disease. Both palliative care nurses, who are based in a local

NHS palliative care unit, and Macmillan nurses, who may be based in a hospital or a hospice, have specialist training in pain control and other cancer symptoms. They will work with other care providers, such as family doctors and community or Marie Curie nurses, to design a package of care for the dying which, *inter alia*, ensures continuity between the hospital or hospice and the home.

Like the hospice movement itself, Macmillan nurses have played an influential role in persuading the health service to adopt some of the techniques and objectives of palliative care. Macmillan Cancer Relief is a nationwide charity, which aims to provide the best information, treatment and care to cancer patients. The charity's 'A Voice for Life' campaign sought to enable people to have a greater say in the care given them, to reduce the public's fear of cancer and to increase the number of experts in the field. Macmillan runs a helpline to advise callers on useful reading and their local support groups and they make grants available in cases where terminal illness has led to serious financial hardship. There are some 200 Macmillan doctors as well, who are involved in both treatment and teaching.

The nursing scheme, which began in 1975, recruits existing SRNs (State Registered Nurses) and gives them specialist training in cancer care. Qualified nurses are then funded by the charity for three years, after which their salaries are generally taken over by local health authorities. (That responsibility will in the future fall to Primary Care Trusts, or PCTs.) In 2000, Macmillan marked the millennium with the appointment of their 2,000th nurse.

Those dying from cancer can be referred to a Macmillan nurse by their GP or hospital consultant or, if they have been admitted to a hospital, by their ward sister. (Patients suffering from other conditions may be fortunate and taken into Macmillan nursing care, but it is not guaranteed and the number of non-cancer patients handled by Macmillan nurses is relatively small.) Nurses will provide advice on symptom control and the use of appropriate drugs and detailed information about other services the dying may require to be looked after at home. They do not do hands-on nursing, but they will facilitate practical caring through liaison with, say, Marie Curie or community nurses. There are now 5,000 part-time Marie Curie nurses, providing round-the-clock nursing for cancer sufferers who are still managing to live in their own homes. Whereas the Marie Curie nurse will change dressings and administer medication, the Macmillan nurse will make practical recommendations and give time to the patient's emotional and spiritual well-being. Macmillan nurses, in other words, play a pivotal role in the overall care of the dying and, as Gill Oliver, Director of Servicing Development for Macmillan, says, 'When palliative care in the NHS is good, it's as good as a hospice.'

So much hangs on the word *when*. There is not much doubt that Macmillan nurses have made a huge and valuable contribution to the management of the dying and their physical welfare. What it is more difficult to determine is how the attention they endeavour to give to the patient's emotional and spiritual welfare measures up to the kind of open-ended care enshrined in the hospice ideal. Macmillan nurses are expected to be sensitive and to have enhanced communication skills, but because of the number of patients they have, the time demanded of them inevitably exceeds the time they have available.

Sue Weatherell, who was a Macmillan nurse in Yorkshire for twelve years, believes that the kernel of good care must be that it is led by the patient. Her experience has taught her that patients want to talk about themselves and want to know the truth about their condition. What varies from patient to patient is how quickly this exchange of frank information can take place. Sue recognizes that her willingness to listen was circumscribed by the pressure of her next appointment and she always made it clear at the outset of a visit, that she 'only had thirty minutes'. When a patient is struggling with personal matters that are too deep or too

personal to disclose to his or her family – Sue recalls stories
of childhood abuse, losing religious faith, cheating on wives
– the 'fixed appointment' is patently not adequate to the
task.

What is the answer in a health service neurotic about
cost? Sue Weatherell was to some extent able to hand on the
problem, by virtue of working in a multi-disciplinary team
that included a chaplain and a clinical psychologist. But
that, in turn, implies a need to establish several axes of
communication and trust, when establishing one is difficult
enough.

Jane Wythe, a Macmillan nurse attached to St Nicholas's
Hospice, thinks that another obstacle to intimacy is the
dying patients' own fear and uncertainty about how long
they have to live. When she first meets patients, she very
often finds that they are angry – about the diagnosis, the
shock of it and the sheer vagueness of the future. 'Probably
the most difficult thing that people find they have to deal
with is the uncertainty of it: when it might happen, how it
might happen, whether it will happen, will there be pain,
will there not be pain, probably particularly when it might
happen – how many months, how many weeks might be
left. Living with that is difficult.'

It takes time for the nurse and the patient to work through
these anxieties, and time is what there may be so little of. In
the absence of a clear prognosis, both parties try to create a
close relationship, but they have no idea whether it will be
for several months or, bluntly, a matter of days. When the
nurse is obliged to move on to other appointments, the lack
of knowledge about how much time the patient may have
ahead can be an additional source of distress.

This seems far removed from the 'touch of a button'
comfort that Cicely Saunders tried to make the mainstay of
hospice care. Saunders always believed that facilitating
intimate conversation was central to the hospice method,
helping patients to 'change from anxious fighting fists into
open accepting hands' and to feel so much 'the security of

love, the simple love that would answer a bell or even come before you'd rung the bell, that they would begin to have a sort of basic trust.' If a patient is seeking to establish sufficient trust to disclose the most private of worries and regrets, the summary nature of some home visits may stifle the very confession that would make dying easier.

If patients are not given the opportunity to speak out and be heard, their vulnerability to depression will increase. Depression, as we now know, is one of the most commonly missed symptoms of dying. One palliative care specialist in Boston argues that it is woefully undertreated because professional carers regard it as inevitable.

> Many clinicians incorrectly presume that depression is normal or expected in advanced illness, rather than viewing it as a biologically based and treatable form of suffering distinct from sadness. The biological signs that usually form the basis of a diagnosis of major depression are often present in a terminal condition but are attributable to the medical illness rather than the psychological state.[10]

There are clearly serious and inhibiting constraints on both the quality and quantity of home care that can be provided by most health service nurses. The pity is that we know what the optimum care should be, but must settle for what is possible within available budgets. Cicely Saunders makes the point that the needs of the dying cannot be bounded by NHS Trust budgets and employment policy. She contrasts the Macmillan service to that provided by the Home Care Team based at St Christopher's:

> Macmillan nurses only do nine to five, Monday through Friday, and we've always done twenty-four hours, seven days a week . . . There *are* twenty-four hour District Nurses, and you *can* get a doctor who's on an on-call service, but they don't know the

patient . . . What I'm saying is you need to be open all hours if you're going to be able to give your patient the best service. You don't stop having urgent problems at five o'clock on a Friday night.

The Department of Health has been saying for some time that there ought to be twenty-four-hour cover for the dying, but at present such provision varies from district to district, and indeed some services that were operating not long ago have been closed down.

Respite Nursing in a Hospice or Palliative Care Unit

The concern to preserve the dignity of the individual patient is under constant threat: from the subversive power of disease; from the patient's own fears and anxieties about the physical chaos they live in and the dark unknown of the future; and from a welling sense that with closure there must be a recognition of meaning in the life that has been lived. The dying patient, then, is a complex and volatile animal to sustain and simple programmes of care, which are not flexible enough to respond to the patient's immediate needs, are doomed to fail.

The onus of care in the home falls, of course, on the principal carer, be it a partner, parent or child. We as a society, however, cannot expect that such carers will keep up the same level of commitment for continuous weeks and months, or that their care will be sufficient by comparison with professional standards. Symptoms such as pain, nausea or vomiting can get out of control at times and, to be good, home care requires not only visits from nurses and family doctors, but also the chance for patients to benefit from direct residential care in a hospice or palliative care unit. As Cicely Saunders reminds us, dying in the home is one thing in the early stages, quite another when symptoms become severe and relatives are exhausted. 'Over half of those who say they want to die

at home change their minds,' she says. 'People want a
sense of safety.'

In practice, the answer to this problem has been to offer day
hospice services and respite care in hospices and palliative
care units. Day hospices are designed for those who retain a
degree of physical independence. They provide access to
medical expertise, but are also the forum for new friendships,
creative activity and a bit of pampering. The terminally ill
meet others in similar circumstances, with whom they can
discuss their problems or, more often, enjoy the freedom from
being preoccupied with dying. The unit will organize classes
in sculpture, painting, writing and other skills that the patients
may never have tried before or thought they were capable of.
There are also hairdressers, beauticians and chiropodists,
together with occupational therapists and physiotherapists.
What is striking about so many of these day centres is how
many people find themselves going into remission, chiefly as a
result of having their spirits lifted. 'You get people in tears,'
Saunders says, 'because they're better and they have to go and
there are other people waiting to come in.'

Dramatic improvement is equally an aspect of respite
care. It can be unnerving for patients and families who were
at the end of their tether, convinced that they had entered
the last phase of the patient's disease, to find that a few days
in the local hospice puts them back to where they were
months earlier. Ellie Bennett, at St Nicholas's Hospice,
regularly admits patients who come in for a few days in
the firm belief that they will not leave.

> People are referred for admission and the GP will say
> 'She's absolutely flat out now. Prepare yourselves that
> she's going to die in a couple of days.' And they come
> in and get good nursing care, and palliative advice
> from doctors and they perk up. Three days later,
> they're sitting up asking for a two-course breakfast.
> That's an awful shock for people who have got them-
> selves into dying mode.

The restorative power of 'good nursing care', and the enhancement of individual dignity it effects, partly explain why patients will often be reluctant to leave the hospice once they have been, as hospices generally put it, 'stabilized'. Carers, too, may try to avoid the awful day when they have to resume responsibility for their dying relative; the respite will have been both welcome and, to some extent, intimidating because it will have shown what can be done if enough time and resources are put into the caring. To try to minimize that sense of inferiority, a hospice may encourage the principal carer to continue his or her involvement while the patient is resident, but it is difficult to insist when the carer is, quite understandably, enjoying the freedom and the opportunity to recover.

The picture that emerges from the complex of provision is that home care for the dying is feasible and can achieve a high quality of care if it is practised in combination with residential services. As things stand, how good the care is and how well coordinated it is, will depend on where in the country the patient lives. Home care is supplied in so many different ways that it is impossible to describe it as one entity, with a single professional standard. The hope for the future must be that the integration and coordination of these services will continue to improve and that national criteria of care can be agreed and fulfilled.

The Future of Palliative Care

The hospice movement is at a critical juncture in its development. The task of meeting rising costs will not be dealt with simply by substituting home care for residential care. Indeed, in January 2001, it was reported that for the first time in their contemporary history, hospices were facing the prospect of having to close beds and dismiss nurses.

St Christopher's has always been in the vanguard of this kind of change, mainly because it was the first modern hospice and has, therefore, tended to encounter problems before other hospices. It faced its own major financial crisis in 2000 and at the time, the cry went up: 'If St Christopher's goes down, what happens to the rest of us?' In fact, the hospice overcame its difficulties by negotiating an improved contract with the NHS. St Christopher's Nursing Director, Andrew Knight, argues that the problem of funding is partly a consequence of the medicalization of hospice care or, put another way, getting rid of an embarrassing reputation for amateurishness has cost money. Knight recalls:

> Many oncologists – cancer doctors, radiotherapists, and surgeons particularly – have always looked at hospices as being slightly Mickey Mouse, in terms of not producing enough scientific data to justify the plinth on which they rapidly climbed. The NHS complaint was that if they had the money hospices had, they too could provide time and nursing of a sustained personal kind.

One can only imagine that the NHS comment was made tongue-in-cheek. The evidence of the last thirty years is that the NHS has been slow to recognize the ideal of personal nursing, and palliative care has been seen as running counter to medical efforts to 'beat' cancer. That said, what Andrew Knight quite rightly highlights is the fact that recent improvements in oncology have informed hospice care and the cost of giving hospice methodology the assured scientific basis that it lacked before has been high. The use of advanced intravenous antibiotics and of blood transfusions, together with new techniques for symptom control and a better audit of care, have all made demands on what has always been limited funding.

From its origins as a subversive, avant-garde and distrusted ideology on the margins of professional health care, the hospice – or, at least, its technique – has moved centre stage. To its lasting credit, it has resolved many of the problems of pain management and it has made possible discussions about death and dying that would have been inconceivable forty years ago. It is now more common – though not widespread – for people to think in advance about death and its implications, about the place and type of burial or cremation they favour, about the 'unfinished business' of relationships and about saying goodbye.

Hospice techniques have also had an enormous influence on palliative care of the dying within conventional medicine, so much so that hospice principles are effectively the mainstay of many geriatric wards and oncology units in mainstream hospitals. In 1990, only forty hospitals in the UK had advisory palliative care services. By 2000, that number had grown to 350. The Labour government has announced that it plans to invest a further £50 million in palliative care by 2004 and £2 million to train nurses in how to care for those living with cancer. Whilst this initiative was primarily motivated by a political concern about the geographical inequity of care across the UK, the techniques that this investment will enhance and develop owe most of their thinking to the hospice philosophy. The success of its approach to palliative care is also internationally celebrated: hospice units of one sort or another have sprung up all around the world.

Much has been done to overcome the distrust of family doctors. As little as ten years ago, there remained a surprising degree of ignorance and fear of hospices in Britain. Some GPs understood that the hospice was intended to complement the NHS, not rival or threaten it, and referred their patients happily enough. Others did not, or they referred their patients too late for the hospice to provide its most effective care.

This was equally the pattern in the USA. Matthew Kestenbaum, at the Hospice of Washington, believes family doctors in the early nineties were guilty of simple prejudice. They took the view that hospices were for 'patient-assisted suicides', which ignored the conspicuous opposition to euthanasia and patient-assisted suicide that had characterized hospices since their beginning. The hospice movement, then and now, has argued that if pain management is of a high enough calibre and patients' needs are listened to and acted upon, the number of sustained requests for euthanasia immediately dwindles.

Dr Kestenbaum's second criticism of family doctors' misunderstanding is that they have tended to believe that they have to give up their patients once they have referred them to hospices. This continues to be a problem in the United States. Kestenbaum is more often than not the doctor in attendance for residents at the Hospice of Washington, but he would much rather local doctors saw fit to continue their care. When I spoke to him in the autumn of 2000, he felt that relations with local physicians had changed since we first met in 1997, and some were following through when their patients were taken into the hospice, although the majority remained distant and disengaged. Here again, the failure on the part of family doctors to find out precisely how a hospice operates has led to a cumulative ignorance and hostility.

This seems to be less of a concern in Britain, where GPs are expected to relinquish their supervision of patients once they are admitted into a hospice programme, but then to resume care if the patients are subsequently discharged. In general, the relationship between GPs and hospices in Britain has improved, partly because some hospices have proposed a more flexible and responsive liaison with their local doctors. Hospice in the Weald, for example, offers a multi-levelled service, which ranges from giving GPs advice over the phone to taking their patients into full residential care. This kind of proposal has undoubtedly eased tensions and removed suspicion. The connection with the mainstream health service is friendlier and more constructive and NHS health workers will now attend courses in palliative care run by hospices.

The development of a closer relationship between hospices and the health service has prompted some commentators to speculate about a merger of the two. Andrew Knight's view is that hospice care must continue to shape the direction and techniques of mainstream palliative care in the NHS, but eventually, he thinks, they will merge into one service for the dying, which will be no bad thing. On the contrary, it promises, in the vogue of modern politics, a 'third way', which Knight welcomes:

> Why should we have these glorified palaces of death really? She [Cicely Saunders] set them up to be ex-emplars, places which would change the medical es-tablishment's thinking about how we should approach death. She has achieved that . . . But we're operating in an imperfect British society that likes its imperfections in its health service. I think the hospice will continue to evolve and transform itself, but with a much smaller 'icon', much smaller in-patient unit, much larger com-munity work and community practice, and hospice care and palliative care have to go arm-in-arm into the future.

But at what cost will these changes be bought? The hospice is perhaps the victim of its own success and certainly of rising health-care budgets. It has always prided itself on its attention to the individual patient, but because so much of what the hospice does has been successful, is there a danger that its methods will become standardized, that the indi-vidual's needs will be shaped by 'the hospice approach' and that something of the individual's crisis will be subsumed under the institution's proven methodology? The establish-ment of a model of care risks the kind of formulaic nursing inimical to the very ideas of flexibility and patient-centred-ness with which hospices began.

Nurses at St Christopher's feel this is already happening. Against the 'third way', there is evidence that experienced hospice nurses see their skills being eroded; they maintain that they are not allowed the time they once gave to listening to patients and to being alongside them. Andrew Knight acknowledges that this may be happening to a degree, but he thinks the nurses' case is exaggerated. The hospice, in its scramble to be accredited and scientific, has not entirely lost sight of its need to get alongside patients and the holistic approach remains intact. The problem, in Knight's view, goes back to training.

If I want a pick-me-up, if I'm fed up with the work on my desk or I've had a bad meeting, I will go on to a ward and I will spend five minutes with a patient or two, and I'll feel so much better because they remind me of what it's all about. And what I see increasingly is nurses coming through the system who don't have those skills to get alongside patients because they haven't been taught them in hospitals and they come here and get caught up with the general business of delivering physical care and don't follow it through by spending time with patients.

St Christopher's annually admits over 1,000 people and it has over 1,200 new patients in the home care scheme each year. It cannot possibly satisfy the overall demand in the south London area it serves, nor is there funding to extend the existing facilities or to build a new hospice. In many countries, notably the USA and Canada, the answer has been to incorporate hospice teams within existing hospitals. The advantages are manifold. There is instant access to hi-tec medical resources, should they be needed. Hospice care can be started earlier in a patient's decline. There is a continuity of doctors, so that when a patient's treatment has not cured him and he faces death, the same doctor can continue to look after him. Within a hospital, a hospice team can be flexible and responsive, caring for in-house patients as they are transferred from oncology wards to the 'hospice department'. Conventional medicine and hospice care are thus better integrated. In return, the introduction of hospice methods into a hospital may have a humanizing influence and go some way towards resolving doctors' sense of failure when a patient dies.

While the main building of St Nicholas's Hospice was being refurbished, the patients and staff decamped to a ward in the West Suffolk Hospital and became, de facto, a hospice unit within an NHS hospital. To Ellie Bennett, it was quite quickly apparent that there were going to be disadvantages balancing, if not outweighing, the advantages. She liked the fact that hospital staff came to her for advice on care much more readily than they had when the hospice was on a separate site. But she was also conscious that, simply because they were on hospital premises, they did many more acute tests – blood, heart and breathing checks – than they would have done in the hospice, and this suggested to Ellie a notable move towards cure and away from care. Moreover, the issue of resuscitation was discussed in three or four cases, notwithstanding that it was a founding principle of the hospice approach that resuscitation was not to be done. (Recent developments, and in particular the new BMA guidelines issued in 2002, have obliged hospices around the country to review their policies on resuscitation, which will now be undertaken in certain circumstances.)

The creeping tendency to seek cures and to go along with doctors' requests to prolong life at all costs may mean that when hospital and hospice are in close proximity, the intimacy contaminates the hospice method. Hospices have been criticized recently from within the radical camp, by those reformers who have supported them in the past and now see some of them undergoing a process of transformation and compromise. The chief concern is that the hospice approach should neither become established nor part of the establishment. A lot does change in thirty years and hospitals have learnt a great deal from hospices, but in many respects hospitals, and their doctors in particular, are unreformed. Doctors remain the gateway to therapy and, as the technology has grown, so that power has increased. Medicine remains a macho game; it's all to do with early detection and cure. Whether doctors, as they cross the corridor to the hospice unit, can make the transition from death-defying hero, with a weaponry of gadgets and drugs, to attentive, consoling hospice doctor, who nurtures the spirit even as the body dies, remains to be seen. Cicely Saunders is sceptical:

> Dying on an NHS ward, as things are at the moment, even with a palliative care team going around, is not good. They will cope with symptom control, but they can't really cope with much more, and we've done comparative studies over the years, and the psycho-social side, the continuity side, the support of relatives side, is better in a hospice than it is on a general ward. So I think we will always be needed for difficult problems, particularly difficult physical problems and dysfunctional families.

Cicely Saunders expects that there will be more hospice units within hospitals, along the lines of practice in Germany, the USA and Canada, but she thinks the drawbacks will be enormous. It will be hard to avoid the reputation of 'the death ward' within the hospital set-up and running home care and day centre schemes will be, in her view, almost impossible.

For an understanding of why this development is a source of serious concern, we have to go back to the origins of the hospice movement. The hospice approach is grounded in ideas that are not cost efficient. Nurses give *as much time as is necessary* to a patient, unlike the busy ward nurse whose job at the bedside has to be executed as quickly as possible. The hospice was designed to be small, to avoid institutionalization. The greater the number of patients, the greater the need for uniform methods and social control. Katherine Froggatt's fear that hospice staff see themselves as the 'parents' and the patients and their families as the 'children' is germane here.[11] As the 'method' is perfected, it becomes more and more likely this criticism will be valid. The staff know what's good for you, and your death, because they've seen it work before. This has always been the prevailing ethic within hospitals and it has lingered on in the hospice, in attenuated form. If the hospice is now returned to the hospital, it is hard to imagine how that condescension can help but re-attach itself to hospice care.

On the other hand, there is some evidence that the NHS itself is trying to instil a new ethos of human interest and understanding. At Southampton University Hospital, they have been educating medical students in palliative care for some time. In the third year, Dr Richard Hillier's students in the School of Medicine learn about symptom control and the need for professional empathy, as well as about communicating with the dying and their relatives. The following year includes training in the ethics of decision-making at the end of life, and both the School's Intermediate and Final examinations usually feature questions on Palliative Care and Ethics. Each week Dr Hillier gets his students to spend time with terminally ill patients in his unit. It is an opportunity for the students to hear what the dying think and, time and again, the patients say the same thing: 'For goodness sake, be honest with us.' Patients try to get over that when the chips are down, they would rather meet the challenge of dying with as full a knowledge of it as it is possible to have.

This excellent initiative, led by a doctor committed to innovation and improvement, is one of the few that compels students to take palliative care seriously. Setting questions in final papers is, in Cicely Saunders's view, an essential requirement of medical training if palliative care is to become part of the mainstream. There remains, she believes, a strong resistance to taking it on: 'Most medical schools don't want to add a whole whack of palliative care to their curriculum, which is overcrowded as it is, and don't

have people on their staffs – other than the people who
come out of the hospice and palliative care movement – to
do it.'

The present, elective method leaves students free to avoid
the subject and, given the many other demands on them,
human nature suggests they will. St Christopher's teaches
Palliative Care and Palliative Medicine to medical students
at King's College, London, but as Andrew Knight points
out, it is not a core component: 'It's not one of the subjects
that they are examined on and it's not a subject that is
mandatory. So they don't come to the lectures. They bunk
off . . . Until it's mandatory, I can't see that we're getting
the message across.'

The new curriculum, however, does show signs of real
improvement. Doctors who want to be GPs are now
required to submit a videotape of consultations with patients, partly in order to demonstrate their safety, but also
to show that they are capable of listening and negotiating
with patients. More recently, in September 2000, the NHS
published its *National Cancer Plan* for Britain. It recognized, for the first time, that communication between
medical professionals and their patients was essential for
high-quality care. But the dramatic change in training that
it introduced was that, by the year 2002, all medical
students were required to evince a competence in communication in order to qualify as doctors. The importance of
this development is not only that it obliges every would-be
doctor to learn about the function of relationships within
effective palliative care, but that it consolidates – and none
too soon – the piecemeal efforts of medical schools around
the country.

There are, then, grounds for hope that doctors in the
future will be more responsive to the needs of the dying and
their families. However, the majority of doctors currently in
practice do, of course, lack such training. Some medical
schools have begun to address the problem by offering
'Higher Medical Training' (HMT), either as a full-time or

part-time course, or by distance learning. The University of Wales introduced a Diploma in Palliative Medicine in 1989 and now offers an MSc degree. The Royal College of Physicians has similarly begun to provide HMT for doctors who have completed two years of General Professional Training. The aim of the Royal College's course in Palliative Medicine is to 'equip individuals to carry the responsibility of a consultant working full-time in a hospice or in a hospital unit or team with responsibility for large numbers of patients with late-stage disease.' The curriculum published in February 2000 emphasized the importance of sensitive communication and 'not withholding information desired by a patient.'

In the USA, too, attempts are being made to re-train practising doctors in the techniques of communication and palliative care. A programme entitled Education for Physicians on End of Life Care (EPEC), uses teaching, discussion, videotapes and role-play to try to familiarize established physicians with the emotional and physical experiences confronted by the dying and bereaved. According to the EPEC website, the curriculum, first published in October 1999, is designed to provide doctors with 'the basic knowledge and skills needed to appropriately care for dying patients'. The course deals with most of the main issues that can lead to crisis: sudden illness, pain management, general symptom relief, feelings of anxiety and futility, suicidal feelings, ethical and legal questions, communicating difficult news sensitively and the character of grief. EPEC relies on a large number of nationally respected medical experts and the intention and structure of the course seem to be well thought through. Although it remains to be seen how popular the course will be and the effect it will have, the emphasis it appears to place on talking to patients and relatives can only be to the good of the dying and the bereaved. But as the detail and formality of these courses demonstrate, telling the truth is a concept that does not come naturally in medical care; it has to be taught. As Richard Cowie reminded me, 'Twenty years ago nurses were forbidden to talk to the dying. If you were asked "Am I dying?" you had to say "I'll get the doctor".'

Is there any other way in which the hospice approach to palliative care can be mainstreamed within acute hospitals? Richard Cowie, at the Hospice in the Weald, is in no doubt that it is essential that integration of the hospice method does take place if dying patients are to avoid segregation and misery on NHS wards. To some extent the approach will remain distinctive for as long as palliative practice takes advantage of external consultation and collaboration. Macmillan nurses were introduced into hospitals on that basis in 1991. Similarly, Dr Caroline Anson from Hospice in the Weald, has an honorary contract at the Kent and Sussex Hospital, which enables her to advise nurses there without becoming a member of the full-time hospital staff. In London, St Christopher's Hospice has a joint project with King's College Hospital to fund clinical research into palliative care and how it can improve. Over time, it has been possible to see the results of this research gradually influencing NHS policy.

The question that the *National Cancer Plan* and its antecedents pose is how far NHS doctors will be prepared to go in accepting patients as their equals. Will they ever allow dying patients an equal right of say in decision-making? Despite their protestations, doctors have not been coping with death as well as they might have thought. Their capacity to look at a body and to prescribe treatment and to witness the death of a patient without becoming upset or horrified is only part of the required duty. Death is patently not merely a mechanical failure, but a complex of responses from the patient and his family. If doctors find these too difficult to negotiate, it is the dying who lose out. No one pretends that informing and collaborating with vulnerable and anxious patients and families will be anything other than extremely demanding and require differing levels of detail and explicitness, but it is an essential feature of a 'good death'.

In the meantime, for the sake of the dying, we have to hope that the hospice hangs on to the social aspect of its philosophy and, by implication, its independence from a highly medicalized health service. What is absolutely clear, from the work that has been done with the dying and their relatives, is that a good death connotes patient autonomy, participation in decision-making, and as much physical and intellectual integrity as is compatible with the management of their symptoms and the natural progress of their disease. It is the hospice movement which has championed these values and objectives and whilst change within the health service is apparent and welcome, it is as yet insufficient to regard merger with hospices as anything other than a threat to dying patients' interests. No doubt there is a shortage of funding, no doubt the gradual restructuring of our society will mean a greater number of elderly and ill people needing terminal care, but it remains the case, that whether the dying are to be looked after in their homes or in residential units, they require patience, kindness, the esteem of the compassionate and, above all, a great deal of nursing time, in which they can speak and be heard.

5

The Need for Ritual

The smaller the society, the more the elimination of one of its members is felt as an attack upon its corporate strength.

Rosemary Dinnage

Forasmuch as it hath pleased Almighty God of his great mercy to take unto himself the soul of our dear brother here departed, we therefore commit his body to the ground; earth to earth, ashes to ashes, dust to dust; in sure and certain hope of the Resurrection to eternal life, through our Lord Jesus Christ; who shall change our vile body, that it may be like unto his glorious body, according to the mighty working, whereby he is able to subdue all things unto himself.

Book of Common Prayer (1662)

Margaret McAfee, one of the Family Support Team at the Hospice in the Weald, recalls her first experience of death when she was growing up in Northern Ireland. It was in 1952 that her brother died, during the big polio outbreak of that year:

For my mother and father it must have been awful, but I remember my father went to collect the coffin and then we all went to the hospital to bring my brother back, and lots of friends came and met us on the outskirts of town and we all came back, and the blinds in the street were down, and he was brought in and laid in Mummy and Daddy's bedroom. The priest would be there and prayers would be said and probably eight or nine o'clock he would go and the rosary would be said. Then the offical wake would begin, and neighbours and friends would bring cakes and all sorts of goodies for the people, to be there for the family and so that the family wouldn't have to worry about doing anything like that. They would all take turns in making tea, and everyone ate their cake and looked at the dead body and said how well he looked. 'He's looking very peaceful,' they'd say, 'he's great to see and he's got a smile on his face.' . . . So then, by ten o'clock most of the visitors would have gone and the core of mourners would settle down and usually some sort of comedian would be there, and then maybe the ladies would go to bed, and the main core of men would sit all night, and occasionally they would go and check that the candles around the body hadn't burnt down – it's called a 'death set', two candles and a little thing of holy water and a little thing for oil. So, as I say, five or six men would sit all night and there would be jokes and carry-on, drinking and coffee and cakes, and they would go away in the morning.

The following day the coffin was closed and the undertaker arrived to take it away. Margaret stood on the doorstep and watched as her father and the other men walked behind the hearse to the local church. Up and down the street, neighbours' blinds were drawn as a token of their respect and people stood in silence as the cortege passed. This was the moment when Margaret said goodbye to her little brother and the long process of her bereavement began.

Perhaps we no longer wish to mark the passing of the dead in this way. The wake is preoccupied with death; it is obsessed with the event and the body in the front room. Indeed, the very notion of a largely unused 'front parlour' owes its existence to the need to have somewhere to lay the dead. I might contrast the wake to the night my father-in-law died in 1984, when we sat around watching a video of Richard Attenborough's film *Gandhi*. Derek's body had been removed from the house. I don't now remember where it was put, though it was presumably with the local undertaker. We watched television as we might have done on any other, ordinary day of the week – except that it wasn't ordinary. Our feelings were vitiated by shock, and *we did not know what to do*. What distinguished the wakes of Margaret's childhood was that the family knew exactly what to do and they were supported in what they did by friends and neighbours who also knew what to do.

This is not to suggest that the Irish wake is a model of grief to be adopted by all western societies hungry for ritual. It is clearly an inappropriate form in a modern, urban context. A wake requires a stable, intimate and familiar population, not a fluctuating society which is highly mobile and frequently exchanged. There are, too, elements of the wake which draw on religious tradition and these would be widely rejected by the post-religious societies of western cities. But the features of the wake that are worth noting and remembering are that it is largely an active event and, secondly, one that is publicly acknowledged. In these respects, it is unlike my family tucked away behind closed curtains and transfixed by a death which was wholly unknown to the television viewers in neighbouring houses.

One of the surprising publishing successes of the late 1990s was a short book about the funeral industry called

The Undertaking. Its author, Thomas Lynch, describes how he rolls around small-town Michigan in his 'Dead Wagon', dispensing annual funeral services to a couple of hundred local inhabitants and poetry to a slightly smaller number. The book recalls his twenty-five years as a funeral director and the long line of fatalities he has had to deal with and commiserate upon. The thrust of Lynch's argument is that we are beginning to lose sight of what funerals are for and, by extension, our understanding of death and how it informs our lives is impoverished. 'We've flattened the gravestones,' says Lynch, 'shortened the services, opted for more and more cremation to keep from running out of land better used for amusement parks, off-street parking, go-cart tracks and golf courses.'[1] Our demotion of death in this way denies us, perhaps literally, the space in which to grieve and adjust and throughout his work, Lynch stresses that it is *our* bereavement, *our* pain and loss, which are the predicament and not the imagined feelings of the deceased. The funeral should be 'an effort to make sense of our mortality' because, as he says in his much repeated maxim, 'the dead don't care'.[2]

> This is the central fact of my business – that there is nothing, once you are dead, that can be done *to you* or *for you* or *with you* or *about you* that will do you any good or any harm; that any damage or decency we do accrues to the living, to whom your death happens, if it really happens to anyone. The living have to live with it. You don't. Theirs is the grief or gladness your death brings. Theirs is the loss or gain of it. Theirs is the pain and pleasure of memory. Theirs is the invoice for services rendered and theirs is the check in the mail for its payment.[3]

To the pre-Reformation world, this would have been an unintelligible and sacrilegious thought. The community of the faithful would pray to God to shorten the time endured in Purgatory by the departed soul; they hoped to improve the soul's afterlife, to influence God's judgement. But Purgatory has gone. It disappeared from the Protestant map at the turn of the Reformation and from the Roman Catholic Church when it was impugned at the Second Vatican Council in the mid-1960s. Funerals, ever since, have been for the living. Irrespective of belief in the afterlife or its denial, the form in which we say goodbye to the dead has been a matter of prime importance to the survivors and of sublime indifference to the deceased. As Philippe Ariès summarized it twenty years ago, once Purgatory went, 'my death' became 'thy death'.

But for many people today, the funeral is a cause of profound dissatisfaction. Seventy-two per cent of funerals in Britain are cremations (in the USA, it is much less: 25 per cent) and the formulaic character of most of them does little to capture the feelings of needful mourners. A service is expected to last half an hour and the presumption is that, unless anything is explicitly planned to the contrary, it will be conducted along more or less traditional Christian lines, with a priest or minister officiating and the Christian liturgy spoken. 'More particularly,' writes Malcolm Johnson, in his preface to the National Funerals College's consultative document *The Dead Citizens Charter*:

it will pass without an informed and thoughtful appreciation of the life just ended. Instead, those who gather will take part in a contentless diluted form of religious service during which the celebrant will provide a scratched together and unsatisfactory account of the dead person . . . Badly recorded hymn music may add to the impression of a synthetic performance. Inappropriate and unheralded disappearance of the coffin may add another layer of discomfort. Such an unsatisfying funeral may, nonetheless, cost in excess of £1,000.[4]

The other funerals, the 28 per cent that are burials, seem equally ineffective. They usually occur in a place of worship and are followed by an interment in a churchyard or, more likely, a municipal cemetery. (Other, non-Christian faith communities do have a number of private graveyards.) These will, on average, cost even more than the cremations. That there is increasing demand for an alternative kind of funeral suggests that people are unhappy and are turning away from both the traditional orthodoxies and the spiralling costs.

This is chiefly the consequence of a decline in religious faith, which is marked in the case of the Christian churches in Britain and is happening in smaller measure throughout the religious community. But it is also to do with the absence of a shared language of funerary ritual and the increasing mobility and fragmentation of society. What people complain about most commonly after a funeral is that the language of the service did not mean anything to them and that the organization and execution of the ceremony was impersonal. Funerals, when they are effective, are highly localized and intimate. Those who are immediately bereaved are able to express their feelings of loss and those who officiate have a personal knowledge of the deceased and, therefore, a loss of their own to acknowledge and voice on behalf of all the mourners. In circumstances in which people lead lives that are remote from the institutions that conceptualize the language of funerals and in which the design of the funerary event is one of a number of pre-packaged options, these qualities of intimacy and a sense of place within a community are rarely achieved.

A Longstanding Problem

Although the arguments have turned on different issues, this discrepancy between 'normative' tradition and the needs of mourners is a problem we have had with funerals for a long time. The history of obsequies is punctuated by a series of crises concerning the rules governing disposal and the dissatisfaction of the bereaved with existing forms. Burials of the prosperous in Tudor England, for instance, were characterized by huge extravagance, but some noble families came to tire of them. When Henry Percy, 4th Earl of Northumberland, left provision in his will for the payment of 2d to any of the poor who attended his funeral, 13,340 individuals turned up.[5] Frequently, people bequeathed funerary rings to the immediate family and a sumptuous dinner would be served to the principal mourners. Funerals amongst the high-born expressed a collective familial and societal grief, but equally they performed a moral and political task: they marked the inheritance of title and property. Elizabeth I seems to have been so alert to that significance she insisted that the funerals of the nobility be administered by the College of Arms. The Church of England, under Edward VI, had simplified the burial service for the edition of the *Book of Common Prayer* issued in 1552 and so these elaborate heraldic funerals were substantially secular ceremonies, superimposed on an abridged religious rite. Not surprisingly, they cost a great deal of money.

The College laid down strict rules governing the burial procession suitable for each rank of the nobility. It was stipulated that the chief mourners must be of the same sex as the deceased and the number of them reflected the status of the funeral. A duke would require eleven principal mourners, a baron only seven.[6] The impression of the whole was that this was a state event, not a personal one and not only was it expensive, but it frequently denied members of the dead noble's family a proper place in the ceremony. The widow of the nobleman, for example, was largely excluded from her husband's funeral by the heraldic protocol.

The College of Arms continued to organize the disposal of the noble dead until the Restoration, but towards the end of the sixteenth century there was growing discontent. That a funeral of this kind marginalized the spouse and other close family members was a source of pain and grievance, and it became increasingly evident that the grandiloquence of these events was excessive and unnecessary. Noble families began to rebel and to hold their funerals at night, in secret. Night burials were free from heraldic restriction and afforded an intimacy between mourners that was appropriate. A woman might mourn her husband's death without interference or disapproval. 'Night funerals emphasised sorrow and loss,' Clare Gittings observes, 'the darkness and torchlight adding to the atmosphere of gloom and reflecting the emotions of grief at bereavement.' James I eventually gave royal approval to the practice of night funerals when he re-buried his mother, Mary Queen of Scots, at night in Westminster Abbey. The etiquette propounded by the College of Arms may have enhanced royal control over the behaviour of noble families, but it bespoke a tradition and continuity at the expense of personal attachment, points which James Stuart, as the son of an executed 'foreign' queen, may not have regarded as in its favour.[7]

When a ceremonial form is emptied of meaning, people will reject it and devise something new. The eschewal of heraldic obsequies was primarily to do with the frustrated desires of mourners and rather less to do with money. These nobles were, after all, the country's richest families; they could afford what the College of Arms charged. It appears, though, that they didn't like what they were paying for. The ceremony did not fulfil their spiritual and emotional needs.

A turning-point of a different kind was the reorganization of urban burial in the nineteenth century. Although the nominal catalyst for change was a practical concern about hygiene in inner cities, underpinning it was the burgeoning diversity of Christian beliefs and their challenge to the monopoly of the Anglican establishment. The conditions of city churchyards in the early years of the century was so poor that they jeopardized the health and comfort of anyone who lived nearby. In London, up to 3,000 corpses might be buried every week, and in the absence of any tradition of secondary interment in charnel houses or ossuaries, this led to appalling overcrowding. The soil in some churchyards was so exhausted from intensive usage that it could no longer stimulate effective decomposition. To make room for the newly deceased, unclean bones were constantly disturbed and a decaying body might be laid to one side under a thin covering of dust. When new mourners attended a burial service, they would often trip over old corpses as they proceeded to the graveside. People who frequented the area near these burial grounds would complain of 'putrid emanations' and it was widely believed that this miasma was responsible for disease and deaths among neighbouring communities. George Alfred Walker described in visceral detail the obscenity of these sites in his *Gatherings from Graveyards* (1839). It was followed by Edward Chadwick's *Interment Report* of 1843, which recommended radical reform as a matter of urgency. In the 1850s, a number of burial acts enabled local burial boards to close noisome grounds and develop new cemeteries funded by the Poor Rate.

These improvements were inspired firstly by anxieties about the nation's well-being and, in particular, the declining health of urban populations, but they were also part of a wider movement to reform funeral practice. Chadwick's report was critical of the millions of pounds 'annually thrown into the grave at the expense of the living.' In 1843, the aristocracy was spending between £500 and £1,000 on a funeral and even the middle classes would have to find over £50. Black feathers, silks and hatbands were all expensive and, for those who really wanted to empty their purses, a funeral procession could be enhanced by the addition of a couple of mutes on horseback. Fear of grave-robbing was then at its height and undertakers happily responded by supplying triple-lined coffins and an iron cage to fortify the burial plot. Undertakers were perceived to be greedy and ruthless in their exploitation of those made vulnerable by grief.

The model of extravagance was bound to have a bad effect on the poor of the cities. They had already been terrified by the Anatomy Act of 1832, which had proposed that unless they could afford proper burial, their bodies could be handed over to medical schools to be dissected. Before the 1830s, the schools depended on illegally obtained bodies and the bodies of murderers, but the new Act stipulated that poor and old internees of workhouses or hospitals who died without the means to pay for a funeral, were not to be buried but sent to laboratories for medical research. Everyone sought to avoid that fate and would make whatever sacrifice possible to purchase a proper burial, a desperation undertakers were quick to take advantage of. At the same time, the wealthier classes were expressing their growing distaste for what they saw as extravagance, particularly when it was to fulfil a social obligation that had no ethical or religious roots. In 1850, the Metropolitan Interment Act called for burials at fixed prices.

The push to create municipal cemeteries, unattached to Anglican parish churches, had come from an altogether different quarter as well. The Church of England had had, in effect, entire control of burial. Since its foundation, it had had the power to stipulate who could be buried and where. Its priests enjoyed the prerogative to permit people to be buried within the walls of the church (banned in 1850) or in a plot in the churchyard, and they provided a religious service for the dead, as set out in the *Book of Common Prayer*. But they had also always had the authority to refuse burial to certain types of dead. They generally did not give sacred burials to excommunicants, suicides and stillborn infants and in the early nineteenth century they could turn away members of non-conformist churches. Even if they did allow a non-conformist burial, they would not usually agree to a non-conformist minister officiating and the family of the deceased would have to assent to the Church of England's liturgy. Clearly, this was not a practice likely to survive the burgeoning growth in non-conformist beliefs throughout the country. Non-conformists did not regard Anglican soil as consecrated, nor did they see the *Book of Common Prayer* as the only rite suitable for Christians. Between 1820 and 1853, 115 private cemeteries were opened, in places as far apart as Truro and Perth. Although 70 per cent of funerals in Britain are still conducted by Anglican clergy, the combined effect of private enterprise and the construction of large municipal cemeteries was to end the Church of England's dominion over funerals for ever.

A second result of Victorian reforms was to promote an interest in cremation. Cremation had long been regarded as anti-Christian, because it posed a theological conundrum: how could the body rise 'incorruptible' at the Resurrection if it had been reduced to ashes? On the continent, there seems to have been less of a Christian anxiety – or possibly a weaker lobby – because by the 1870s when the cremation movement began to exert an influence in Britain, there were already ten official crematoria in Europe.

If people in British cities wished to opt for a swifter, cleaner, cheaper means of disposal, it was hardly surprising given the intimacy in which they had come to live with the dead and their reek. *The Lancet*, pursuing a keenly hygienic line, seemed to agree. But the medical journal had not reckoned with the strength of Christian objection. Even though church attendance was in marked decline, its influence was sufficient to make *The Lancet*, in the closing decades of the century, ping-pong back and forth, supporting and then opposing cremation until it finally decided it was a good thing. The turning point was a trial in Cardiff in 1884, which found that cremation was not illegal.

Crematoria began to spring up around the country – Woking (1885), Manchester (1892) – and the industry was then regulated under the Cremation Act of 1902. This did little to persuade the churches, however, which remained adamantly opposed. The Church of England took until 1944 to conclude that since the practice was not having an adverse effect on people's beliefs, it should no longer offer resistance to it; and the Roman Catholic Church did not approve cremation until 1963.

What unites these historical moments of change is the determination on the part of individual mourners to wrest control of funeral services from the state and its appointed institutions and to make the ritual serve *their* needs. The personality of grief and the demands it makes on existing funeral etiquette are sometimes obscured by the sociological and economic facets of change with which they coincide. Pat Jalland, writing about the impact of World War One on social behaviour, has observed that funerals were simplified and made less conspicuous soon after the casualties began to mount in Flanders. Some historians have attributed this to a shortage of men to work within the funeral industry and of vehicles to serve as hearses. Others have argued that these more chastened obsequies reflected a widespread concern about public morale. The sheer number of funerals was enough to demoralize a whole nation and Jalland notes that many were impressed by the dismal note struck by the Eton *v* Harrow cricket match of July 1916 when so many men wore black in token of their losses.[8] But above all these, people eschewed ornament because it offended. It was insensitive to the many mourners who could not hold a funeral, who had no bodies to bury. Funerary ornament dignified with pomp and a dark beauty an event that was, for some of the bereaved, sullied and diminished by the absence of any honour, triumph or redemption.

The Need for a New Turning Point

That we occupy now what Thomas Lynch sardonically describes as 'a difficult space in the history of obsequies' is perhaps less remarkable given this background of conflict between the needs of the bereaved and the prevailing conventions. The bereaved have always had to struggle to achieve the forms of service they believed would help them through their grief. In fact, Victorian women had to fight to secure a place at the funeral at all. Women were excluded from funerals because they were considered to be unable to control their feelings and it was only in the 1870s that they succeeded in obtaining the right to attend the church service, if not the committal. Form, almost invariably, mitigates against the show of emotion and the individual's grief has been routinely subverted by a rigid protocol that we imagine to be older than it probably is.

When a ritual is the subject of a compact between the organizers and the organized, as for example when it is grounded in shared religious conviction, the individual may willingly subordinate his or her sensibility to the tried and tested formula. The problem is that the compact is under constant threat of breaking down and without an innate capacity to change, the ritual is soon discovered to be out of step with the society it serves. It is in the nature of modernity that the individual will be exposed to critiques and parodies of the ritual, and will accrue odd shreds and whole parcels of new philosophy which, intentionally or not, traduce and overturn the old. Thus, the possibility of a traditional Christian funeral service meeting *all* the needs of today's bereaved is slim, and the reason that so many mourners wish now to speak at funerals is that the officiating priest or minister is not saying what needs to be said.

Because the event of death is awesome and intimidating, it is inferred that the procedures for disposal of the dead are

highly regulated because they need to be. Certain institutions contribute to this impression, notably the Church of
England. It is a much repeated complaint, of Anglican
communicants and parishioners alike, that the rules governing the funeral service and the churchyard are too strict.
At one funeral company I visited, the director told me of
three recent cases when the Church of England had refused
the most simple and unobjectionable requests regarding the
design and wording of gravestones. The family of a wheel-
wright was not allowed to put the image of a wheel on his
stone; a man who had been a shepherd was forbidden a
shepherd's crook. Perhaps more ridiculous than either was
the case of a family who were told they couldn't include the
word 'Dad' within the name of the deceased, even though
this was the tag by which he had always been known. *The
Churchyards Handbook* makes explicit the reason why:
'Nicknames or pet-names ("Mum", "Dad", "Ginger") in-
scribed in stone, would carry overtones of the dog-cemetery
unsuitable for the resting-place of Christian men and women.'[9] This sounds like an attitude struck in 1888, not
1988. As a regulation, it takes no account of a mourner's
need to stay close to the dead through the use of an intimate
language.

The failure to acknowledge the right of mourners to
record sentiments appropriate to their personal experience
arises out of a concern about the public status of gravestones. The Church appears to equate freedom of expression with a cheapening of the churchyard and there is
nothing new in this. Dr Johnson objected to the inflated
language of epitaphs in the eighteenth century. He accused
their authors of a total want of discrimination. Few humans
deserved the general order of praise bestowed on them in
epitaphs, he argued, and furthermore people were too alike
to be distinguished by such encomiums. Rather mordantly,
Johnson added 'the greater part of mankind have no
character at all.'[10] Whether the good doctor can be said
to have stuck to his principles when he came to bury his

own wife is a moot point. The epitaph he wrote for her was short, but not short on praise:

> Here lie the remains of Elizabeth, descended from the ancient house of Jarvis at Peatling in Leicestershire; a Woman of beauty, elegance, ingenuity, and piety. Her first Husband was Henry Porter; her second, Samuel Johnson, who having loved her much, and lamented her long, laid this stone upon her.[11]

Later in the same century, Wordsworth disagreed with Johnson. In his own essay on the subject, he pointed out that although epitaphs are a public statement, 'open to the day', the sentiment is designedly personal: 'It is a truth hallowed by love – the joint offspring of the worth of the dead and the affections of the living.' Wordsworth enjoined the use in an inscription of 'the general language of humanity as connected with the subject of death,' so that all who passed by could read and learn from it, be it the stooping man or the newly literate child. It is not in our nature, he wrote, to analyse the character of those we love or weigh up their merits and defects, particularly when 'under the pressure of sorrow'. Rather, the business of the gravestone is to strike a tone 'which shall sink into the heart . . . and the stranger is introduced through its mediation to the company of a friend.'[12]

This is scarcely likely to be achieved for as long as the language permitted remains reductive and impersonal. Gone are the days when an intimate story of accidental death could be summarized on a gravestone in this way:

> Beneath are deposited the remains of Thomas and George Weller of this parish who on the 18th of November 1834 suddenly passed into eternity by incautiously descending a well before the foul air was expelled.
> Thomas aged 62
> George aged 45

The loss of the two Wellers was no doubt felt by everyone who lived in the village, and the manner of their dying was so unusual and alarming that they wanted to record it for posterity. Had the mourners been denied the right to describe it, something of their grief would have been thwarted and something of the village history erased.

A Rebel from within the Ranks

So what can an individual mourner do in the face of institutional antipathy and bureaucratic rigidity? One answer is to fight back. Now more than ever, it is possible to do a great deal both to determine the form a funeral takes and to design a memorial in such a way that it is a statement of the bereaved person's grief and not the reproduction of someone else's idea of appropriate sentiment.

In recent years, popular frustration with the obstructiveness of the Church has driven people to take advantage of the artistic and literary freedom that municipal cemeteries afford. Harriet Frazer became so exasperated that she decided to set up Memorials by Artists, which alerts the bereaved to the range of designs that can be used in local authority cemeteries and then introduces them to artists willing to carry out such commissions. Images abound of teddy bears, pheasants, cars and bicycles, things that had been of importance in the life of the deceased. Memorials by Artists has completed over 600 stones since it started in 1988.

Bev Sage and her children were another bereaved family frustrated by the hidebound stance on gravestones adopted by all but one of the Anglican churches she consulted. Her husband, Steve Fairnie, was a painter and had signed all his work with a symbol of his own design, representing 'Man & Woman'. Bev wanted to incorporate this motif in an inscription on a Celtic cross. The churches refused. Many widows might have been deterred, but Bev wouldn't take 'no' for an answer. She had the confidence of her own profound Christian faith to know that there was nothing in what she proposed that was un-Christian or unreasonable. Eventually, she found a church which agreed to both the cross and Steve's 'signature'.

The advice seems to be: persist. Bev had met with mild opposition to her plans for the funeral as well, but there too she overcame it by force of will. Steve was a young man when he died and Bev was determined that his funeral would be as much a celebration of his life as a lament. He had died suddenly. On 22 February 1993, the day after his birthday, he took a party of his art students on a study trip to Devon. Steve was an asthmatic and when he rang Bev that night from the fishing village of Brixham, he complained about being a little short of breath, a bit off-colour. It didn't seem too serious, but he died later that night from a massive asthma attack. He was forty-two.

A friend of theirs had died of epilepsy three weeks before and Steve had remarked at the funeral that when his turn came, he would rather four beautiful women with fishnet tights carry his coffin than men from the Co-op. Bev decided she would do what she could to give Steve the funeral he had inadvertently requested. It took place at the Bristol church of Christchurch in Clifton on 2 March and the service was led by James Jones, later to become the Bishop of Liverpool. With the help of friends, Bev organized every aspect of it. She helped design an invitation card and an order of service beautifully illustrated with some of Steve's designs. She styled the event a 'ceremony' and invited everyone to bring a candle. There were to be no flowers, but people were welcome to make donations to pay for a sculpture that Bev had commissioned in memory of Steve. When the coffin entered, it was carried on the shoulders of six peroxide blondes. Each held a candle and as they processed up the aisle, they paused to help people in the congregation light theirs. The service itself did include traditional prayers and hymns, but there were also readings from Steve's own writing and pieces specially written for the funeral by friends. Others spoke about their memories of Steve and some of his favourite music was played, including *One* by U2. In the meantime, the children were allowed to play in the sandtrays where the candles had stood.

Steve Fairnie had a good funeral, or rather his widow did. 'The funeral can be the best moment for the widow,' Bev suggests, ' because all your friends make you feel special and loved.' One year on, Bev and the children held a commemorative party, in the week of Steve's birth and death, 'to continue the celebration of his life'. She called it Fairnie's Feast (The Feast of Stephen). In February 1998, with seventy-four guests assembled and James Jones once again leading the prayers, Bev and the family marked the fifth anniversary of Steve's death around the newly erected Celtic cross. This is a funeral that is, in a sense, ongoing. Although Bev now visits Steve's grave infrequently – she might go for months without going there – his death is remembered each year.

Too often the bereaved are frightened to ask for the funeral they want. They make the assumption that the things they might cherish, things likely to give joy or comedy or simply sentimental memories, will disrupt the sombreness of a traditional ceremony and will, therefore, be unacceptable. This may be true in certain circumstances, but increasingly churches and funeral directors are asked to accommodate all sorts of requests as part of an effort by the bereaved to make the event distinctive, personal and memorable.

Dorothy Waterhouse (no relation) runs a funeral service called C. Waterhouse & Sons in Burwash, East Sussex. She joined the firm when her father needed extra help and over the last twenty years she has increased the business tenfold. Dorothy now arranges 250 funerals a year and has clients from Burwash down to the Sussex coast. Her company is independent and she plans to keep it that way. Like many funeral directors, she sees her first re-

sponsibility as 'the care of the living' and that can mean
persuading the bereaved to do things that at first they
would rather not do. Dorothy believes we have lost touch
with death. It is now possible for people to die in hospital,
be removed to a funeral director's chapel of rest and end
up six feet under, or in an urn of ashes, without their dead
bodies ever having been seen by relatives or friends. This is
ill-advised, in Dorothy's opinion, and she encourages all
her clients to spend time with the body before the funeral.
She takes great care over the embalming of her bodies and
is sure that by the time the family comes to 'view', the
deceased is presentable:

> You're not going to have any odours that are distres-
> sing. Sometimes, when we move people, they're leak-
> ing from every orifice and it's nasty. That's all cleared
> up. It's not a full embalming, as the Egyptians did it, it
> just sanitizes the body. It gives it a good colour because
> sometimes people are blue if they died on their side or
> face down. We wash them and men have a shave and
> their hair is washed and blow-dried and then their
> clothes are put on. We call it the 'Temporary Hygienic
> Treatment'.

Not everyone agrees with embalming and the Office of Fair
Trading has warned against 'unnecessary embalming' on
the grounds that it can be both unsightly and expensive.
The OFT has now stipulated that it should only be done
with the consent of relatives. It can alter the appearance so
dramatically that the bereaved would rather not have seen
the body at all. When Dorothy took me backstage into the
chapel of rest, she showed me three bodies – two men and a
woman – which had been embalmed and laid out in coffins.
What struck me was how un-lifelike they looked and
Dorothy appeared a little upset when I suggested they
might be waxworks. But that is what they most resembled.
The hands were whiteish, with a fake yellowing, particu-

larly around the fingernails. There was a white rim to the mouth and I remarked that it was pleasing to see that one of them was smiling. Dorothy explained that the corpse had no choice but to smile. In most cases, the mouth falls open after death and it has to be sewn up. Apparently, it's as easy to create a smiling face as a grumpy one.

The abiding impression these bodies left on me was that they appeared to be imitations of human life. There was no sense in which these embalmed images might be confused with a living form asleep. But whatever view is taken of embalming, the experience of viewing the body, if it is deliberate and for some time and not a snatched and anxious glance, does seem to be more beneficial in its effects than not. This is especially true when it is a baby that has died. Babies have been known for so short a time that their features are difficult to fix in our memories.

Dorothy recalls the parents of a baby boy and how they chose to bring their young daughter to view her dead brother:

> They all sat there for nearly an hour. We'd designed the coffin like a teddy bear, with teddies in it and birds and things. And the little girl had written a letter to him and she put it into the coffin. And they'd brought photographs of everybody, including the dog and a teddy bear, and we put them in as well. And she was sad, that little girl, and she cried, but she knew what she was doing, and she'd done what she needed to do.

The value of these moments of strange intimacy is perhaps best evinced by a story Dorothy told about a couple who refused to see their baby, Coral. Coral's mother had supplied Dorothy with clothes in which to bury her, but she simply did not wish to view her child in the coffin. Dorothy intuitively felt this was a mistake and, risking offending the parents, she took a photograph of Coral. She then told the mother that she might have the picture whenever she liked.

The funeral went ahead and the parents were reluctant to participate in any practical way. They did not want to carry the coffin and they were clearly too traumatized to appreciate that these moments might have a lasting value. Some weeks later they returned to Dorothy's office and saw the photograph. 'You would have thought I had given them the Crown Jewels,' Dorothy told me. 'They were over the moon about it.' Coral's parents then went on to have another child, Oliver, and they sent Dorothy a piece of the christening cake, together with a note from the mother that simply said, 'I wouldn't have known that Oliver looked like Coral if I hadn't had that photograph. Thank you.'

This is very much a modern approach to funeral provision. The style is personal and responsive, and the service may extend beyond the funeral itself and into the ensuing weeks or months. Dorothy receives many letters commending her work and appreciating her kindness. 'When we said goodbye at the crematorium,' one client wrote, 'you put your arms around me and said keep in touch any time I was around your area. I was really touched by your warmth, your genuineness . . . My friends all comment on what must be your uniqueness. Certainly no one has ever heard of a funeral director with your qualities of genuine empathy, understanding of the needs of the bereaved (whether they acknowledge them or not) and your comprehensive efficiency.'

Dorothy Waterhouse recognizes that many people today want to conduct their own funerals and, if not to conduct them, to devise their appearance and content. It is quite common now for her to record the funeral on audio cassette, which would have been unthinkable a generation ago. An approach that might have seemed eccentric, even ten or twenty years ago, can now be understood to play an important role in grief resolution. Dorothy is happy to arrange a funeral which is attended by a large number of dogs and horses belonging to the deceased, if that is what will enrich the event for the bereaved.

She also remembers a particular man of twenty-eight who died suddenly from leukaemia. His girlfriend, who had known about his condition, had wanted to marry but had failed to discuss it with him. She decided to make the funeral into their 'wedding'. White ribbons were laced around the hearse, the young woman carried a wedding bouquet and the mourners wore buttonholes. The family carried his coffin to the grave and let off fireworks at the graveside. The would-be bride had made two souvenir boxes in which she had put things of sentimental value to them both. She placed one box in the coffin and kept the other.

The episode smacks of Miss Haversham and her failure to come to terms with sudden reversal, but in fact this woman has not since suffered from 'arrested grief' and appears to have made a new life for herself. Perhaps we are too quick to assume that people do not know what they are doing when they depart from tradition. Dorothy is sure that the key to a successful funeral, by which she means one that fulfils the needs of the bereaved, is participation. She encourages the family to take part in the planning and to design an active role for themselves during the proceedings. Some people may be prostrated by their grief, but most, she believes, can be helped to do something.

Commercializing Death

It remains to be seen what will emerge from the conflicting trends in today's funeral industry, whether we will be forced to purchase the expensive packages that much of the industry provides, or whether the smaller companies will survive to become a more flexible and responsive service, reflecting many of the individualistic fashions and methods of the 'alternative' sector of the trade. At the moment, the continuing success of the conglomerates is uncertain. Service Corporation International (SCI) is the largest of a number of huge funeral chains that have been buying up funeral businesses around the world. As of December 2001, SCI owned 3,099 'funeral service locations', 475 cemeteries and 177 crematoria in 11 countries. The SCI 'empire' is not what it was, however, the company had, until recently, 527 funeral companies in Britain, and serviced one in eight funerals; in the USA, the figure was one in five. But in February 2002 SCI sold up most of its holdings in Britain, and its share of the market in the United States fell to around 10–12 per cent.

There is a lot to play for. According to a survey commissioned by the friendly society Oddfellows, and published in April 2000, funerals went up in price by 25 per cent over a period of two years from 1998 and they doubled during the 1990s. A burial in Britain in the year 2000 cost an average of £2,048, whilst a cremation averaged around £1,215. Funerals are currently worth £700 million a year in Britain. Furthermore, the death rate is set to rise, which means that in the USA, the number of deaths per year will increase from 2.3 million to 3 million. That is a big and attractive market.

The prime criticism levelled against some of these large funeral chains is that they go for the 'hard sell'. They have been accused – as mid-century undertakers in Victoria's reign were accused before them – of using unreasonable pressure to persuade those who are poor, vulnerable or old, or all three, to part with money they can ill afford to buy unnecessarily extravagant funeral services. In particular, they have been criticized for the 'pre-need' sales pitch, employing a crude rhetoric of fear to convince people that if they didn't arrange a satisfactory funeral now, it would be a burden upon their – by implication – feckless children, who would ensure that the parent's last rites were more or less cheap and nasty.[13] SCI's departure from Britain may be a sign of changing tastes.

The implication is that 'pre-need' funeral arrangements

are either odd or wrong, but the wisdom of thinking ahead is recognized by respectable charities such as Age Concern. A joint venture between SCI Pre-arrangement Ltd. and Age Concern to sell pre-paid funerals – ranging in cost from just over £1,000 to nearly £2,000 – began in 1997 and continues. Considering in advance what kind of funeral ceremony you would like is recommended with equal conviction by funeral directors at the other end of the spectrum, the idiosyncratic *à la carte* services associated with green burials and the protection of the environment. One distinctive feature of small progressive companies is that they charge a good deal less. Large funeral chains can exploit a general ignorance about funerals and what is permissible. Most people are anxious to do the right thing and a funeral is seen as, amongst other things, an act of loyalty. But people do not, by and large, know what choices they have and they tend to opt for what appears to be straightforward and easy, such as the services of the leading high street funeral director and one of the funeral plans in the firm's catalogue.

Ancient Playgrounds

Much of our inhibition about making even minor departures from sombre custom – accepting, thereby, that we are spectators rather than actors at a funeral – arises out of a belief that the dead are best respected by our silence and stillness. But this kind of estrangement from the dead is a relatively recent notion in western cultures. Clare Gittings has pointed out that throughout sixteenth century Britain, and into the nineteenth century in certain northern districts, the act of watching the corpse, the night before the funeral, was usually accompanied by drinking, card playing and even 'sexual' games, often versions of Blind Man's Buff.[14] They symbolized a kind of licensed chaos, which made the death more tolerable and asserted the continuation of life in the face of death. Graveyards, too, were centres of communal activity. In the eighteenth century, it would have been common for any visitor to a church to see cattle grazing amongst the gravestones, children playing games and women hanging their washing out to dry, as well as fights, plays and fairs.[15] (In parts of Ireland today, tinkers and gypsies still hold parties in graveyards.)

In this way, the living maintained their contact with the dead and, by their presence, preserved them in memory. Wordsworth's poem *We are Seven* (1798) depicts just such a rustic churchyard in which the poet encounters an eight-year-old 'little Cottage girl', who explains that she is one of seven children, two of whom are buried in graves nearby. The poet is intrigued to know how there are seven children in the family when two are dead.

> 'You run about, my little Maid,
> Your limbs they are alive;
> If two are in the church-yard laid,
> Then ye are only five.'

> 'Their graves are green, they may be seen,'
> The little Maid replied,
> 'Twelve steps or more from my mother's door,
> And they are side by side.

> 'My stockings there I often knit,
> My kerchief there I hem;
> And there upon the ground I sit,
> And sing a song to them.

Again, the poet tries to impress on the girl that she is mistaken, but she won't have it:

> 'How many are you then,' said I,
> 'If they two are in Heaven!'
> The little Maid did reply,
> 'O Master! we are seven.'

> 'But they are dead; those two are dead!
> Their spirits are in heaven!'
> 'Twas throwing words away; for still
> The little Maid would have her will,
> And said, 'Nay, we are seven!'

For Wordsworth, her adamant belief that the 'life' of her two siblings persists in some sense is evidence of our innate trust in the immortality of the soul. Without that truth, our memorials, he believes, would be meaningless.

That we have abandoned our graveyards as arenas of domestic and leisure activity may, then, be allied to our abandonment of religious traditions. (Interestingly, traditional Muslim families continue the practice of inviting guests to share a meal at the graveside.) By and large, graveyards are now places of solitude, irregularly visited by friends and relatives of the people buried there, and only then as part of a continuing act of mourning. Sadly, this has left these beautiful retreats vulnerable to desecration. The Mill Road Cemetery in Cambridge, for example, was attacked by vandals in the early hours of New Year's Day 1999. They went in with sledgehammers and broke up headstones and crosses and mutilated the figures of angels. Ironically, although burials ceased there in the 1950s, this was a cemetery that had, in a distinctly modern fashion, clung on to its social function as a public park. Local residents used to walk their dogs there and groups of men were often seen hanging around, drinking, smoking roll-ups and listening to portable radios. The cost of repair is said to be beyond the means of the local authority and, like many similar Victorian cemeteries, it may have to be locked up to prevent further damage.

Doing Your Own Thing

The growth in alternative funerals reflects this detachment from the traditional places of rest as much as it does an objection to the high costs and impersonal style of large funeral companies. The choice of alternative funeral, however, is often hedged about by ignorance of what is legally permitted and what rights we, the bereaved, enjoy. Many people are unaware that you can bury a loved one in your garden if you own one. If you live in an area where the 1847 Burial Act applies, you may have to ensure that the corpse is covered by at least thirty inches of soil, but there is no other legal constraint. And although the Natural Death Centre suggests that it is sensible to establish with the National Rivers Authority that the body will not contaminate the water table, it is not obligatory. Further, you do not have to place the body in a coffin or put lime in the grave. Indeed, the Ministry of Agriculture (now part of DEFRA) advises against the use of lime.

There is similar confusion regarding possession of the dead body and where funeral services can be held. It is illegal for a funeral director to refuse to release the body to the next of kin, and hospitals, too, must release the body unless acting on a coroner's instructions. A doctor can stipulate that the body be taken directly for burial or cremation, but only if he has a reasonable concern about infection. People can request that the funeral service be held in whole or in part in their own home, and there is no requirement that the funeral be conducted by a member of the clergy. Indeed, anyone may lead a funeral and it can be entirely without religious content. In short, people have more discretion in their choice of funeral than they tend to imagine.[16]

This is a point stressed by Heaven on Earth, Paula Rainey Croft's alternative funeral company in Bristol. Heaven on Earth was set up in 1995, first to sell what might be called funerary furniture, bookcases that doubled as coffins (or maybe it's the other way around!). They were substantially cheaper than those offered in a conventional funeral directors' catalogue and available in highly decorated patterns. Within six months, Paula found herself being drawn into providing a full funerary service. She has no doubt that people started to come to her not out of an eccentric desire for the new, but because they could not satisfy all their needs elsewhere. Commonly, they said they didn't want a 'rota vicar', who hadn't a clue who the deceased was. 'They'd rather have nobody talking, and just have music,' Paula says. Those without religious faith complained of feeling distant from the traditional funeral service and yet they had a deep yearning to mark the event, to recognize its importance as part of a grieving process.

Paula regards every funeral as ad hoc and *à la carte*. She brainstorms with her families about what they really want. 'You can do whatever you like,' she tells them. Heaven on Earth funerals take place everywhere: at churches and crematoria, at sea, in remote woodlands and private gardens. She reduces the cost by using cheaper services and cheaper materials, although the process, she is quite sure, is one of enrichment. She is happy to pick up a coffin from the mortuary in her VW Passat. Her coffins cost much less than those generally available in the high street because they are made of medium-density fibreboard (MDF), reconstituted oak, or even cardboard (a material frowned on by funeral directors and some crematoria) and the handles are usually made of rope. Or, if you wish, you can have a 'Ghanaian' coffin in the shape of a boat. The tradition in Ghana is to be buried in a coffin emblematic of your trade or skill, so a fisherman is buried in a canoe coffin. In Britain, this idea has led to some bizarre requests. Paula supplied a 'Red Arrow' coffin to a woman in Glasgow and she has also created one in the shape of a chess piece.

Like Dorothy Waterhouse's funeral service, Paula Rainey Croft places the emphasis on participation. 'If they've got friends who want to bear, or if they want to paint the coffin or line it, any of the bits they think they can handle, I encourage them to.' The result is a more intimate, more active kind of funeral. Often the deceased is placed in much closer physical relation to the mourners to underscore that intimacy: 'We've done them with a great big photo of the person who is in the coffin, a great big poster on a stand. The coffin comes in and then people come and touch it. We don't have it on the catafalque but on trestles within the congregation, and people have stood around and put flowers on it.'

Currently, Paula arranges over 100 funerals a year and, undoubtedly, her work is fulfilling a need, but it raises an important question about the function of ritual within a society. Can the self-designed cremation or the do-it-yourself burial provide the same sense of closure, the same rite of passage, as funerary ritual that is collectively approved and practised? Thomas Lynch thinks not. He observes that we are 'making up new liturgies to say goodbye' and that this degree of subjectivity in a ritual will eventually distort our understanding of death itself.[17] The problem arises because there is an implied disparity between the death of the individual and the death that is our common lot. Although the traditional liturgy may no longer serve the collective good, its virtue as Rosalie Osmond has remarked, is that it:

> avoids the severance of the particular and the general. We celebrate a particular marriage, but we also celebrate marriage as a whole. We mourn an individual we have loved, but we accept this death as part of a universal pattern of growth and decay – or more specifically of God's plan of birth, death, and regeneration for humanity. Again, it has the function of asserting order and through it meaning.[18]

What many people face today is a conflict between their lack of religious belief – what they may regard as a rational discarding of superstition – and their anxiety about how to mark the end of a life they have loved. So, can we learn anything about the values of continuity and participation

from other people's funeral rites? We have, after all, been
exposed as never before to examples of non-western cultures and how they honour their dead. Hindu women are
intimate with the dead to the last, anointing the corpse,
dressing it and then weeping over its departure as it burns
on the funeral pyre. For Mexicans, the dead are a part of
their lives. On the Day of the Dead, they bake bread for the
dead (*pan de los muertos*), leave it in the family grave and
then consume *what the dead have not eaten*. In fact,
examples of active rituals rooted in a tradition of participation are myriad. Some we may find attractive, others crude
and repellent, but could they help resolve our own need for
a ritual that has spiritual content but is not compromised by
an orthodoxy that no longer serves?

Whether the United States will face the same anxiety
over ritual that Britain is beginning to confront is unclear.
The USA may be able to devise new, crossbred rituals as a
consequence of its growing multiculturalism. The racial
composition of the country has never been so varied. In
1980, 1 in 5 Americans belonged to an ethnic minority;
by 2000, it was 1 in 4. Moreover, during the last
twenty years, the growth amongst ethnic groups that bring
to the States the funerary rituals of other religious traditions has been enormous: Vietnamese (135%), Korean
(125%) and Laotian-Hmong (1,600%) to mention only
three. The Hmong raise pigs and chickens in order to
sacrifice them in ceremonies designed to appease the spirits
of the dead! Who knows what kind of obsequies might
arise out of the cultural interaction of the next twenty
years?

It seems unlikely that we in Britain will cherry-pick other
people's practices and make them ours. These rites are
culture-specific for historical reasons; they are underpinned
by a system of belief. In a society where the belief system is
crumbling – perhaps has already crumbled – ritual will
inevitably fragment. But the importance of the funeral
remains beyond question. As the *Dead Citizens Charter*

so clearly puts it, 'An individual's funeral will take place just once. It is the principal means by which people can gather together to say goodbye and honour the dead, to comfort the living and to address the mystery of life and death.'[19] Under circumstances in which there is no agreement that death *is* transcendental, what kind of spiritual ritual can we sustain that will help us to grasp that mystery and begin to settle the trauma of death?

That there is no imminent prospect of western societies developing a belief system to which all of us will subscribe is beyond question. Rather, we witness the growth of idiosyncratic and eclectic beliefs, which are determined by individuals and shared amongst small groups. In the same way, funeral reform seems to be occurring at a private level. Ultimately, there may be a problem with the DIY approach. The loss of any collective ritual will mean the loss of any collective understanding of death. In the meantime, whilst the abandonment of orthodoxy has left some of us bereft, it has freed others to meet the challenge of marking the passing of human life in an active and participatory manner, organizing the form of their funerals and performing in them. It would appear that it is these people who, by crafting their own rituals and liturgy, derive the most benefit from the funerary event.

What unites many of these alternative ceremonies is the emphasis placed on the life-story of the deceased. In much the same way that palliative care has sought to lend meaning to the lives of the dying by encouraging patients to recall the story of their lives, these new funerals recount the dead person's life through a combination of narrative, music and symbol, which together summon up the memories of those present. To some extent, story or biography has always been a feature of traditional funerals, but the alternative ceremony may take the responsibility for storytelling away from the officiating priest and give it to the mourners. This process of devolution, or deprofessionalizing, of ritual allies the new kind of funeral to, on the one hand, the hospice approach to dying and, on the other, a new approach to grief, which, as I shall try to show in the next chapter, could enable the bereaved to gain some control over what is happening to them and to feel slightly less helpless at a time of enormous suffering.

6

Dealing with Grief

A hundred years ago no one was silent or tongue-tied, as we are now, when death was in the room. They had not yet muzzled grief or banished it from daily life. Death was cultivated, watered like a plant. There was no need for whispering or mime. Let the hubbub drive the devils out, they'd tell themselves. Let's make a row. Let's shout.

Jim Crace

Since some 650,00 people die in Britain every year, it is perhaps surprising that we are not more aware of the bereaved amongst us and not better able to accommodate their pain within our daily lives. After every one of those deaths, two or three people, perhaps more, will have their lives turned upside down as they face the awful prospect of a life *without*. As we travel the tube or buy bread in the supermarket, there will be around us and unknown to us, hundreds of people struggling to turn their feelings of devastation into a sad reconciliation. They will be striving to reconstruct a life that still has pleasure and fulfilment in it, together with tolerable memories of the loved one they have lost. And as they undertake this unequal contest, they will be generally ignored by the rest of us. Although we have a vast literature of consolation, offering models of mourning and lists of organizations from which we can seek help, it seems that bereavement remains a disease without remedy and that the open display of grief is still a solecism that society won't forgive.

Our grasp of how to deal with the bereaved at a personal level, and particularly over a long period of time is very poor. The tendency of modern responses to the bereaved is to demand precisely the kind of 'staged' recovery that psychiatric theory has abandoned. Those who have lost their loved ones should cry for a bit, preferably at the graveside or in their own homes, and then maintain a dignified, if sorrowful, restraint when in public. They should move from shock to anger to resignation and not make too much fuss. Although the workplace has come to recognize an obligation to the bereaved and compassionate leave is now the norm, it is usually too short to begin resolving a problem that often lasts for years. So many bereaved people are asked to go back to work within a week or two and to carry out their duties effectively when they do. Forcing those who are burdened by an extreme, emotional disorder to behave 'normally' on their return does no service to a section of society that must be, in the nature of things, quite large.

The absence of codified signals in our culture does not help and leads to countless blunders. In the past, a man or woman who wore mourning, or a simple black armband, made their condition evident and they would have been treated with caution and sensitivity. Mourning dress or mourning emblems, correctly understood, are not designed to silence but to ask for a sympathetic handling. The bereaved today cannot easily show that they are in mourning, and without any convention of dress or gesture, their vulnerability goes unacknowledged.

Empty Women

We may not wish to strap our widows into widows' weeds, and perhaps the bereaved do not wish to advertise their grief, but equally it is absurd that people sometimes behave towards a bereaved person in a way that suggests that they are the ones with an emotional problem, not the bereaved. Is it the responsibility of those in deep anguish to be sensitive to the possible embarrassment of others? Is it the job of the widow to alleviate the awkward feelings of an acquaintance casually encountered in a shop?

Grief is, in Colin Murray Parkes's phrase, 'the cost of commitment'.[1] But the cost for widows, in a society like Britain, seems to be particularly high. What is striking about many widows' accounts of their experience is how isolated they were made to feel by people they had come to regard as friends. Jeannette Kupfermann's powerful memoir of what happened to her after she lost her husband, Jacques, suggests that she was largely abandoned by the very people from whom she expected her greatest comfort. She had children and friends, but she presents grief as an experience that was suffered without any support from her surrounding society. She found that compassion was short-lived (about six months) and she estimated that she was dropped by 30 per cent of her friends and acquaintances. She recalls a dinner party when a couple, who knew her and her husband quite well, appeared to be unaware of Jacques' death.

> I felt angry, shocked, and hugely embarrassed at having to divulge at that very moment, at a social gathering, in front of strangers, the details of Jacques' death and of my own circumstances. Even more surprising was the reaction of all present. A total silence fell over the table for about two minutes, and then the conversation simply switched abruptly to the publication of someone's latest book, and everyone got on

with their meal as if nothing had happened. I never heard from any of the people present again. I felt rather as if I had announced that I had contracted some 'social disease'.[2]

No wonder that when she went out in the first few weeks after the death, she felt a sense of shame and wanted to avoid anyone who knew her. Furthermore, as bereavement counsellor Vincent Gordon makes clear, the act of re-stating the facts deepens the pain. 'Bereaved people have said to me,' Gordon recalls, 'that it is very distressing for them not to know what to say when they meet people they don't know well. In telling them what has happened, you are also having to tell yourself again, and in telling yourself, you're confirming the reality. In the early stages of grief, that's still very hurtful.'

The ill treatment of widows has a long history. By the Victorian era, an attractive young widow had come to be seen as a threat to the sound practice of primogeniture and might through contracting a second marriage, disperse a good family fortune. But according to Pat Jalland, up to 30 per cent of women were widowed by the time they reached their fifties and the majority were not, of course, left in charge of family fortunes. Instead, they were expected to wear mourning black for two years and faced a future in which they had a diminished income, could not work and would be frowned on for re-marrying. The result of all this social anxiety was an attitude to widows that can only be described as oppressive.[3]

Widows continue to be regarded as appendages in many societies around the world. It is as if they have ceased to serve a function and the word we use confirms that redundancy. The Indo-European *widh*, from which 'widow' derives, means empty or separated and the Sanskrit *vidh* adds ideas of lacking and destitution. As Sally Cline puts it, 'The taint of death that attaches to widows marks them out as a socially abhorrent group, as surely as stigmata upon their foreheads.'[4]

Undoubtedly there are widows who have not experienced ostracism of this kind – it is noticeably less common in the United States – but whilst there is evidence that widowers are treated with greater kindness in Britain, the silence at the dinner table that Kupfermann encountered is widely reported by many widows. Too often, and utterly misguidedly, it is supposed that the grieving individual is best supported by a discreet avoidance of the subject. The absence of an adequate language of condolence, and of a convention of useful and practical assistance for the bereaved, seems to induce a hapless negligence at the time when the bereaved are most in need.

The Job of Grieving

Grief around the world exhibits a remarkably high degree of uniformity. As Colin Murray Parkes and others have pointed out, 'Crying, fear and anger are so common as to be virtually ubiquitous.'[5] It is commonly accepted by most cultures that these feelings will sometimes be expressed in public and western inhibition about openly displaying feeling seems, in this light, anthropologically peculiar.

Most newly bereaved people will experience a loss of appetite, palpitations, weakness and sleeplessness, searching and restlessness, a kind of absent-mindedness and an indifference to routine sources of stimulation such as friends and television. They may question the value of everything, including life itself. All these symptoms tend to weaken the immune system and the bereaved are much more susceptible than the rest of us to bouts of cold and flu. Very often this can become a cycle, albeit temporary, of despair, loneliness and ill health. It is important to recognize this misery for what it is, however. In the early phase of grief, we do not *want* to change and it is this inability or resistance to change that determines, and deepens, our suffering. We have very little choice in the matter. We cannot, simply through an effort of will, adapt overnight. It has to be a gradual process of transition.

Early grief is often accompanied by a sensation that the deceased is present in the bereaved's life. The presence cannot be seen and it cannot speak, but the bereaved person has a distinct awareness that the loved one is in the room, on the back seat of the car, in the next shopping aisle, somewhere near. Parkes has argued that those who feel such a presence, like those who succeed in expressing their grief, do better than others.[6] The presence may be an illusion, but it performs a beneficial function. It keeps the dead 'alive' as the bereaved negotiate the important and difficult onset of grief. The dead remain in the world, even if it is by force of imaginative will. Their story, in this sense, continues.

Parkes also draws attention to 'imitation' as an early feature of grief.[7] In the case of a couple that has lived together for years, this is doubtless an extension of something that characterized their life together. Using each other's phrases and reproducing each other's gestures and habits are an inevitable consequence of close partnership. But in grief it can be pronounced and even sinister; it is as if the bereaved is trying to reconstitute the deceased by acting out the part, by mimicking that life which has gone. The dead person is made to live again in much the way that Hamlet is revived in each new performance.

A common emotion is guilt, usually about being responsible for the death. In cases of cancer, for instance, this is a needless reproach, but it is perhaps indicative of a widespread conviction that given the right treatment at the right time, the patient could have survived. Again, death is seen as something that should not happen and, if it does, it is to punish the living for their shortcomings. In Isabel Allende's *Paula* (1995), she gives an account of how her twenty-eight-year-old daughter fell ill and entered what turned out to be a long terminal coma. She recalls Paula's husband, Ernesto, and how he was racked with guilt about causing Paula's death by 'loving her too much'.[8] Jeanette Kupfermann, too, who also lost her father soon after her husband died, found herself similarly vulnerable to primitive superstitions: 'Somewhere in the dark recesses of my mind was the notion that I myself was responsible for all the bad luck, that I had somehow *caused* two deaths, and was being punished.'[9] She became convinced that she could have detected Jacques' illness earlier and, therefore, saved him.

Equally, guilt can arise when a carer has simply witnessed too much suffering. There are illnesses such as Motor Neurone Disease which strip sufferers of their dignity and their autonomy and put an enormous strain on those in charge of their care. Undoubtedly, death can be welcome in these circumstances, because there is no reasonable hope of improvement – let alone recovery – and the best outcome is a release from suffering sooner rather than later. But whilst death is welcome and the bereaved may comfort themselves with the thought that things could only have got worse, some of those bereaved by conditions such as MND feel guilty about the ambivalence of their feelings. They have gone through the experience of anger and loss already: because there was no prospect of a cure, the carer would have begun to adjust to the idea of death as the disease progressed. This 'anticipatory grief' as it is called, mitigates the affliction of post-mortem grief, but it does not do away with it altogether. People bereaved in this way very often enter a period of bewilderment, guilt and dislocation of a kind other grievers may not undergo. They have, after all, lost their role in life.

Guilt, then, has been added to the list of racking and irrational symptoms that students of grief have come to recognize as 'normal'. It is part of the substantial knowledge we now have of how people grieve. We know what the purpose of grief should be and how it should proceed. But today's model is psychotherapeutic rather than a social etiquette. The aim of grief is to find a place for the dead in our memory, with which we can feel comfortable. The dead thereby achieve what John Bowler terms 'the stable condition of ancestors'. It sounds so simple, doesn't it? Yet it involves a harrowing of our being which, when it first occurs, is unlike any other experience we are likely to have had. In order to resolve that torment, we shall have to become, in a sense, different people, who are adapted both to the absence of someone we still love and to the intention to live on without them. To begin with, that seems impossible.

The Tasks of Grief

There are, according to contemporary psychotherapeutic theory, four 'grief tasks' that, in some shape or form, the bereaved will undertake before their feelings will begin to improve. These tasks were outlined by J. William Worden in 1991 and they supplanted the previous 'stages of grief' theory. At one time, psychiatrists and others who work with the bereaved spoke of grief resolution as a series of states of mind and feeling, at the end of which the bereaved could be said to have 'got over' their grief. The length of time the bereaved remained in any one stage could vary, but its limitation as a model was that it suggested a progressive pattern, which started with 'shock' and ended with 'acceptance'. Those whose grief did not conform could feel that they were deviant or chronic, or simply 'stuck'. By contrast, Worden's 'tasks' make very few stipulations. They do end with an acceptance of the loss, but there is no assumption that all the tasks will be undertaken and no prescribed order or duration for them. Thus, this theory appears less daunting; there is not the same risk of implied failure. Indeed, it provides an informed therapeutic model which has proved successful in the treatment of many bereaved adults.[10] Tasks, according to Worden,

are much more consonant with Freud's concept of grief work and imply that the mourner needs to take action and can do something. Also, this approach implies that mourning can be influenced by intervention from the outside. In other words, the mourner sees the concept of phases as something to be passed through, while the tasks approach gives the mourner some sense of leverage and hope that there is something that he or she can actively do.[11]

That bereaved people can respond actively to their grief is the key idea at the centre of contemporary grief theory.

Worden begins with the task of accepting the reality of the death, of recognizing that 'reunion is impossible'. People who have not experienced the death of someone close might assume that this act of recognition is simple and easy, that one couldn't do otherwise than to realize that a death has occurred. In fact, when death strikes, the impact is often sudden, shocking and, above all, incredible. This was even true in my own experience of my mother's death from a terminal illness. The death was, for a time, beyond the scope of my belief. There is, then, a sense in which our intellectual awareness of the event is temporarily without meaning, whilst our emotional responses to what has taken place are stunned, reduced to a summary shock. This is why, quite often, when those who are nearest to the person who has died learn of his or her death, they do not howl or cry, but stand in a kind of stupefaction of denial and incredulity. Everything within is saying, *This is not real. This is not going on. This information is untrue. It has not happened.*

In the days that follow, denial can lead to behaviour that continues to repudiate the facts. The bereaved may decide to keep the dead body in the house or, more commonly, keep the clothes and possessions of the deceased or, in the case of a child's death, leave the child's bedroom exactly as it was at the time of death. These responses are typical of the first wave of grief, and it is the moment when the mind becomes fully sensible of what has happened, of the loss, that 'grief work' really begins.

Along with knowledge comes pain, all the keening and anger and crying and sadness that go to make up the profound emotional trauma of grief. Worden maintains that there is no substitute for this task. If death has put an end to the sufferings of a loved one, these symptoms of loss may be attenuated in some degree but, in general, they are a necessary condition of bereavement.

Life goes on, however, and the children have to be fed, the house has to be cleaned and the mortgage has to be paid. As days succeed to weeks, Worden's third task of adjusting to new circumstances will be seen more clearly. Of course, it began very soon after the death, with the first shower and the first tooth brushed, but the adjustment is more evident after a time, because at the core of it is a routine of practical living which is undertaken in the absence of someone who was once part of it. In particular, the bereaved begin to acknowledge – perhaps for the first time – what the role of the deceased was in their lives. If it was a partner who died, the loss can present the bereaved with all sorts of duties and jobs that they had scarcely given a thought to in the past.

Julian Bond, Bereavement Service Coordinator at the Hospice in the Weald, believes that Worden's fourth task – which, broadly speaking, describes the process of 'moving on' – is really two tasks, or one in two parts. The first is to integrate the dead person into the bereaved's new life. Essentially, this is the Freudian concept of 'reinstatement' of the deceased within the ego, or locating the deceased at a convenient distance, such that he or she can be comfortably remembered without overwhelming distress. The second, the forming of new attachments, is perhaps the most radical step taken by a bereaved person on the way to recuperation. Worden agrees with Freud that the bereaved have ulti-mately to detach their hopes and memories from the deceased, but he does not believe that that means forgetting. Indeed, trying to rid oneself of all sense of the dead is potentially damaging. To move on is to find 'an appropriate place for the dead in their emotional lives – a place that will enable them to go on living effectively in the world.'[12] In other words, you don't have to give up the dead to form relationships.

Moving on does, however, entail an acceptance of the possibility of loving again. 'Some people', Worden claims, 'make a pact with themselves never to love again.' His contention that not completing task four is tantamount to 'not loving' is frequently misunderstood. Being prepared to show love is, in this connection, an indication that the bereaved person is willing to resume a role in society. According to Julian Bond, the idea is often rejected as soon as it is proposed: 'You say to a widow or widower anything about a new relationship and they instinctively think you are talking about finding someone else to go to bed with, but it's not about that, or not exclusively about that.' This last task acknowledges that the bereaved individual remains a social animal and that his or her need for companionship and purposeful activity continues. Commonly, there will come a point when the bereaved person will join a new organization, or take up a sport or hobby, or renew contact with someone not seen for years. Indeed, people sometimes find themselves doing things they'd always wanted to, but never got around to.

The danger with any formula, and not least Worden's tasks, is that it will sound glib and not recognize the struggle that bereavement is from hour to hour and day to day. Julian Bond is in no doubt about the effort required. 'I see it as work,' he says. 'I like the concept of "grief work". We go to work to earn money. We work at our relationships. We work at our marriage. Why shouldn't we work at our grief?' In other words, grief is not a passive experience, but something we *do* – to which the immediate retort of the bereaved might be: 'But how do we do it?' Knowing how to manage grief and how to gain some degree of control over it are probably two of its most difficult and most elusive aspects.

We have then, from Worden, the intellectual theory to deal with our bereavements, but do we have the personal apparatus? The evidence of therapists and writers on bereavement is that although it is possible to generalize about the common symptoms and likely progress of grief, when it comes to coping and acting out our bereavements, we are individuals. We are individuals not only in the obvious sense that we bring to grief our own particular skills and weaknesses, but also because the character of our grief is so much determined, as the examples below hope to show, by the nature of the death that took place and the treatment we received at the hands of others.

Sudden Death: the Vanished Horizon

Montaigne took the view that we die when we are supposed to. 'No man dies before his houre,' he wrote in the 1580s. 'The time you leave behinde was no more yours than that which was before your birth.'[13]

Few statements could be more opposed to contemporary thinking. Whenever someone close to us dies, we tend to see the event as premature and wrong. Even if the deceased had 'a good innings', we feel he deserved a little longer. To resist the idea of due time, of death occurring appropriately, seems to us a natural function of our grief. Death is never right, or as the French philosopher Jean Baudrillard put it, 'it is not normal to be dead'. By implication, our lives should be longer than they are and death denies us something which is rightfully ours to enjoy. The earlier it strikes, the more unnatural and unjust it is, and if it is a sudden death, it overturns our understanding of the world and disturbs the natural order. Sudden death implies a residuum of life to which we were entitled and which cannot now be lived. In whatever circumstances it takes place, it is a catastrophe.

About 10 per cent of us die suddenly. For those who are left behind, the experience is unlike any other kind of bereavement. There is no time to adjust or to understand. The bereaved are rendered clueless and disoriented. They struggle to make sense of what has happened to them. *There was nothing wrong a moment ago – why should there be now?* The horizon was there and now it has gone. To be bereaved by a sudden death is to be lost, not knowing where you are, or where your loved one has gone. The shock is profound and enduring.

That we don't fear sudden death today is a direct reflection of the safe environments in which most western people live. Ill health is not usually life-threatening and, a few bouts of illness notwithstanding, we anticipate that life will continue much as it has done. For my sister, Clare Houghton, and Simon, her husband, that was not what happened. They were both in their thirties, and it would not have occurred to Clare that a man of Simon's age *could* die. Then one October morning in 1995, she was woken in the early hours by the sound of Simon's coughing. She quickly discovered that she couldn't rouse him. 'I can see myself waking up and touching his body, talking to him, trying to get him to wake up – then going to the window and crying out "Oh my God! What is happening?" Then phoning. The ambulance. The police.'

I asked Clare if she had realized that Simon had died:

No. Actually, I didn't think about death at that point, even though I was thinking *he doesn't appear to be breathing* and *I can't feel a heartbeat*. The worst I thought was *he's gone into some kind of coma*. It all happened so quickly. I was saying *this can't be right, this can't be right*. That moment on my own with him, waiting – it's vivid. Then seeing the ambulance arrive and the men coming in and saying he's gone and attaching him to the heart monitor, and I was absolutely screaming and seeing the bodybag go down the stairs and being questioned by the police – it's all very, very vivid.

What is striking about Clare's account is the desperate psychological crisis she describes, in which shock and denial were vying with the evidence of her own eyes. Even the place where Simon died, their bed, appalled her in all its ambiguity. In a moment, the place of 'togetherness and love' had become 'the most horrific place as well'.

It is widely accepted that grief work after a sudden death takes a lot longer than recovery from other deaths. In cases of death following terminal illness, the rule of thumb is between two and four years to restore a high degree of normality and control to everyday life. After a sudden death, it can take, on average, between four and seven years and the initial phase of shock will probably last longer too. During the first six months after Simon's death, Clare 'searched' for him. She likens it to a previous feeling, when splitting up with a boyfriend, that they might get back together again.

> There is some shadow of hope there. I know that sounds ridiculous because you know logically that there isn't, but you still think *well, we might . . . this might be resolved somehow*. Or you hope that some- how he might walk through the door, or if I drive far enough, I'll find him. Perhaps he's away, abroad. Because you just can't believe that this is reality. You don't feel as if you're living on the planet.

Holding out hope in this way expresses a kind of loyalty to the loved one. Rather than letting go, the bereaved continue their commitment, as if they were saying *I'm still here, I'm still yours*.

Successful resolution of grief is frequently accelerated by an intellectual understanding of what has happened. There are only three organs whose failure can cause death and usually damage or disease in the heart, lungs or brain is detected at the post-mortem. If the evidence is not apparent macroscopically, it is generally found once tests have been done of blood and tissue. The presumption is that people do not die for no reason. Simon's body was retained not for one post-mortem examination, but two. They could not find anything wrong with him, except that he was dead! At the coroner's inquest, a consultant pathologist informed Clare, rather tentatively, that the coroner proposed to record a death from 'Sudden Death Syndrome'. When Clare asked what this was, all that she could be told was that it was a way of acknowledging that he had not died of any known condition or failure.

SDS, as it is beginning to be known, is a relatively new verdict for coroners to return, and there has been an understandable reluctance on the part of coroners' courts to acknowledge that death can be of such uncertain origin. Until the mid-nineties, the medical profession refused to accept that it could not explain these deaths. Pathologists attending inquests would give an acute cardiac condition, such as myocarditis, as the cause of death rather than admit ignorance. Partly as a result of research conducted in Germany and partly due to the efforts of Professor David Wood at the Royal Brompton Hospital in London, doctors have begun to accept that people do die suddenly, leaving not a single pathological clue.

New forms of death, particularly of this indeterminate character, are few and far between and research is currently underway to verify the circumstances in which sudden adult deaths occur. We know that they tend to occur amongst people under fifty and predominantly amongst males. Rather oddly, one coroner has noticed that they are most likely to take place in September or October. The distinctive factor in Simon's life, which his family believe may have played a part, is that he was under a very considerable amount of stress in his job as a schoolteacher and deputy chaplain. Whether stress does have a contributory role in Sudden Death Syndrome, research has yet to show.

Simon was a fit young man, who ate a healthy diet and followed a balanced routine of moderate exercise. On the day he died, he spoke of a feeling of discomfort in his chest, but he had no history of heart trouble and none was identified at the post-mortem. That the coroner's inquest was wholly unable to arrive at a comprehensible cause for his death has created deep and lasting complications for Clare and her grieving process:

> After that, I started getting physical symptoms – stress, panic. I found that I was getting things like starting to shake. It usually happened in the evening or at night when I was quite tired. The more extreme version was involuntary shaking from head to foot, and I just couldn't stop myself. It was almost like shivering, but it was a horrible sense of being out of control – which I wasn't used to at all because I'm not someone who has suffered from stress in that way. Then I was getting illnesses. I had two very nasty sort of gastro-enteritis bugs, with very high temperatures. There was no getting run-of-the-mill flu. Everything was extreme.

Clare also had to move house. Most people are advised not to make any significant decisions in the period following a bereavement, but she had no choice. The house she and Simon had lived in belonged to the school, so Clare and her baby, Emily, moved out and went to stay with her father. The school authorities had given her six months' grace in which to make new arrangements, but that proved too short a period for someone reeling from an emotional disaster.

The next April she came back to clear out their belongings. She managed to pack up without obvious signs of worry, but towards evening she began to feel nauseous and complained of chest pains. Eventually, she went to see an emergency doctor, who prescribed beta-blockers. The day had been all too much. She'd arrived to find that the house had been stripped and re-painted. This had been their first marital home. She had lived there with Simon and their baby daughter for scarcely a year, and here were people painting over the friezes she'd made for Emily's bedroom and tearing up carpets that they had laid less than twelve months before. Memories of having to wait until Emily was asleep before she could start stencilling the friezes, of all the effort of creating a family home, came flooding back. It seemed like these decorators were 'painting over my life'. Their time together had been reduced to the dozen black plastic bags which now stood on the doorstep.

The decision to keep or throw out each of Simon's bits of clothing was particularly momentous:

> They were so representative of him. He chose them and they were what he wanted to wear. They were part of his style and it doesn't matter how good or bad that was, it was *him*, and I think our clothes and possessions do say an awful lot about us. If you get rid of those, you have nothing! You can't hold on to the body, so all you can hold on to are possessions because everything else is gone.
>
> And there's the smell, of course, the sense of smell. It's just the smell of that person. It's not necessarily aftershave or anything like that, it's just a smell. If you give that shirt away, you've lost the memory, you've lost the smell. I felt that the minute Simon was pronounced dead, I lost so many things all at once, everything that was attached to him, and you can't let it all go at once. You just can't. It's not emotionally possible to do it.

Clare's experience epitomizes that of many people bereaved by sudden death. As Therese A. Rando has observed, in an American book entitled *Living with Grief after Sudden Loss*, 'The mourner's coping abilities are assaulted by the sudden and dramatic knowledge of the death, and the adaptive capacities are completely overwhelmed.'[14]

Clare's grief was complicated by so many factors. She had been unable to say goodbye, which left so much unsaid and unshared – the 'unfinished business' recognized by psychiatrists and counsellors. She lost any sense of control over her life, of there being safety in her life, and then she suffered the more familiar grief symptoms of guilt, about the possibility that she might have saved Simon, and anger that he'd just upped and died and left her alone with a baby.

> Simon's death contradicts all my previous thoughts about life, i.e. you don't die in your mid-thirties, you don't die if you are seemingly fit and healthy and you don't smoke and drink and debauch. You don't die if you exercise regularly. You don't die without warning, with no seeming history of anything. It contradicts all that, and so, if that is contradicted, then finding any kind of sure-footedness about anything is very difficult. That's why I panic about little things because – I keep using this analogy – the rug's been pulled from under my feet. It's the best way of describing it, because it's that sense of a slippery floor. You thought you were on firm ground, on a nice safe rug, and it's whipped away and you are just floundering.

In the immediate aftermath of Simon's death, Clare received enormous support from her friends and, especially, from her father. She did seek counselling, but perhaps too early because it was not at the beginning very helpful. In retrospect, she realizes that she wanted counselling from someone who would understand the specific nature of her bereavement. This one event we call death is suffered in a variety of ways, and very often the bereaved will speak of wanting to talk to someone who has been through *their* experience. The young widow of someone who has died from an indeterminate complaint may not find it easy to share thoughts and feelings with a counsellor who has largely dealt with elderly people and common causes of death. That said, when Clare subsequently saw a professional counsellor in 1997, she found it extremely beneficial. In particular, it helped her construct a plan for the future. Counselling, in her case, has been something she has returned to when her bereavement has become too much; it is as if the need for it builds up over a period of time: 'I'm not like Woody Allen. I can't talk about myself for ever. I run out of things to say. But every so often I've got into mental knots and wanted to talk to someone who wasn't my father or my brother, a complete stranger, so that I can, if you like, go back to basics and tell the story all over again.'

Clare sought counselling a third time, in 1999, on this occasion from her GP practice, and the particular value of this consultation, so long after the events, was that she was reassured that it was 'all right' to feel awful. She'd begun to feel that she ought to be over her grief, or at least making more progress than she felt she was, but her counsellor spoke of '*only* four years', as though it were not long at all.

Alongside counselling, Clare has relied heavily on anti-anxiety drugs and although bereavement specialists like Parkes claim that these can be effective in the treatment of post-traumatic depression, much of Clare's grief has remained unresolved. When I interviewed her for the first time in 1997, she described her grief as less 'painful', but 'sadder'. She contrasted the routine of her current feelings, in which Simon's death was 'woven into the fabric of life', to the intensity of immediate loss. On the other hand, she had felt *closer* to Simon during that first wave of shock and agony, and she missed that closeness: 'When you get to eighteen months, it's beginning to fade, even the memory of those last few moments together, so you are losing all the time.'

Simon's absence in a social setting had become less troublesome, less debilitating, and Clare was less self-conscious about being alone at a social gathering. There had been a time when she had felt that presenting herself alone at a dinner party was not 'enough', that people wanted them together or not at all. That anxiety had waned. Similarly, when in the past she had been asked by an unknowing hairdresser if she was doing anything with her husband at the weekend, Clare would be completely nonplussed and unable to think of an answer. By 1997, she was used to such awkward moments.

> You think *shall I say yes, or no?* It's such a light, throwaway comment and she's really not that bothered. And you think, *shall I actually say 'my husband's dead'?* You don't want to lie, but on the other hand there is no reason why she should know, and she'll only feel apologetic, as if she should have known by the way I walk or something.

What seemed to be unchanged was Clare's anger: 'I am raging about how my life is so different from other people's and it's not how I want it to be. There's nothing I can do about it. I don't know whether that will ever totally go away.'

Outwardly, there was a growing stability in her life. She had bought a house in Cambridge and settled down there with Emily, and she had embarked on a law course, training to be a solicitor. Emily had been too young to be aware of her father's death and was still below the age at which she could recognize a loss of her own. At first, this had frustrated Clare and made it difficult for her to find time to grieve, but in the long run caring for Emily has been a source of sustenance and, naturally, of love.

Today, at a distance of seven years, Clare gives an impression of strength. But she remains on the drugs that help her cope with her anxiety and her attempts to give them up have not been successful, attended as they are by a renewed fear of the external world and a sudden loss of confidence in her own worth and competence. Perhaps it is simply too soon for her to have recovered. The rule of thumb may be four to seven years, but that is only as reliable as any average prediction and Clare still has a way to go. This was never going to be a grief to get over quickly.

Post-traumatic Stress Disorder

Jeremy Howe's wife, Lizzie, was stabbed to death on the campus of York University in July 1992. She was running a summer school for the Open University and that afternoon she was in her room preparing a lecture. Her attacker had a room on the same corridor. It appears that around 4.00 p.m. he started knocking on adjacent doors, trying to find someone in. Lizzie's was the first occupied room he came to.

The police telephoned Jeremy later that afternoon. Before he'd had a chance to assimilate what had happened, he was required to identify Lizzie's body and attend a police interview, in which he was clearly regarded as their first suspect. Since murders are more often than not committed by someone the victim knew, enquiries start with the nearest relatives and friends. The police acknowledge that they are dealing with people pulverized by shock, but they feel they have no alternative. The perpetrator must be caught – as indeed he was, in this case six hours after the attack. Robin Pask, a laboratory technician who had been attending another OU course, was arrested later that night and charged with murder. He had been having, it seems, a bad time with his wife. He'd bought a knife on his way to the university, perhaps with a view to killing himself, but in the end he turned whatever feelings of anger and aggression he was harbouring on Lizzie Howe.

One of the strangest aspects of it all for Jeremy was the publicity of what was, for him, a private agony. As his interview with the police drew to a close, the officer said, 'What do you want to put in the press release?' Jeremy hadn't a clue. Press release? Whilst he had thought this news was nobody's business but his own, the world was busy taking possession of Lizzie's story and turning it into an issue of public interest. The following day, as he drove down from York to Norwich, where his sister lived, he began to hear versions of Lizzie's death broadcast across the nation, first on Radio York, then on ILR stations throughout Yorkshire. By the time he was approaching East Anglia, it was a national news story on Radio 1. He listened with mixed feelings. He was, after all, in a state of profound shock. He didn't feel pride exactly, but hearing it on the radio did make Lizzie's death more real and there was a peculiar sense of gratification that the importance of the event was being recognized.

The loss was so enormous, the pain so complete, that Jeremy couldn't begin to understand it or to put his life into any kind of order. Lizzie had been his wife, his lover, his best friend. They'd met at Oxford University towards the end of the seventies, when Lizzie was in her second year at St Anne's College. He'd known her virtually all his adult life. She was the woman with whom he'd had their two children – Jessica, who was six at the time, and Lucy, who was four. How were they all to cope? Jeremy describes his own condition then as 'wrecked'. He remembers Jessica being 'very difficult to gauge', while Lucy was 'very, very angry', especially when he started to interview applicants to be their nanny. The woman he eventually appointed was the only one to whom Lucy had not said, 'Go away! I don't want you! I want my mummy!'

In fact, it was from bringing up his family that Jeremy was to derive his principal consolation. At first, it had seemed he wouldn't. The recognition that he was 'in charge', that he was Jessica's and Lucy's only parent, had felt like a part of the trauma. He had found initial consolation elsewhere, in consultations with a family psychiatrist, in the company of his friends, and in literature – Wordsworth's poetry, the book of Job and, especially, *The Winter's Tale*. As time went on, though, his daughters turned out to be his real solace: 'I couldn't get enough of the children. There was nothing more comforting than comforting the children.'

At every turn, his grief was complicated by the criminal justice system. It comes as a total surprise to the bereaved that, in a case of traumatic death including suspected murder, the victim's body belongs to the state. Murder is considered a crime against the state, not against the person. When Jeremy wanted Lizzie cremated, the police advised burial, 'in case they needed to exhume'. It was effectively an injunction. The police became the sole conduit of information regarding the cause of death and they controlled access both to the body and to Lizzie's possessions. Jeremy repeatedly asked them to release at least some of her things, but they were incredibly slow about it: 'Eventually, I had to go to Police Lost Property and queue, as it turned out behind my neighbour, who was picking up a stolen bicycle. He got the bike. I got Lizzie's wedding ring.'

Jeremy spent months trying to recover Lizzie's suitcase. In the end, it was returned and it stood in Jeremy's office 'like an unexploded bomb'. When he later transferred it to his home, it remained untouched, but it was reassuring to know it was there. What the authorities often underrate in these circumstances is the bereaved's attachment to anything that belonged to the person they have loved and lost. As Jeremy says, these were Lizzie's 'last things'; they were 'the closest you get to her being alive'. He didn't have her briefcase back until 1996, four years after her death.

Colin Murray Parkes compares grief to a physical injury – it is a 'blow' or a 'wound' – which gradually heals, but there are often complications along the way that delay or problematize the healing process.[15] In Jeremy's case, there was the man who did it to consider. What attitude to him should Jeremy adopt? It is common for survivors of murder to fantasize about torturing the murderer, but Jeremy decided he wanted to know as little as possible about Robin Pask: 'If you know the man responsible, you may have to confront deep, unpleasant feelings, tribal feelings. I wanted to see him as a kind of juggernaut which just ran her over. The evil you don't know you can't picture clearly. That's how I wanted it.'

Pask's first trial for murder took place in July 1993, almost on the first anniversary of Lizzie's death. Jeremy was not informed of the trial date, but he had in any case decided not to go. 'I didn't go because I didn't want to be in the same room as the man who killed Lizzie.' A Detective Chief Superintendent rang him afterwards to tell him that the trial had collapsed. Pask had been deemed unfit to plead and had been sent to Ashworth Hospital. It took nearly three years for Pask to be tried again.

In the spring of 1996, Pask was passed fit and a trial date was set. Again, Jeremy decided against attending. Quite apart from not wishing to see the face of his wife's killer, he was aware that the courts made no special provision for the families of victims and he would have been forced to find a seat in the public gallery, alongside strangers curious about the case. He also had very low expectations of the trial itself. It would only record a 'story' of Lizzie's death, and the adversarial system was likely to prejudice further the truth of what had happened as he understood it. In the event, the prosecution reduced the charge from murder to manslaughter with diminished responsibility. The defence eventually agreed and Pask was despatched back to Ashworth to be detained there 'at Her Majesty's pleasure'. Although Jeremy now says he spends '99 per cent of the time' not thinking about him, the impact of the trial, even experienced at a distance, was undoubtedly damaging. It was partly to deal with his deep frustration with the legal process that Jeremy decided to make a film about what he had been through.

Jeremy had worked for the BBC for many years, chiefly in radio drama. After Lizzie was killed, the Corporation was 'incredibly solicitous'. A personnel officer took him out to lunch every week and at the time of the first trial there was always someone on hand for him to talk to. They helped him make decisions about his career and when he thought he needed a different kind of job, they gave him the post of Head of Radio 4's Serials and Series. He buried himself in the work – he didn't want any 'space to grieve' – but in due course he ran out of interest. He felt 'burnt out' and he decided that, if he could, he would leave London and move to a job in television at the BBC's base in Bristol. Shortly after getting there, he directed and presented a film about his experience of losing Lizzie for the documentary strand *Picture This*.

Jeremy's hope was that the film would enable him to define the experience he had lived through. He remembers interviewing the psychiatrist who had treated him and when he spoke of 'post-traumatic stress', Jeremy suddenly realized that that was what he'd had. The phrase had not been used during their meetings, but it now gave a shape to his grief and explained the feeling he'd had that all his 'systems were shutting down'.

One motif that recurs again and again in the film is Jeremy's sense that he needed to 'find' Lizzie. This was more than a deep desire to have her alive and back in his life. It was an obsession with recovering her *for his bereavement*, giving her a place in his memory where he could be both intimate and comfortable with her. The whole trauma of her death and the drama of events which followed it had put Lizzie at a distance. Even if he accepted that she was dead, he wanted her back with him, in the same sense that childhood can be long over and yet remain vivid and close in memory.

This yearning had begun early on. When he returned from visiting his sister in Norwich, Lizzie wasn't at home. She was not there in the obvious sense that she had died, but she was also not there as a feeling, an atmosphere, a presence. This was the driving reason behind Jeremy's desperation to recover her belongings. 'I can't find her,' he says in the documentary and what he means is that all that made up the person he knew as Lizzie, what she was, had vanished, without trace. He revisited the campus at York, the corridor stalked by Pask, the room where Lizzie was killed. The film is at its most moving when it engages with this struggle to redeem Lizzie through exploration of every detail and every place of Jeremy's grief. It becomes a memorial to her and to the survivability of love. If Lizzie is 'found', she is found in the closing image of Jeremy and his two girls standing on a windswept path. Lizzie, we are left to imagine, is alongside them, invisible in the wind, 'roll'd round in earth's diurnal years' like Wordsworth's Lucy.

'The tempest is over,' Jeremy says, 'but I'll always hear the wind in the rigging.' Lizzie lives on in Jessica and Lucy, and Jeremy has discovered that he is a better father than he'd ever thought he could be. He has emerged from the long, dark tunnel of acute bereavement into something more tolerable and more compatible with living. 'There are moments of pain, but they're not so agonizing and don't last as long,' he says. He is still confused by his loss, still baffled. He does not think he has been damaged by Lizzie's death, but he was certainly changed by it; and there remains a natural anxiety about the future and what it holds: 'The real fear is that if it's happened once, why not again?'

That fear has not prevented him from establishing a new career in Bristol and a new home in Bath. After years of grief, he has also found happiness in another relationship. In November 1996, Jeremy met and fell in love with Jennie. They married in 1998.

A Destabilized World

That Jeremy came to recognize that he had been suffering from post-traumatic stress disorder gave a degree of meaning to his grief, which it had lacked before. PTSD has been accepted as a psychiatric diagnosis since the late 1980s and it has helped improve the lives of many people bereaved by sudden, violent deaths. It was first acknowledged by the Americans – they face 20,000 murders a year, compared with 600 or so in Britain – and it is now a feature of most psychiatric practice in Europe. Although many of its symptoms are exaggerated or acute expressions of general bereavement behaviour – anger and irritability are common, as are feelings of guilt – someone bereaved by a murder has to deal with other, often disturbing, influences or intrusions upon their grieving process. Not only will the bereaved have to conduct their grieving in the glare of publicity, but they will have to endure police interviews and the more or less unwieldy machinery of the criminal justice system.

Unfortunately, the procedures of the police often appear brutal and insensitive to the recently bereaved. When several family members have to be interviewed, they may be separated and not be reunited for several hours. Denial of access to the body is particularly trying for, say, grieving parents, whose first inclination on hearing the news of their child's death will be to want to see and, more often than not, touch the body. Certain police departments in the USA are experimenting with the use of photographs to enable parents to have some sight of the deceased. These pictures may depict the results of extreme violence, so the protocol is that the parent bring someone with them, who views the pictures first and then describes them to the parent. The parent can then decide to look at them, or not.

In Britain, too, efforts have been made in the last few years to recognize that the legal process can be very distressing for relatives. The Crown Prosecution Service now sets out standards of care for the treatment of families bereaved by murder or manslaughter. The police should inform relatives when someone is charged and should appoint a Family Liaison Officer, who will advise relatives about the progress of any trial and its outcome. Since the end of 1995, Crown Courts in England and Wales have also provided a Witness Service, run by the charity Victim Support, which aims to provide free and confidential advice to families who need it. The service can mitigate some of the disturburing aspects of attending court. It can arrange a visit to the court prior to the trial, a private room for relatives on the day of the hearing and, on occasion, special seats can be allocated in the courtroom. Perhaps most valuably, a representative from Victim Support will sit with family members during the trial.[16]

In general, though, in both Britain and the USA, until relatively recently, the rule has been that the personal feelings of the bereaved play second fiddle to the requirements of police procedure. Close relatives can be made to feel that they have only a marginal relationship to their own murdered loved one. What Jeremy Howe discovered was that information from the police and other authorities could be scarce and inconsistent, and others report that they were told not to worry about the coroner's inquest or the dates and outcomes of trials. The implication is that these events are no longer their business. Paradoxically, the relatives may come to feel that their loss is seen as insignificant precisely at the moment when the state is attaching greatest importance to it.

This is one of many respects in which the bereaved can undergo a dramatic loss of autonomy. As one American widow of the 1988 Lockerbie bombing (Pan Am 103) has put it, 'The addition of media, attorneys and the judicial system into the lives of homicide survivors is so overwhelming and confusing that it prevents families from regaining a sense of balance and control in their lives.'[17] Much of our sense of reality – the 'assumptive world' as it is sometimes called – depends on a continuity of existence and behaviour, which we internalize and habituate ourselves to. Sudden deaths shatter that entirely and we can lose our trust in what we see. 'A sudden loss', writes Kenneth Doka, 'may make one feel that the world is a very dangerous place so that even simple acts now cause anxiety. In short, sudden loss assaults a sense of safety and predictability.'[18] In this context, the loss of an ability to influence the behaviour of institutions such as the police or the media will only serve to confirm an intuitive perception that our assumptive world has been destroyed.

Jeremy's 'search' for Lizzie, as Clare Houghton's for Simon, is characteristic of all those who are suddenly bereaved and desperate to regain some hold on a familiar reality. Colin Murray Parkes believes that bereaved adults may know that searching is fruitless and irrational, yet feel compelled to do it.[19] It is something we share with other social animals, he thinks, and the search for 'where' the deceased might be is only one of many questions – When? How? Why? – that we will repeatedly ask after a sudden death. There are, however, no answers that will satisfy.

A Massacre

Our reactions to certain kinds of sudden death can be complicated or eccentric, and our grief may be delayed for a more or less extended period. After the massacre at Dunblane on 13 March 1996, in which sixteen children and a teacher were brutally killed by an intruder at their school, people in the community started to behave in ways that were out of character and disturbed. A woman teacher from another school suddenly developed a phobia about children. For six weeks she was unable to teach or go near schoolchildren, indeed near any children, including her own grandchildren. A little girl who had been fired at by the killer as he chased her along the school corridors, appeared to be coping. Then she fell during a gym class and that night she became temporarily paralyzed. She described the fall as 'the worst shock of my life'.

These experiences were typical of a wide variety of suffering and deranged behaviour that characterized the community during the first few weeks. People complained that they were unable to cry, that they'd lost their feelings. Some went to all seventeen funerals, just to be close to those who had lost most. Others had nightmares and flashbacks to the interminable wait outside the school when they were unsure what had happened and who had been killed. People would drive to the shops and walk home, forgetting they had taken their cars. They bought food they didn't like. They fell out over whether a child's birthday party should take place. People said they had lost their powers of concentration or that they were afraid to talk to anyone from outside Dunblane in case they raised the subject of the massacre. When shopping in another town, they would pay for things in cash rather than sign a cheque that would reveal where they were from. Everyone was overwhelmed by emotions they could scarcely begin to understand.

Rhona Campbell, who had set up a SHEN clinic in Dunblane some years before the tragedy, treated many people from the community for a period of twenty-two months. SHEN, which originated in the United States in the late 1970s, is a hands-on form of therapy, which uses touch to raise memories and emotions, the 'core wounds', into consciousness. Rhona had never felt bodies like these before. They were 'rock hard with tension'. She frequently observed that her patients spoke of a feeling of 'safety' after a treatment. Their sense of safety – what we might otherwise call their assumptive world – had been blown away by the killings and the kind physical contact began to allay their fears. Rhona also found that there was commonly a constriction of the throat and a difficulty in swallowing, or lower back pain, which SHEN theory associates with feelings of inadequacy and powerlessness. After a SHEN session, people would experience 'a huge outburst of emotion' – panic attacks, crying, anger or terrifying memories of the gunman.[20]

The value of Rhona's evidence is that it testifies to the longevity of the shock and acute psychological disturbance that sudden deaths can induce. That intentional or accidental deaths of this kind are relatively rare is something for which we may be grateful, but it does mean that the experience of the minority is little understood by the rest.

Anger against the outside world was a widespread problem in Dunblane. It affected everyone. In the first few days, they were filled with anger at the barbarous invasion of their lives, at what this man had done to their children and their community. Then they had to contend with the attention of the media. They were angry at seeing Dunblane prominently featured in newspapers and television reports for weeks on end. They became furious when reporters repeatedly asked how they were, as if they might feel differently, 'better' even. Many of them wanted to lash out and some families eventually left Dunblane because they could no longer tolerate the media interest. The effect of this anger, Rhona believes, was to 'shut in' all other feelings, to postpone grief in other words. SHEN was helpful to some. Others found that their emotions were only released when another subsequent event touched them; it was like a locked door suddenly flying open. A pet dying, a relative dying of a terminal illness, ironically even a television documentary about injured children, could trigger an emotional outburst that was desperately needed.

The Effect of Personal History on Grief

We bring to bereavement all our experience of previous bereavements and previous moments of emotional crisis. This is why handbooks advising us on how to handle our grief will be of only limited value. If I failed to resolve my grief when last someone close to me died, the accrued feelings of loss may well prostrate me the next time I am bereaved. The historian Pat Jalland detects this pattern of incremental grief in Queen Victoria's life. There was in the nineteenth century a prodigious literature of consolation to comfort the grieving, but works such as John Keble's *Christian Year* (1827) and Tennyson's *In Memoriam* (1850) would have done little to protect Victoria from a personal crisis that had been accumulating over a number of years:

> Queen Victoria's father died when she was a baby and her search for a father-figure included Lord Mel-

bourne and culminated in the Prince Consort. Her love for Albert was overwhelming, involving powerful dependency, even in matters of state. Victoria was highly emotional, prone to what Albert called 'combustibles' and temperamental nervousness. Her response to her mother's death in March 1861, aggravated by guilt and remorse, led to a nervous breakdown. She nursed her sorrow in isolation, her 'unremitting grief' arousing rumours that her mind was unbalanced. Victoria had barely begun to recover from her mother's death when Albert died suddenly of typhoid in December 1861. The doctors had concealed the gravity of his illness from the Queen, so 'this frightful blow has left her in utter desolation', as Mary Ponsonby noted.[21]

Victoria went on to mourn Albert's death for twenty years!

If the bereaved person was unable to grieve properly on the first occasion, for whatever reason, it can complicate later experience of loss enormously. Vincent Gordon, Family Support Director at the Hospice in the Weald, told me of a case of delayed grief that produced the kind of neurotic symptoms that would have sat well in Freud's *The Interpretation of Dreams*.

I was in the psychiatric department at St Thomas's and I got a woman referred to me from her GP. She'd been to him with constrictions in the throat. He could find nothing wrong, but sent her to a specialist. He couldn't find anything either, so she was sent to me. It turned out that when she was twelve, her mother had died, probably of cancer of the throat, she wasn't sure. She saw her mother die and be buried, then she was sent away to a boarding school. She learned that this was something that was frightening and she mustn't ask about it. When she tried to ask, people said, 'Don't talk like that. It's morbid.' So she grew up with her personal life darkened. She married, had a daughter herself. Everything was perfectly normal until her daughter reached twelve, and then she began to produce the symptoms in her throat. For me, this was a classic example of how when children are little, they need to be involved.

Those who are responsible for giving bereavement support at the Hospice in the Weald are alert to the possibility of postponed or complicated grieving of this kind. Julian Bond considers the likely impact of bereavement on all the families who have relatives dying in the hospice. He fills in an Ongoing Risk Factor Assessment for each. The categories of risk are partly defined by the nature of the death – how sudden or dramatic it was – but also by the individuals' backgrounds. If the bereaved have had a bad experience of death in the past, have difficulties communicating now or are in a troubled relationship, if they have suffered depression or other health problems or financial hardship, Julian will note it down and make a point of ringing them to find out if they would like his help. He is all too aware of how accumulating grief can become a chronic condition.

The Consolations of Faith

That grief engages our ability to resolve crises in the past raises the question of free will. Are we helpless victims of our own histories? Is our capacity to deal successfully with a bereavement solely determined by the skill with which we met crises in the past? Or can we learn new methods of grief resolution, whose efficacy is not so easily compromised by subjective weaknesses?

The value of religious belief is interesting in this connection. Does religious belief help those who are bereaved? There are several practical respects in which religious believers may be at an advantage. Grieving members of a congregation are often well provided for by their religious community in ways that are not strictly dependent on the consolations of faith. The Methodists' *vigil*, held in the presence of the dead body the night before the funeral, and the Jewish tradition of *shiva*, a period of seven days during which the bereaved are regularly visited by relatives and friends, are two examples of how religions support and organize grief, subsuming individual responsibility under an approved ritual. But it is the afterlife on which much religious thinking is focused during a bereavement, and the concept of the afterlife, whilst it may provide the comfort of continuation, is in fact an assertion of the separation between life and death.

Belief in the afterlife – and today, that means a spiritual eternity of some description – is declining but variable. Some western countries report that over 70 per cent of their populations believe in a life after death, but it is as low as 26 per cent in others. (In the highly religious United States, where 96 per cent of people espouse a belief in God and 92 per cent claim to be affiliated to a religion, only 42 per cent attend a religious service weekly, or almost weekly.) The desire for immortality beyond the grave can be as tenacious as – and is doubtless a consequence of – the desire for immortality here on earth.

Undoubtedly, religious belief is taxed and exercised by bereavement, but it can also prove an impediment to the progress of grief. From her experience of counselling those bereaved by suicide, Jo New has come to regard religious faith as a potential threat to recovery because it is so often implicated in the process of blame and distrust: 'I think a belief system can help, but I also think that it can hinder, when Catholics, for instance, get involved in blaming God. It [suicide] knocks your faith in other relationships, so it can also completely knock your relationship with God.'

In fact, the information we have concerning the value of belief to the dying and bereaved is puzzling and sometimes contradictory. When Clive Seale and Ann Cartwright did research into belief and dying in 1994, they concluded that the evidence in Britain was ambiguous. Interestingly, only one in six people they interviewed had no religion at all. In broad terms, the very religious among them were more accepting of death and talked more freely about it, but there was also some indication that to be moderately religious might cause more anxiety about dying than being very religious or not religious at all. Seale and Cartwright found that a belief in the afterlife did not make it easier to die, although uncertainty about the afterlife was, without doubt, a source of anxiety during the final weeks of a patient's life. Overall, their report suggested that faith was more helpful than unhelpful, and that the worst off were those who were uncertain of their beliefs and worried about issues such as God's mercy and the afterlife.

By contrast, two hospice professionals I talked to thought that being 'very religious' was a problem for the dying and, subsequently, for the bereaved. At the Hospice of Washington, nearly all the patients and their relatives believe in some form of afterlife, according to the Reverend Valerie Chillis, a minister in the African Methodist Episcopal Church and one of the very few full-time hospice chaplains in the USA. The patients and their families are predominantly Christian or perhaps have come from a Christian background and ceased to be part of a faith community.

Washington DC is unusual in the United States – Valerie Chillis prefers the word 'unique' – in boasting a huge number of churches and quite a few mega-churches, which attract younger people. Chillis is convinced that people with a solid faith, a God present in the bad times as well as the good, cope much better than those with no faith at all. They are often able to maximize on the time left to them and not dissipate it in anger or bitterness. These patients and their families want to be affirmed in their religious belief and will seek reassurance from Chillis that God isn't punishing them, especially if the person dying is young. Their faith sustains them, but Valerie Chillis is all too aware that faith is but one factor amongst many. If the dying patient has lived through poor family relationships, faith will not entirely override those anxieties.

Valerie Chillis has noticed, with interest and some surprise, that amongst those who do not cope well with death and grief are fundamentalist Christians. She contends that this arises from not having a full understanding of what it is to be a Christian. When they are vulnerable, she conjectures, they grab on to Christianity as a clear set of beliefs. Faith brings with it comfort and certainty. Chillis thinks this kind of faith is too focused on outward show – not smoking, not drinking, sexual fidelity – to provide the soul with the nurture it needs to deal with life's adversities: 'If the soul isn't nurtured,' she says, 'the individual Christian can't endure the struggle of dying and grief and still hold on to his faith.'

'Fundamentalist Christianity' is an unsatisfactory term. It doesn't describe a known group or a denomination that meets in a certain way or in an identifiable place. Instead, it is a catch-all term for those Christians who eschew drink, drugs and sex, who believe in the literal and unmediated truth of the Bible, and who consider themselves 'chosen' above others. However, a faith that promises the faithful that they are 'chosen' – and, by direct contrast, everyone else is not and will go to hell – is frequently misunderstood to imply that 'if you're good, nothing bad will happen to you'. It is this misunderstanding that can cause serious anxiety for some Christians living out the last weeks of a terminal condition and the relatives who survive them. If something bad like this can happen to a devout person, they reason, it must be a punishment. It seems unfair, at odds with the life of continence and abstention which that individual so consistently led. They find themselves wrestling with anger when they can least cope with it. Above all, they don't want to say God is to blame. That admission would cast aside months and years of what they may see as sacrificial faith.

These are the conclusions of a chaplain in one hospice in the United States, but her observations are echoed by the experience of hospice staff in Britain too. Angela Warton was the Service Development Director at the Hospice in the Weald. In her time there, she found that most of the patients had a belief in the afterlife. Where her experience differed from that of Valerie Chillis in Washington was on the issue of religious practice. Very few of the families connected with the Hospice in the Weald were part of a faith community. Many had had a form of Christian upbringing and most did not wish to define too closely what their notions of God and the afterlife might amount to. Angela Warton was convinced that this group, the majority, fared better for imagining there was an afterlife than those who didn't. But, without prompting, she went on to say that 'fundamentalist Christians' – she used the same term – did face problems with dying.

For Clare Houghton, the sudden loss of her husband led her to reconsider her faith but not to abandon it. Although Simon's death forced on her questions about God's intention for her and the extent to which he was a protective force in her life, she nonetheless found that the support of others was evidence that God was continuing to work within the world and to act through the love and generosity of people around her.

I have felt sure-footed about my religious faith but my faith has had to change and grow up quite considerably. I don't think I ever really believed that you became a Christian and God would make everything all right, that He somehow protected you from the nasty things in life if you were a Christian. But I think there was an underlying feeling that God would look after me. I never thought we would have very much

money, because I married a minister, but somehow
we'd get by and trusting in God, trying to follow His
way of conducting oneself in life, would mean that life
wouldn't be too traumatic. There would be ups and
downs and problems and things to face, but I had
Simon and our beautiful daughter, and life would be
pretty ordinary. Then, cutting through that, this splen-
did minister, who everyone thought preached marvel-
lously, whom I admired enormously, died. So I've had
to review God's view of me, God's view of how things
will progress and I'm still doing that. I think at my
lowest ebb, it would be inaccurate to say I hadn't
doubted, but I've had so many confirmations that He
is there that I know that's not real doubt. It's a bit like
a relationship with a person you love. You misunder-
stand each other – *How could they say that? I thought
they loved me!* – but you don't really think that person
is vicious or horrible. And the confirmations come
through other people, what other people have done for
me, and every time I've cried out, there's been an
answer of help.

The consolations provided by religious traditions are ready-
made. Although this can inhibit a deeper consideration of
what has happened, it is clearly valuable to have a convenient to-hand means to express grief when it first deluges
all one's defences. In later grief, too, religious formulae can
ritualize a memory that the bereaved fear is losing its shape
and definition. Bev Sage has found that her faith provides
her with a framework for thinking which usefully supple-
ments the memorial parties she has held and the sculpture
she commissioned in memory of Steve. Before he died, Bev
used to wonder occasionally whether her faith was simply
something to lean on in times of crisis. But, as she says,
death, when it came, was 'too big for my faith to be an
effective prop.' It didn't protect her from the pain of loss; it
didn't make sense of Steve's death; it didn't reassure her

that their parting was temporary. She maintains that she didn't feel any anger towards God because she had always believed that people have a destiny, and she'd felt even at the time of his death, that Steve's life had been 'completed'. She had been angry about their parting, however, and it took some time for that resentment to soften into acceptance. What faith has done, she has come to realize, is to deepen her conviction that life is better led with it than without it and that, in a way she cannot describe more precisely, 'the love we had lasts somewhere.'

The Worst Death of All

What perhaps lies at the heart of the religious comfort is a sense of being in contact with a group of people and a system of belief that tries to offer an understanding of death. For some bereaved people, however, the generalized consolation offered by a theology which has only one perception of death's meaning is too narrow. Some kinds of loss have an intensity and a particularity which make them unlike others. If there is to be comfort for these mourners in the company of other people and in a system of belief, both must take account of the precise nature of the mourners' experience.

Perhaps there is no grief more acute than that caused by the death of a child. The seventeenth-century theologian, Jeremy Taylor, whilst advising his readers on how to prepare for death, reminds them that 'Nothing is intolerable that is necessary.'[22] But the implication that God requires our deaths, that death is part of a natural, immutable and moral order, is not easily reconciled with the ending of a life that has scarcely begun, a life that has had scant chance to think or do anything. That sort of death seems *unnecessary* and without meaning or intelligence.

Whether grief over a child's death was very different in Taylor's time is hard to say. What is undoubtedly true is that all of us, children and adults, now survive longer and enjoy better health. According to Ralph Houlbrooke, pregnancy and childbirth before 1750 were 150 times more dangerous than they are today.[23] Between one-quarter and one-third of all children did not reach the age of fifteen and this rate of child mortality remained little altered up to the nineteenth century. Pat Jalland's work on the Victorians suggests that children accounted for one-quarter of all deaths. In 1840, 154 out of every 1,000 born were dead within one year; in 1860, the figure was 148; in 1880, back up to 153; 154 in 1890. Even in 1900, 25 per cent of the children born alive were dead by the age of five.[24] People were expected to be affected by the loss of their children, but they did not regard these deaths as unnatural or, in the general sense of the term, premature. This is perhaps most clearly evinced in the recommended mourning periods to be observed in respect of each member of the family. As late as 1899, people were advised to mourn for nine months if the deceased was a grandmother, three if it was a child.

There is an all-too-easy tendency to suppose that because people were more familiar with death in the past, it hurt less. Even experienced writers on bereavement persist in the belief that parents in previous centuries underwent a less painful process of bereavement when their children died. 'During early days,' writes Parkes, 'when most parents would expect to lose up to half of their children in infancy or early childhood, they accepted their losses more readily than we do today. Hence Montaigne can write: "I have lost two or three children in their infancy, not without regret, but without great sorrow." '[25]

Montaigne's particular interest in promulgating stoicism in the face of *all* death notwithstanding, the testimony of those who have left us journals, letters and diaries paints a rather different picture. Many historians have seen the emergence in the eighteenth century of a new sense of individuality as the turning point in personal and familial affections, but Ralph Houlbrooke has amassed substantial evidence to show that we have underestimated the quality of personal grief in earlier periods. Reactions varied, of course, as they do in any era, and factors such as the age of the child, whether there were other children in the family, the pre-existing relations between the child and the parents, and – at least among the upper classes – the need for a male heir to survive, all modulated the tone and depth of parental grief. But the general conclusion is plain: it has always been a profound and agonizing experience to lose a child.

In some cases, the bereaved parent was inconsolable. The seventeenth-century diarist, John Evelyn, took a special delight in the bookish interests of his son, Richard, and clearly hoped they would have much to share as he grew up. When Richard died, on 27 January 1658, at the age of five, Evelyn was devastated and suffered 'inexpressable grief & affliction'. On St Valentine's Day, he wrote to his father-in-law, Sir Richard Browne:

> God has taken from us that deare childe, yr grandson, your godsonn, and with him all the joy and satisfaction that could be derived from the greatest hopes. A losse, so much the more to be deplored, as our contentments were extraordinary, and the indications of his future perfections as faire and legible as, yet, I ever saw, or read of in one so very young.[26]

William Wordsworth lost his third son, Thomas, to measles, when he was only six and a half. Thomas had developed the disease one Thursday and by the following Tuesday was dead. Wordsworth's letter of 2 December 1812 to his fellow poet, Robert Southey, is suffused with a sense of inescapable agony:

> . . . For myself dear Southey I dare not say in what state of mind I am; I loved the Boy with the utmost love of which my soul is capable, and he is taken from me –

yet in the agony of my spirit in surrendering such a treasure I feel a thousand times richer than if I had never possessed it. God comfort and save you and all our friends and us all from a repetition of such trials – O Southey feel for me![27]

Pat Jalland has found similar accounts of distress amongst Victorian families ruined by smallpox and scarlet fever. The mortality rate from scarlet fever doubled between 1840 and 1870. Entire families could be wiped out in a matter of weeks. One of the most moving stories Jalland tells describes the affliction of Campbell Tait's family as the fever repeatedly struck them in the 1850s.[28] Tait was Dean of Carlisle – he later became Archbishop of Canterbury – when it began to desolate the city during March and April 1856. 'Five little weeks', Tait later wrote, 'did the work of more than fifty years.' In a matter of two months, the fever robbed Tait and his wife of five daughters, one by one. It seemed that with the announcement of each death, there came news that another child had contracted the illness. Chattie died first on 6 March, aged five and a half, then on 10 March Susie (1), and later Frances (4) on 20 March. The fourth death was that of ten-year-old Cattie. Her mother, Catherine, recalled the misery of waiting for the inevitable to happen: these were 'hours which burn into one's soul', she wrote in her journal.

Exhausted, Catherine went to bed and left her husband to stay with Cattie.

Dean Tait watched his child die at last at 4 a.m. on Easter Tuesday, and then went to tell his wife, noting in his diary 'the unspeakable agony of that announcement'. He thought of rushing into the Abbey grounds and shrieking aloud in his grief, but instead lay down on the floor of Mr Gipp's dining-room, underneath the room where Mrs Peach and a maid dressed Cattie's body. The father noted sadly in his journal: 'The

Sunshine was gone for ever from our earthly life. Oh
may God grant us a happy meeting in a better world.'

Dean Tait's own grief was lengthy and complicated by the
widespread belief that children's deaths were a sign of
divine retribution. Twenty years later he lost his son and
his wife within a year. His pain was unbearable. Nonetheless, he was finally sustained by a faith which survived
his doubts, and the memorial volume he subsequently
wrote proved to be one of the most popular books of
consolation of the late Victorian era.

At the beginning of the twenty-first century, our assumptions about child survival are in marked contrast to those of
a century ago. Today we take it for granted that obstetric
care in hospitals is of such a high standard that our babies
will be delivered safely, irrespective of prematurity, breech
positions, entangled cords or holes in the heart. We adopt
the view that scanning procedures will alert us to most
difficulties and intensive care will cure them. In a child's
later life, too, we remain confident that the continuing
improvements to the sanitary conditions in which we live,
together with the systematic inoculation of our children
against everything from whooping cough when they are
babies to meningitis when they are in their teens will protect
them against what we used to call the killer diseases. Of
course, we retain some anxiety. An outbreak of meningitis
in Gloucestershire or Cumbria will have all British mothers
and fathers sprinting to their 'what to look out for' cards
describing the tell-tale symptoms. We similarly worry about
increased road traffic and exhaust fumes, drugs, random
muggings and child molesters, but on balance the parents of
children in western societies entertain the sanguine prospect
of a relationship with their children lasting well into their
old age. So secure are the lives of the young that when
something does go wrong and a child dies, it is anathema
and the families of the dead may come to feel that they are
themselves taboo.

The transformation in survival rates has been remarkable. In 1983, only 16 out of every 1,000 infants were dead within one year, one-tenth of those who died in 1880. But there is something curiously opaque about mortality rates expressed as a proportion of a larger whole and, if we examine the simple number of deaths, the picture seems a lot less rosy. In today's Britain, for example, 4,000 babies die each year before they are 12 months old – 9 deaths per 1,000 – but that is 50 per cent more than in Scandinavia and 20 per cent more than die in France and Germany. They appear to die of neglect, infections or of developmental problems. These deaths are generally attributed to the prosperity gap between rich and poor, which is thought to be widening more rapidly in Britain than elsewhere in Europe. Poor children eat a worse diet and live in inferior housing, indisputably factors that contribute to a higher mortality rate.

But all is not happy in the households of the prosperous either. British children eat fewer vegetables and fruits than they used to and far too much salt. They face illness and early death, according to a government report published in June 2000, and in August of that year *The Lancet* printed a study which showed that there has been a substantial increase in cases of child leukaemia precisely because of the unprecedented prosperity of British families. Children aged one to four are 75 per cent more likely to develop leukaemia than their counterparts twenty years ago. The children's immune systems, it is argued, have been weakened by improved sanitation and their reduced exposure to diseases. If children can die of prosperity, what hope is there?

Perhaps the value of these statistics is that they throw a little light into a dark corner. Although we do not anticipate that our children will die and do not in general experience the deaths of our friends' children, the truth is that children do die and not necessarily for the reasons we might imagine. In the USA, 228,000 children and young people die each year. In the UK, the figure is 12,000. Until recently, I would have conjectured that most of these were due to fatal car crashes or drug abuse. In fact, one-third of the children die on Britain's roads today that died in 1922, when there were relatively few cars and the speed limit was 20 mph. Drugs similarly account for very few deaths. Although the number of teenage deaths from drug-taking has risen steadily over the last twenty years, it remains remarkably low. Between 1991 and 1995, there was a total of 67 deaths from opiates and narcotics. Things are not what they seem.

By contrast, a particularly alarming statistic is that for stillbirths in Britain. According to government figures produced for 1991, there were 3,249 stillbirths out of a total of 702,134 births that year. 'Stillbirth' is defined as a birth which occurs when, after the twenty-fourth week of pregnancy, the child is taken out of the mother's body and there are no signs of life. A stillbirth is, therefore, to be differentiated from a 'neonatal' death, when a baby is born alive and dies in the first few weeks, and a 'perinatal' death, which occurs when a baby is born between the seventh month of pregnancy and full term, but fails to survive the first week of life. Taking the three types as a whole, the principal causes of death in new babies are asphyxiation, an incurable physical abnormality or insufficient development at the time of premature birth.[29]

That stillbirth is occurring on a scale of this order, and is so little discussed, is surprising and suggests that it remains a taboo subject. In *Love, Labour & Loss*, a study of stillbirth and neonatal deaths, Jo Benson and Dawn Robinson-Walsh recall that twenty years ago hospitals in Britain treated stillbirths as pregnancies which had never really taken place. Doctors and nurses did not regard counselling of the bereaved as a part of their work and encouraged bereaved mothers to bottle up their feelings and forget that it had happened. The view taken by the Church of England was not much better. Funerals for unbaptized stillborn infants could not be held inside the church, and their coffins were generally buried at the side of the building without a headstone to mark the grave.

In so far as attitudes to stillbirths and neonatal deaths have improved in the last few decades, it is in large part due to the establishment of a support group, SANDS (the Stillbirth and Neonatal Death Society). SANDS gives bereaved parents a first port of call, which they lacked before. Through a network of self-help groups, it provides a telephone befriending service and opportunities for similarly bereaved mothers and fathers to meet. The society raises funds to assist parents when they are in hospital; they might equip a quiet room where grieving parents can be allowed some privacy or relatives can stay overnight. SANDS also has a political dimension. It lobbies for greater recognition of stillbirths and, in particular, it campaigned for the reduction of the age of viability of human life from twenty-eight weeks to twenty-four weeks. When the law was altered in October 1992, a baby born at twenty-six weeks was no longer a miscarriage. Terms that are commonly employed within hospitals can be not merely insensitive to the mother's feelings of grief, but they can demean the status of the loss as well. Miscarriage and spontaneous abortion may not carry a derogatory implication when used by doctors among their colleagues, but to a recently bereaved parent, they convey the idea that what has been lost was not a proper life, a baby's life that but for asphyxiation or an organic abnormality, might have continued. The change in the law acknowledged for the first time the quality of loss experienced by parents bereaved at twenty-four to twenty-eight weeks.

The use of the phrase 'proper life' is germane here. What many bereaved parents object to is a tendency, on the part of both society and medicine, to equate the length of a life with its significance. Thus, an adult's death means more than a child's because the adult lived longer; and a child's life is correspondingly of greater worth than a baby cut off in its first week. The emphasis of much contemporary counselling for parents is to reject these relative values and to insist on the individuation of the dead child's personality, its significance in the lives of those who knew the child and, above all, its irreplaceability.

Of all the issues raised by the death of a child, the need for society to continue to recognize that the child had an existence, however short his or her life, is paramount. Whilst hospital staff are now more openly compassionate than they were, there is evidence according to Benson and Robinson-Walsh that more could be done to train staff in the skills appropriate to the care of suffering families.[30] If parents are not treated with sensitivity, their already complicated feelings will be further problematized. Following a stillbirth, for example, mothers commonly experience a sense of revulsion from the idea that death could occur inside their own bodies.[31] This may lead to a reluctance to see the baby, to take a lock of hair or a photograph at the critical juncture when this is possible. The hospital staff can encourage the mother and father to give the child a name and make a print of a little hand and thereby create a stock of memory, for which both parents will be grateful in the future. At a time when many parents, especially mothers, are in a state of complex denial, it is essential that every effort is made to show the parents that they did have a child, that the child was 'someone' and that, therefore, their sense of grief and loss is appropriate.

When Paul and Isobel's daughter Nicola died in 1989, at the age of seven, it was the tragic end to four and a half months of hope, struggle, resilience and despair. Throughout that time, Paul feels that he and his wife had the full co-operation and affection of everyone who loved their daughter and tried to help her, from the doctors and staff of the hospitals they visited to Paul's brother and their local vicar.

Nicola died on 13 April 1989 from a tumour in her spine. It had been discovered suddenly. Nicola had been in good health until the autumn of 1988, when she developed a slight limp. The family GP thought it was a sprain. No one made too much of it. But after a week in which there had been no improvement, Isobel asked for a referral to their local private hospital. On 1 December, they saw a neurologist at High Wycombe Hospital. He quickly decided that there was a neurological impediment of some description and that Nicola should see a paediatrician. It emerged that there was a problem in her spinal cord and she was immediately sent to Great Ormond Street for tests. Paul and Isobel had tried to remain calm, but there was something about the reactions to Nicola that worried them: 'From the sheer urgency and the mention of Great Ormond Street, we started at that point to realize that it was a serious situation.'

Nicola was admitted on Sunday 3 December. She was given a scan on Monday, and they were told that there was a tumour in her spinal cord. Paul and Isobel kept Nicola appraised at every stage. Together, they agreed that the hospital should proceed with an operation to remove the tumour. When the operation took place on 22 December, it appeared to have gone smoothly, but Paul had the impression that the consultant was surprised by what had been found. He described the tumour as 'of an irregular type' and on 29 December, sent away a sample of it for tests.

The results came through in the New Year and they were shocking. The tumour, it turned out, was both malignant and very aggressive. Nicola might have only a year to live. Within a matter of weeks, her problem had developed from a minor sprain into a fatal cancer. The whole family was reeling.

January 1989 started with the grim prospect of radiotherapy for ten weeks. Nicola would have loved to have continued at school – she missed her friends and teachers – but it was not practical for her to do more than make a couple of short visits there. The treatment had had no impact on the tumour and it continued to grow. Paul and Isobel discussed the possibility of chemotherapy with the consultant, but he was of the opinion that conventional chemotherapy would not do any good.

By 10 March, Nicola had started to decline. She had been at home for several weeks, but when she developed hydro-cephalus, she was re-admitted to Great Ormond Street to have a valve inserted in her cranium to reduce the pressure in her brain. Once again, the operation appeared to be successful and an MRI scan was done to confirm it. The scan, however, revealed something else – a new develop-ment: 'The cancer had started to affect the brainstem. Time was running out suddenly and early in April the prognosis got much worse. We were told that she had up to three months to live.'

At this point they thought they would like to take Nicola home. No one opposed the plan and, in fact, the Liaison Sister encouraged it. Paul and Isobel had had no experience of death before and they did not know what to expect. Although she was very weak, Nicola did not cry or com-plain and in the end death came quickly. They arrived home on Monday 10 April and she died quietly the following Thursday.

It was the day they had dreaded. With her death died many of their hopes for the future. Paul and Isobel had another child, then twelve, who would inevitably become the focus of their aspirations and anxieties, but in those first weeks their loss was unique, without equal, without miti-gation. They would never see Nicola sit her GCSEs, go to college, or have a partner and raise children. They would never again cook Nicola a meal, take her on holiday or pray with her. Whatever had happened to her – and it was hard enough trying to understand – was irreversible.

They decided to keep Nicola's body at home for the next few days, a decision which they are now grateful they took. It gave them time to be with her, to say goodbye and to begin to get used to the idea that she had finally gone. Afterwards, Nicola was cremated, but it took a further three years before they felt ready to have the ashes committed. Then they buried them in a cemetery ten minutes away from their home. 'I don't believe she's there,' says Paul, 'so there's no great yearning to visit the grave.'

When a child dies, the event stirs the well of superstition. Other parents clutch their children to them and look on in horror as the bereaved flail and weep. In the weeks that followed Nicola's death, Paul and Isobel watched as people crossed the road to avoid them or stood in front of them 'literally stuck for words'. They heard that some of their friends had taken their own children to have scans at hospital, just in case. Did they think it was catching? Paul returned to work after a week or so. He was told by a colleague that his boss had expected him back within a couple of days of the funeral. There was very little understanding of what he was going through. Above all, Paul wanted everybody to know of Nicola, to remember her and say her name, but it was as if the world wanted to silence him.

In Dennis Klass's view, this is a typical experience:

> For a significant number of parents, the pain they experience is not felt within their communities. It often seems to them that neither the child nor the child's death has any social reality. They find people will not mention the child's name in their presence, that inquiries about how they are doing imply that it doesn't hurt as bad as it does, that the child can be replaced by a new baby, or that God loves the child in heaven better than the parent could have loved the child here. When a child dies, it seems to the parent that their lives have stopped while other people's lives go on. The sense of isolation can be bitter.[32]

This has certainly been true of Paul's bereavement. 'Part of me is frozen in that time. For me, there's a timelessness about Nicola's death, but others move on so quickly and they behave almost as if nothing has happened. There will always be a hole that nothing will plug. Learning to live with it is a very difficult thing to do. I miss her terribly.'

Eleven years on, some therapists would regard Paul's attachment to the moment when he lost Nicola as 'being stuck' and would ascribe it to a sense of persistent anger that death has robbed him of what he believed to be the most precious property of his life. But perhaps we presume to know grief too well. It could be that there is no choice between retaining a memory of Nicola and 'missing her terribly'. If Paul wants to feel a continuing presence that is meaningful, every recollection has to be vivid. Thus, the pain of intimate memory is a function of not losing her altogether.

Perhaps the most ill-judged and hurtful remark that is commonly made to parents who have lost a child but have other children is 'Oh well, at least you've got the others.' It seems to imply that the other children can, in some way, make up for the loss, as though children have a collective personality that can be shared around and re-apportioned. Similarly, the well-intentioned may celebrate the birth of a child born after a loss as if the newborn were a substitute for his or her dead sibling. What friends of this kind fail to grasp is that the business of bereavement for many parents is to clarify and retain as much as they can of the detail and particularity of their child's short life and not to allow it to be confused by the characters of their other children and the passage of time. To achieve this distinctive memory, a parent struggles against the brute force of a society determined to obliterate the child from the social record.

Paul is sustained by the belief that he has not seen the last of Nicola and that they will be reunited in heaven, but in the meantime he struggles to integrate her into the continuing life of the family. They mark the anniversary of her death by taking a day's holiday from work and doing 'things that are consistent with memory and reflection'. The pain of grief ebbs and flows, diminishing behind the quotidian routine and resurfacing on her birthday and at Christmas. In this way, Nicola's life and death have become features within a continuum and not spectres from another world.

Support Groups for Parents

Whilst many parents do not wish to give up their grief because they associate it with forgetting their child, they are left wondering what they can do to make their feelings tolerable. It was partly to keep the memory of Nicola alive and to keep talking about her, that Paul helped start the Child Death Helpline at Great Ormond Street Hospital in London. The service now operates jointly with the Alder Centre in Liverpool, and the helpline provides a confidential listening service to anyone affected by the death of a child. Volunteers are all parents who have lost children themselves and applicants must have been bereaved for at least four years before they will be considered for training.

Laurie Didham, who is now the Development Officer, joined as a volunteer in 1994. She remembers that when she first rang up, 'It was liberating. I was able to talk to someone who was on the same wavelength. No one, in the six years since Rebecca's death, had given me the opportunity to talk for that length of time.' Laurie had found that although she continued to be invited to mothers-and-toddlers groups, to socialize with other mothers, there was a tacit silence surrounding her daughter's death: 'People didn't know what to say, because they can't say "she had a good innings" because she didn't. Many people said "Never mind, you still have Elisabeth, you must look to the future now." It was as if they wanted to forget that Rebecca ever existed.'

A close friend of Laurie's has recently admitted to her that she too hadn't known what to say at the time. 'I thought if I mentioned it, I'd upset you and if I didn't, I had no idea what you'd think.' This belated apology, over ten years after the event, has made Laurie more aware of the difficulties everyone around her must have been experiencing.

Laurie sees the helpline as an opportunity for people who have been isolated by their loss, and know no one around them who has experienced anything remotely similar, to talk to friendly people who know exactly what they have been through and will not say to them 'You'll get over it.' The parent-callers can feel confident that when they have contacted a volunteer, there will be no skirting around the subject.

The average length of a call is forty-five minutes. When a parent phones, it is usually because he or she has a great deal to say. Sometimes callers want to know about their rights: *Can I spend as long as I like with my dead child in the hospital? Am I entitled to a full explanation of my child's death from a doctor? Is it acceptable to ask for photographs of my child if I don't feel sure about seeing the body?* More commonly, the helpline shares in a simple act of memory, confirming the child's existence prior to death. Parents can talk intimately and at length about the child they have lost and, very often, the telling of the story, the biography of their child's last days or months, is all they want to do. Their stories differ, but as Laurie observes: 'The story provides the structure, a vehicle for the theme, because it is the re-telling of the story that's the therapeutic thing. I can remember being on what I would describe as "constant spool", telling it over and over again.' The theory is that the bereaved parent will tell and re-tell his or her story until there is no longer any need to tell it. That may take a very long while.

The majority of parents seek straightforward consolation in the company of people who will understand what they are going through. For some, the willing listener at the end of a phone – a volunteer at the Child Death Helpline, say – is enough; others need more and want to be in the same room as grieving parents. This was something that Simon Stephens recognized in 1970 and it resulted in him setting up Compassionate Friends, another support group for bereaved parents. As a vicar, Stephens had witnessed the isolation of parents who had lost children. He felt the inadequacy of what he had to say to the parents of children killed in road accidents or parents whose children had recently died of cancer. They clearly needed to be with people who *knew* the experience. Simon Stephens' wisdom was to put the parents together, and from there sprang up a network of regional branches of Compassionate Friends, each with its own coordinator, whose responsibility is to bring together bereaved parents to talk about their children and their loss.

Today, Compassionate Friends operates in Britain and the USA, and it is a much more sophisticated organization now than it was thirty years ago. On both sides of the Atlantic, it has been recognized that losing a child may not be enough common ground *per se* to unite parents in their grief. The group has had to acknowledge that losing a baby of six months to SIDS (Sudden Infant Death Syndrome) may be a very different grief from losing a child of ten in a school massacre. The two sets of parents may have very little to share. Compassionate Friends has created a number of sub-groups, such as the Infant-Toddler Group and Support After Murder and Manslaughter (SAMM),[33] to try to cater to these varying experiences.

Inverting the Natural Order

Our confidence in our children's survival will inevitably build up as they grow and develop their own strength and wisdom. We begin to think that it is more likely that they will go on than not. It is perhaps for this reason that the death of adult children has always been so alarming and amongst the most distressing of all bereavements, as indeed it was a century ago.

The Victorians anticipated that children would frequently die at birth or in their infant years. But deaths over the age of twenty would have been, as Pat Jalland has observed, 'harder to cope with because of greater emotional investment, a stronger bonding process, and half a lifetime of memories.'[34] To denizens of a western culture imbued with the Dickensian sentiment that the death of a young child is the death of all hope and affection, Jalland's argument might strike a discordant note. But heartbreaking as the deaths of Little Nell and Paul Dombey are, it is the death of an adult child which consistently seems to have wrought the most ruinous effects on parents' lives. This is testified to by psychotherapists today and the rigour of this kind of loss is evidenced in the bereavement literature of the last 400 years. In *Holy Dying* (1651), Jeremy Taylor observed that parents who had survived the deaths of infants with fortitude, might later be broken by losing older children, who were 'hopeful and provided for'.[35]

Of course, people are cut down in road accidents and muggings, by heart attacks and bullets, raving or abseiling. Nonetheless, common sense dictates that the old must die before the young and we store in our hearts the notion that our children will survive to nurture us in our old age. So powerful is this sense of propriety that when it is contradicted, we commonly react by demanding an explanation, someone or something to blame.

Sue Smith lost her younger son in August 1996. Giles was electrocuted at the precision engineering company where he was working as trainee. He was twenty. Sue was away at the time, on a walking holiday on Dartmoor with her partner, Norms. Her other two children, Jay and Kate, heard the news first and drove down to find them: 'I thought "How lovely, they've come to take us out to dinner!" But then I saw their faces, and I knew something had happened because they didn't smile and wave. They told me Giley had been killed and you just don't take it in. Norms let out this prehistoric scream because he saw the future without Giles.'

Jay was a doctor and he arranged for Sue to see the body at the Bristol Royal Infirmary. It was then thirty-six hours after the death, so Jay warned his mother that Giles 'would be starting not to feel very nice'.

> I wish, I wish, I wish I had had him at home up to the funeral. But I went to see him every day at the funeral parlour and I am really glad I did. But I can understand that some people don't like it. It must be very upsetting if your child has been damaged in the process of death. I now realize that I didn't see Giley's hands – they were tucked away – and I imagine perhaps they were burnt, and I wonder that now. That picture of Giley in his coffin is the thing that stays with me.

What precisely occurred and who was responsible for Giles's death took some time to be determined. According to Sue, the engineering company had been closed during August in order that it could be 'cleaned down'. What she understands to have happened is that Giles was operating a machine to suck up water from the warehouse floor. The machine had metal wheels and a metal handle, and it was plugged into a mains supply that used industrial voltage. Giles himself was standing in water and holding the handle. When the wheels came into contact with exposed wires in the mains cable, he received a massive shock.

At the coroner's inquest, a verdict of 'unlawful killing' was returned and the engineering firm was subsequently prosecuted under Health and Safety legislation. The court heard that the circuit breaker, which should have saved Giles, had been 'quite deliberately and cold-bloodedly overridden' so that it would not trip in the event of an electrical fault. The company was fined and the judge commented that 'the state of electrical wiring, the fuses and circuit breaker were appalling'. Nonetheless, despite four contraventions of the Health and Safety Act, the fine was reduced on appeal in the High Court and Sue was left feeling frustrated and disgusted.[36]

Sue's real concern, of course, had been that Giles hadn't suffered. 'Some awful man came up to me at the funeral – he wasn't really an awful man, I think he thought he was being kind – and he said " I was with your son when he died and he only suffered for about five minutes." Five minutes! That was the worst thing to say to anybody.'

The disorder created by Giles's death was dramatic. Sue's eyesight went temporarily and she was unbalanced by the wild behaviour of her hormones. At the suggestion of her partner, she turned to her faith for help. Norms had been extremely supportive throughout, 'like an oak tree', and it was he who had recognized that if Sue wanted to continue to feel close to Giles, she must 'get close to her God'. Instinctively, she knew this was right. She had been brought up in a convent, and although her faith had 'withered away' while she was bringing up children – Pony Club seemed to be a greater priority on a Sunday morning than the 10.30 service – it had never been lost. Now she would say her faith was strengthened by the experience of bereavement: 'I'm not angry with God. I believe if you've got a force for good in the world, you've got also to have a force for evil, haven't you? God can't make it rain on us because we need it for our gardens and shine next door because they're having a party. I don't think God pointed a finger at Giley and said "You've got to come." '

Sue decided she wanted Giles buried near where she has a weekend home in Somerset. She was fortunate to have a vicar who was entirely open to her suggestions for the service and happy to cooperate in any way he could: 'We sat on the grass outside the church, choosing where Giley's plot would be – and mine too, because it was going to be a double plot. And I wanted to read a verse from *The Prophet* over his grave. I wanted him to hear my voice as the last thing before he was covered up. Then we let balloons off to take his spirit off to heaven.'

In the months that followed the funeral, Sue struggled with a pronounced sense of guilt, about her divorce from Giles's father and the effect it had had on Giles, and about her failure to protect him from harm. However much she tried to rationalize events and acknowledge that she could not have been responsible, and that if blame was to be placed anywhere, it should be at the door of Giles's employer, she could not help but feel that she had not done her duty. She had not brought him up to be an adult.

> For a mother, you've just spent your life nurturing and rearing your child. You feel totally responsible for them. In the teenage years they grow away – love is in the letting go – but a mother still worries about her son. It's such a deep, deep, deep thing looking after a child, and so you feel you've failed. Giles was twenty, so he didn't make it to being a man.

This was Sue's first bereavement and she was taken aback by it. She hadn't realized how much grief hurt physically, that you feel as if there is 'an incredible void opening up inside you', and perhaps above all, that you come face to face with your own mortality. She wishes that the wearing of armbands were still the rule, so that others could acknowledge her bereavement and treat her accordingly gently. At the very least, it would save embarrassment: 'If you see somebody and they've got a black armband, you know they need a hug or something. I find myself meeting someone in Waitrose and having to say "Did you know my son had died?"'

After five years, Sue's grief remains acute. Giles is in her thoughts every day and she always visits his grave when she is staying at her cottage. She would not wish to give up these thoughts, even though they can be painful, and it is important to her that she remains 'close' to Giles. On Friday nights she and Norms attend Evensong in Wells Cathedral. The names of deceased loved ones are read out in the course of the service and, on each anniversary of Giles's death, they make sure that his name is announced and they all say a prayer for him, which Sue likes to think remains as an echo long after the cathedral has emptied. Although the occasion of this remembrance is, for each mourner, infrequent, Sue values its formality. She recognizes that it cannot be a substitute for all the private ways in which she grieves and remembers, but her religious practice very successfully complements the conversations, the grave visits and the work she has been doing with other bereaved parents through Compassionate Friends. For Sue, her prayers are a token of love:

> He was my youngest. He was the one I fussed over. Giving love is the thing, isn't it? It's as good as receiving it really. Giles used to love being loved.

For Sue, the issue of criminal responsibility for Giles's unlawful killing has still not been satisfactorily resolved. There is part of her that continues to hope that one day the death of her son will be 'explained', that an organization will be held *properly* to account for it and, importantly, punished for taking his life. What that punishment might entail is hard to imagine. As Sue said at the time of the trial, no matter how big a fine was imposed on the engineering firm, it was never 'going to bring my beautiful boy back'.

The need to blame is widespread amongst parents whose children have met violent deaths. They may not acknowledge that the pursuit of blame and punishment is a function of their grief, but that in essence is what it amounts to. This behaviour is evidenced in Stephen Lawrence's parents' tireless quest for the murderers of their son, who was killed in south London in 1993, and in the even longer campaign for justice pursued by the families who lost children and loved ones in the Lockerbie bombing. The bereaved in these cases were particularly distressed by a feeling that they had both been abandoned by the authorities and that insufficient was being done to identify those responsible and bring them to trial. At times, they suspected that they were simply not being taken seriously and that the authorities would rather they just shut up. But campaigning for justice was an aspect of their grief. As Caroline Garland has remarked, in a BBC documentary, 'There is no such thing as an accident in the unconscious. We always attribute what happens to a somebody or a something.'[37] The need to blame clearly provides a purpose for parents who have lost a large part of their purpose. It is an alternative to helplessness, but it is also an alternative to parenting.

Occasionally, the fruition of these campaigns is a trial and, even less frequently, a punishment. Whether such a conclusion fulfils a need in the bereaved parents, still less mitigates the pain of their grief, are moot points. Bud Welsh, for example, who lost his daughter, Julie, in the Oklahoma bombing of 1995, found that after a year of heavy drinking and a passionate desire for revenge, he was destroying himself. He came to the conclusion that no punishment could sublimate his grief and began a campaign to save Julie's killer, Timothy McVeigh, from the death penalty.[38] Perhaps the value of a legal procedure, however, is that it provides an ending, a sense of closure analogous to the cause of death announced by the coroner. The different elements, which together constitute a 'reason', are thus put in place and the bereaved can move on.

The death of a child is unfair. Parents will wrestle with their memories and beliefs, the literature of consolation and the conjectures of their friends, colleagues and counsellors in an effort to deny this. They will struggle to find a reason for death that will attenuate its simple cruelty. In explanation, they will conjure up extravagant ideas of divine punishment, for their neglect or their excessive love, or their betrayal of God. But nothing will do. At the end of a very long and dark tunnel, which is full of spikes and ghouls, they may find a peaceful clearing.

It is inconceivable to newly bereaved parents that they will ever feel anything but distraught and without hope. Jane Swire, whose daughter, Flora, was killed in the Lockerbie bombing, maintains that for a long time she envied the dead. 'I wanted to have shared her end just as I had shared her beginning,' she said, in a BBC programme in 1996. At first, she could think about nothing other than Flora and she dwelt on every vivid image of her life. There was, she believed, no possibility of recovery, or even of a lesser pain: 'People say trite things like "Time cures everything." No, it doesn't. Nothing could cure the ache and the heartache, and that loss of the relationship. I mean, Flora isn't here to share our life and she was a very big part of it.'

It took Jane between two and three years to acknowledge that she still wanted to carry on living. In all that time, she had not been prepared 'to commit myself to life again'. Whilst she is adamant that time does not cure, the wound has begun to heal. There comes a moment when 'you start to feel the sun warm on your back again and feel there is yet a meaning in life itself.'[39]

Parents, it seems, do survive. They do get through. What their crisis demands of the rest of us is greater imagination, greater forbearance and greater care. It is too much to ask them to bear it on their own. Above all, we are asked to remember their children and not to consign them to oblivion.

A Convenient Distance

What is the aim of grief and, in pursuit of a 'good death', what is 'good grief'? Is grief, in any sense, 'resolved' or is it simply ameliorated degree by degree until it has become an aspect of habit? These are the large questions.

Most grief therapy emphasizes a satisfactory detachment of the bereaved from the dead as the desirable goal. But what all the bereaved people in this chapter reveal is a process of grieving that is in constant flux. As their anguished minds try to achieve equilibrium, they negotiate and re-negotiate how much of the past they will retain and how much discard. Their 'new normality' is a psychological settlement which includes the life of the deceased as it was lived and, at the same time, allows them to live reasonably contentedly without the physical presence of their loved ones. This Janus-like relationship between the bereaved and the deceased is something that psychotherapy has come to value only recently and it is beginning to supplant the emphasis previously placed on abandoning the past.

Other voices, chiefly from a sociological discipline, have begun to say similar things. Perhaps a fully resolved grief will not so much separate the dead as balance separation with a kind of transformed intimacy. Tony Walter, in what has proved to be a provocative article called 'A new model of grief', written in 1996, claimed that grief resolution could be as much about the 'preserving' of memory as 'letting-go'. Walter recalled his own experience of the death of a woman friend and how he derived his principal consolation from talking to her other friends and sharing recollections of her with them. By this means, he confirmed some impressions, modified others and discovered entirely new things he had not known about her. Walter's aim was to settle her in his memory, but that required active discussion and re-modelling of the idea of her he already had. 'If her place in my life is to remain stable,' he wrote, 'it has to be reasonably *accurate* and this requires testing it against the views of others who knew her.'[40] In a subsequent essay, in 1997, Walter withdrew the word 'stable' and further qualified his original assertion by arguing that, in fact, the image retained of the deceased does not have to be accurate; it has simply to be credible enough to the bereaved to function *as if it were* a reliable memory, and the memory is then enriched and deepened by conversation with others.[41] Preserving and letting-go are thus not, finally, in conflict; they are a fragile marriage.

It's All in the Doing

Implicit in the idea of shared recollections is the idea of storytelling. The use of storytelling has made a vital contribution to the theory of grief resolution, much as it has to the hospice approach to dying and the evolution of alternative funeral rituals. One of the valuable elements of Walter's 'new model' is that, like Worden's Tasks, it makes grief active. The bereaved act upon their loss and seek out the company of others who are also bereaved; together, they act out a therapy of storytelling which functions both subjectively and collectively.

Storytelling, in its broadest definition, does seem to offer a way forward. In the USA, it has become a key feature of what therapists call Traumatic Incident Reduction, or TIR, which is specifically aimed at those bereaved by murder, but has, I suggest, a much wider application. As has already been noted, it plays an integral part in the support given to bereaved parents by organizations such as Compassionate Friends and the Child Death Helpline. The bereaved person is asked to tell and re-tell his or her story, in a variety of circumstances to a variety of people, until he or she finds what is called the 'end point' and feels an enormous sense of emotional release. There is then no longer any need to tell the story, or it need only henceforth be told from time to time.

Rather than being seen as a peripheral counselling technique, storytelling could be usefully placed at the heart of the grieving process. For the bereaved, the story might begin with the dying person's own recollections. Then there will be the story told at the funeral, which is both the story that is a formal part of the funerary ceremony and the story that is shared informally among the mourners. All these successive narratives serve to adjust the balance between 'preserving' and 'letting-go'.

Such ritual need not occur in language alone. Storytelling can equally make use of images, motifs, possessions and souvenirs. Mourners may choose to come back, to assemble at another time or times, simply to tell again the story of their dead and recall memories of them. A practice that seems to work well for the bereaved and to play an essential part in their long-term grief, is the periodic observance of the death. Whether it is organized formally, as the prayers for the dead at Evensong, or informally, in the way that Bev Sage has held annual parties to remember her husband, the prolongation of ritualized or semi-ritualized remembrance, beyond the funeral and for several years thereafter, seems to be a healthy and beneficial custom to develop. The bereaved wish to continue to talk about their loved ones, but there comes a time when they begin to feel inhibited about doing so. Rituals of anniversary storytelling can enable them to overcome that.

Today, we have no name for the tradition of annual remembrance, but in the middle ages, it was known as 'the twelvemonths mind', an *obit*, or yearly commemorative service, when those with life were mindful of the day they lost a family member or friend. It is a practice well understood within non-Christian cultures. The 'twelvemonths mind' is closely akin to the Jewish tradition of *Yahrzeit* – literally, the 'time of year' – when the anniversary of a relative's death is marked by fasting, the recitation of the funeral prayer (the *Kaddish*), lighting a twenty-four-hour memorial candle and visiting the grave.

Another declining, but as yet still observed, practice involves more regular visits to the grave. Egyptians will mark the loss of loved ones for four days after the death, and then after forty days, but the most orthodox will return to the grave every Thursday. In the past, people have built small structures over the grave – *apartments* is the only adequate word to describe them – in order that they can spend hours or even days 'in the company of the dead'. Some of these are quite elaborate, with kitchens and running water, and outside Cairo they occur in such large numbers that the cemetery has come to be known as 'the City of the Dead'. Once the housing shortage in Cairo reached a certain crisis point, the homeless moved out to the necropolis and took over some of these 'grief apartments'.

In Tibetan tradition, the marking of the passage of time since a death is intimately related to the Buddhist belief in reincarnation. The living can influence the fortunes of the dead by following a routine of spiritual practice. It is an idea familiar to us from the doctrine of Purgatory. During the first seven weeks after the death, and especially in the first twenty-one days, the dead have 'a stronger link with *this* life, which makes them more accessible to our help'. By their spiritual practice – contemplation and prayer – the living can improve the deceased's chances of 'liberation, or at least a better rebirth'.[42] Those who are able to will repeat their spiritual practice every day for seven weeks. Others will practice every seventh day. By the end of the forty-nine-day period, the living will have done all they can for the dead; one year after the death, they will celebrate the re-birth of the deceased with an 'offering ceremony and feast'.[43]

From the perspective of a secularized and sceptical wes-tern culture, these beliefs may seem fanciful. But their value is transparent. Bereaved people, in their first year of grief, are given an active role, which formalizes their behaviour and discharges much of their intense feeling through a scheduled meditative practice. They do not avoid the sub-ject, nor do they repress emotion, and though we in the west may not buy in to the theology, the utilitarian benefit of these rituals must be obvious.

Waving in the distance

This process of storytelling and periodic observance might be described as a staggered farewell. Staggered farewells can take many forms. After the Oklahoma bombing in

1995, the state brought in car registration plates commem-orating the victims. The profits from the scheme have paid for some of the injured and the children of the dead to receive a college education. Every time an Oklahoma state licence is seen, the story of that massacre is, in some degree, re-told.

Bev Sage also continued the narrative of her loss when she began an MA course at a local art college. She felt strongly that she had lived with 'a profoundly creative person and needed to surround myself with creativity.' Her final project was a photo-study of aspects of death. But Bev also sought the help of a counsellor, and it may well be that counselling or psychotherapy adds another dimension to the storytelling that the bereaved need to continue. In a society that discourages the telling of the grief story after only a few weeks, therapy may provide one of the few remaining havens where the bereaved can tell their tales.

The value of an active grief is that it restores the bereaved to centre stage, which is where they belong for the duration of their mourning. Too often they are hovering in the wings, uncertain whether they should be part of the action at all. Not everyone will be as active in their grief as Bev Sage, but even those who are laid low by bereavement have lines they want to say. That they often lack a proper time to voice them and a proper audience to listen is in large part due to the inhibition the rest of us impose.

The best a society can do for the bereaved is for those who are friends, neighbours and work colleagues to create a supportive environment in which they can grieve actively and in a way that is most fulfilling *for them*. Not everyone will want to cry or to confide. In Britain, we inhabit a culture that has sought to inure itself to pain by means of self-restraint, and so for some people, it may not be helpful to try to buck that natural containment of feeling. Equally, of course, supporting the bereaved does not mean a simple compliance with their traumatized instincts. What the bereaved may initially want may not be what is ultimately right for them. Their stiff upper lip may be induced rather than innate, and they may have to be reassured that they can open up without cost to their dignity or intactness. Nervous actors, after all, still need to perform.

Colin Murray Parkes has argued that we would all benefit from a set of rules governing the open display of mourning for a prescribed period.

> An accepted mourning period provides social sanction for beginning and ending grief, and it is clearly likely to have psychological value for the bereaved. While it is true that social expectations concerning the duration of mourning cannot correspond closely to all individual needs to express grief, which vary considerably, the absence of any social expectations, as is common in Western cultures today, leaves bereaved people confused and insecure in their grief.[44]

Parkes's appeal to the churches to take a lead in determining an etiquette of grief is closely allied to his conviction that there comes a moment when grieving should stop and the bereaved rejoin the mainstream of life. It is hard to imagine the churches wielding that kind of influence any more, either in Europe or, frankly, in the United States. We are so far removed from a prescriptive behaviour for mourning that it would require a church leader with the power and charisma of an ayotollah to effect such a sea-change in our social behaviour. What may have to substitute for institutionalized rules is a repeated call for tolerance and recognition of the bereaved. Western societies expect grieving people to 'recover' too quickly. When the bereaved return to work or step back onto the street, they are treated to a litany of inappropriate clichés designed to protect the speaker from close contact with the bereaved's raw hurt. As the young woman widowed by the bombing of Pan Am 103 angrily replied – when friends insisted on speaking of her husband's violent death as 'passing away' – 'I guess he passed away like the Jews 'passed away' under Hitler.'[45] The attempt to soften the murder maddened her, as did the assumption that since she was young, she would marry again. The implication was that, on the one hand, *everything will be all right* and, on the other, *there is no need to speak further about death*. That silence is, of course, the worst reaction of all to the bereaved's predicament.

All the signs are that we are beginning to re-examine our attitudes to dying and bereavement and that there is an inchoate acknowledgement that we do not handle death well in the west. At the same time, there are fears expressed that we are in the process of de-socializing, partly as a result of the changing nature of work. Margaret Thatcher notoriously stated that there was no longer such a thing as society, at least in Britain. For the experience of dying and bereavement to improve, every element of truth in that contention needs to be expunged. There *must* be societies and, furthermore, if there are to be any social rules governing death, one should stand above the rest: that we all have a duty of care to those we know who are dying and to those we know who are bereaved.

7

Conclusion

But when that last part of death, and of our selves comes to be acted, then no dissembling will availe, then it is high time to speake plain English, and put off all vizards: then whatsoever the pot containeth must be shewne, be it good or bad, foule or cleane, wine or water.

Michel Eyquem de Montaigne

Most things will never happen: this one will,
And realisation of it rages out
In furnace-fear when we are caught without
People or drink. Courage is no good:
It means not scaring others. Being brave
Lets no one off the grave.
Death is no different whined at than withstood.

Philip Larkin

Fleeing to Teheran

Death, as Viktor Frankl knew, can be postponed, but not avoided. In *Man's Search for Meaning*, written shortly after his time in Auschwitz, Frankl recalls a traditional fable of the Orient:

A rich and mighty Persian once walked in his garden with one of his servants. The servant cried that he had just encountered Death, who had threatened him. He begged his master to give him his fastest horse so that he could make haste and flee to Teheran, which he could reach that same evening. The master consented and the servant galloped off on the horse. On returning to his house the master himself met Death and questioned him, 'Why did you terrify and threaten my servant?' 'I did not threaten him; I only showed surprise in still finding him here when I planned to meet him tonight in Teheran,' said Death.[1]

Optimists are said to live longer and so perhaps on the basis that it is better to travel in hope than to arrive, we may be able, through a combination of rapidly advancing medicine and a scrupulous diet, to prolong the journey a little. If the scientists who in 2000 reversed the ageing process of six cloned calves can reproduce their results in humans, some of us might even reach 200!

The refusal to accept that things are as they are and will always be as they have been is innate. It is what has motivated us to discover, innovate and change and whilst it may be a function of a stubborn and inflexible egoism, it is born equally of courage and idealism. Why shouldn't we live as long as we can? In the past, our religious traditions attributed death to a culpable error on the part of our ancestors, but today the error is biological. Death is 'a series of preventable diseases', according to one scientist, and so the logic goes: *let's identify each one, extirpate the lot and thrive!* We have always thought of death as a mistake that should not have happened, and perhaps medical science is simply catching up with human intuition.

Yet immortality on earth, which is what the death-as-disease model prognosticates, is a daunting prospect. It is the 'vast, obscure unfinished masterpiece' to which Nabokov said human lives are now just 'footnotes'. That we might attain immortality seems as improbable as it is desirable, but to imagine for a moment that we did, would it not be as fraught with new problems as it would be the solution to the old? If life is infinite, it takes on a loose and indeterminate shape, full of endless promise and precious little achievement. The old accumulate in their droves, with mixed health and varying degrees of sanity. People experience the death of a loved one with growing infrequency. The bereaved feel and appear peculiar. Those who are slowly dying, as a result of injuries sustained in an accident or a fight, or for no reason at all, become the failures of the Human Life Project. As a minority, their care comes to be seen as a specialization, attracting poor funding and poor public awareness. Immortalism is quickly made inimical to palliative care.

This is, of course, a fantasy. We are not about to increase life expectancy very substantially and indeed some estimates suggest that, should we succeed in eradicating the common killer diseases, the average length of life might improve by as little as twelve years. The serious point, however, is that we in the West inhabit a culture that is committed to the extension of human life and the avoidance of death. Modern medicine is preoccupied with the defeat of death and thereby fosters a hope that it can be done. Television and newspapers, too, nurture the belief that with the approved combination of meat and drink, exercise, potions, pins and prayer, we may live on beyond, as it were, our due. Failing all else, we can be frozen.

But common sense tells us that what we are seeking from these regimens is a bit more of what we've got and not immortality on earth. Eternity is a 'pleasing, dreadful thought', as Addison said, and in that phrase he summed up the contradiction of humanity.

Why Do We Fear Death?

Death is 'a site of paradoxes'.[2] It is a place where opposites collide: freedom and captivity, anguish and relief, body and spirit, being and non-being, meaning and the void, order and disorder, joy and anger, the beginning and the end. Death can be the termination of one person's suffering and the commencement of another's. It is the 'easeful Death' that Keats was half in love with or it is Lear's howl as he carries on Cordelia's body, 'dead as earth'. Death comes as a laughing skeleton or as a bride, as an angel or as Satan, as a syphilitic seductress of the demi-monde or as 'the gentle nurse that puts the children to bed'.[3]

A large part of our problem with death results from our attachment to our physical being. We are exercised by the thought that death will damage and corrupt that aspect of ourselves which we know best, our bodies. All the images above struggle to understand death as a physical force, which transforms our bodies, and each new image places itself on one side of the dichotomy or the other, the curse or the nurse. Attachment to the body is latent in our culture – rarely have human beings been so preoccupied with the physical form – and that partly explains the fastidious sensitivity we have concerning the ill-treatment of corpses.

Thomas Lynch's contention that funerals are for the living and that, therefore, what we do to the corpse is a matter of concern for us, and not for the dead, holds good only up to a point. Of course, he's right – 'the dead don't care' – but there is an important sense in which we the mourners hypothesize the thoughts and feelings of the dead. The resistance to the re-use of graves is one example of how we endow the grave with a sanctity that should not be dishonoured. But still more is the breach of a coffin, which is an outrage against the dead themselves. In their book *Death and Representation*, Sarah Goodwin and Elisabeth Bronfen recall the desecration of the Jewish cemetery at Carpentras in France. In 1990, vandals broke up headstones and wrote graffiti on them, but what disturbed us most was their violation of the grave of an eighty-one-year-old man, who had died two weeks earlier. The coffin was torn open and the man's corpse was pierced with an umbrella. Goodwin and Bronfen quote a comment made at the time in the *Frankfurter Allgemeine Zeitung* by the veteran war crimes campaigner, Serge Klarsfeld: 'to injure the dead is to declare total war, total hatred.'[4] When the dead are dishonoured in this way, the insult goes deep and touches the core of our moral propriety.

People were similarly appalled when the sculptor, Anthony-Noel Kelly, conspired to take body parts from the Royal College of Surgeons to use as models. He was helped by a junior technician at the college, Neil Lindsay. The two men stole a number of heads, torsos, arms and legs. They stuffed them into black, plastic bin-liners and travelled home with them on the tube. Kelly and Lindsay were later prosecuted for theft and, in April 1998, they were sentenced to nine months in prison, with half the term suspended. Anthony-Noel Kelly's defence was that he had taken the heads and limbs for artistic purposes; his intention was to model sculptures on them, which would capture Kelly's feelings about life and death.

The appropriation of dead bodies has a long and disreputable history. Everyone has heard of the body-snatching from cemeteries that caused such a furore in the early nineteenth century. The anatomy schools' constant demand for fresh corpses led to an iniquitous trade that was only brought to an end once the bodies of the destitute were made available to hospitals. Less well known is that the seizure of bodies for research still goes on today. Under the Anatomy Act (1984), if people die in a hospital or a nursing home and they are not recovered by their families, their bodies, too, can be sent away for 'anatomical use'. That this continues is shocking to many people. In key respects, it differs, for example, from an individual's freely made decision to donate his body to medical research. One body laid out on a table might look much like another, but in the public's perception the means by which they ended up there have different moral resonances. First, the dead of the hospital and the nursing home exercise no choice over their disposal, whereas the donor has made a gift of his body for the benefit of others. Everything about his action stresses its individualism and its integrity. Those, by contrast, who have not given their consent and wind up on a slab are depersonalized by their appropriation. They become specimens, the fodder of the dissection lab.

When people are made fully aware of practices of this or a similar kind, there is usually a public outcry. A recent example followed the child organs fiasco at Alder Hey Children's Hospital in Liverpool at the end of 1999. The hospital was found to have a collection of over 2,000 hearts, which had been removed from children during post-mortem examinations and not replaced. In general, the parents of these dead children had not been consulted and had therefore buried their children unaware that their bodies had been eviscerated. People found it hard to understand the explanation, given by a former senior pathologist at the hospital, that the organs had been needed for research into cot deaths and that they had accumulated as a result of a shortfall in research funding. However accurate, the official account was dramatically out of kilter with the distress of parents who felt that their children had been totally mutilated. The hospital staff were accused of breaking the law, of arrogance and of a complete disregard for the rights and sensitivities of grieving parents. The children had been treated, it appeared, as nothing more than a resource.

A year later, it was revealed that organ retention without the consent of bereaved families was much more widespread in Britain than had been first supposed. Amongst other organs stored in over 100 hospitals across the country, were an estimated 11,000 hearts and in October 2000, the government announced that it would investigate the unapproved removal of over a million body parts from dead patients. The practice was defended, on the grounds of humanitarian concern, by Professor James Underwood of the Royal College of Pathologists: 'In the past,' he said, 'if relatives were left ignorant, it was done with the best of intentions. Doctors acted to protect the bereaved at a time of great upset. Now it is clear that opinions have changed and the public expects more information. If that is what is demanded, we will change our working practices.'[5]

So what is it that lies at the heart of our fear that if an old man can be stabbed in his grave or a child gutted on a pathologist's table, the same might happen to our bodies or to our children's bodies? Why does it matter? They are dead. We forget too easily that much of our identity is vested in the body. It is the first sign of our individuality which the rest of the world encounters. Pierced, amputated, deprived of a lung or a heart, we are less than that whole, less than that individual person. Perhaps the 'total hatred' of which Klarsfeld wrote was another way of saying that nowhere was safe for that individual Jew. Even the 'selfhood' of his body lying in a grave was not protected from the destructive hatred of his violators. They wanted to mock his wholeness, make him less than one.

For some commentators on death, like Samuel Beckett, who could not accept that anything continues beyond corporeal life, the body generates whatever purpose it can within its lifetime, and death is consequently 'meaningless and valueless'.[6] But for others, the body is a much more ambivalent dimension. William James, for instance, argued that the body may produce life or it may, as religious writers contend, reflect life. Thus, the body is understood either as the vehicle of life or its progenitor.[7]

This kind of ambivalence is conspicuous within the Christian tradition. The resurrection promised by Jesus Christ is a resurrection of the physical body, which explains the churches' longstanding antipathy to cremation. But although the body is implicated in the life of the soul, Christianity has also supported the view that the body is base, corrupted by crude desires for food and sexual union. By implication, a superior life, born of disgust for the physical existence, would be one in which the body's lusts are suppressed and the flesh is mortified for its sins.

For most of us, the body is the index both of life's continuation and its quality. We can only picture resurrection if it includes the persistence of *self*, which, crudely, we understand as the face that looks back at us in the mirror. The life we value presupposes an intact body, which functions correctly and affords us sensual pleasure. Religious culture has struggled against this conviction, promulgating the view that the death of the body represents the liberation of the soul to enjoy the life of the spirit. (Hindus, for example, see death as the moment when worldly illusion ends and the self begins to reveal its divine nature and in some traditions, such as Islam, this is symbolized by the transfiguration of the soul into a bird.) Yet the spiritual life is not characterized simply by freedom and peace; it is often set amid trees, grass and flowers, in other words sources of sensual stimulation for the physical being. 'Paradise' derives from the Persian *pairadaeza*, a royal park or garden, and is found, *inter alia*, in the Judaeo-Christian story of Eden, in the Elysian Fields of Greek myth, the 'happy fields' of ancient Egypt and the 'fields of heaven' where Tibetan Buddhists reside between death and reincarnation. These, then, are stories that perpetuate the idea of the body as restraint, the body as gross matter in conflict with the refinements of the spirit, but also describe immortality in terms which emphasize the entertainment of the senses.

With such a philosophical history, it is hardly surprising that the death of the body evokes a complicated unease. Although our own experience of physical life is generally mixed – the body is a matrix of pleasure *and* pain – we are not inclined to give it up. On the contrary, the body is one of the most important means by which we secure our identity in relation to others. Whatever view we take of the Christian resurrection, if we wish to live on in the minds of those who survive our deaths, it is our bodies – every bit as much as our personalities – that we expect to be remembered and respected.

The Threat to the Individual

The second source of our fear, both of dying and of death, has to do with the primacy of the individual personality in western culture since the Reformation. Freud, in *Beyond the Pleasure Principle*, quotes Hartmann's dictum that death is 'the termination of individual development'.[8] True selfhood inevitably eludes the present – we never achieve all we are capable of – and we therefore die uncompleted. This concept only carries weight, of course, in a culture which esteems the individual and, as Clare Gittings has pointed out, many cultures do not. The primacy of the individual is an idea that is not shared – and is even derided – by 'most of the earth's population'.[9] Western culture, by contrast, has experienced what Norbert Elias has called a 'spurt of individualization' that has produced 'individual immortality-fantasies'.[10] These are rooted in the Reformation, as Gittings makes clear. Once the individual could enjoy a personal relationship with God and, indeed, manifest the divine in his own personality, the importance of the individual soared.

A society that prizes the individual so highly will fear death more than a society that prizes the collective, and for two reasons. The first is obvious: the individual has been made unique and 'one who is unique can, by definition, never truly be replaced'.[11] Secondly, any structure of belief that explains death and promises the survival of the spirit gains meaning and substance when it is supported by the collective. That is how orthodoxy is shaped. As the individual's ideas, sanctified by conscience, become progressively separated from other people's ideas, the 'meaning' of orthodoxy diminishes. The individual is left with less and less that is collectively agreed to protect him from his own fears. Ultimately, individualism finds itself at odds with orthodox salvation.

This brings us to the present crisis. Because improved sanitation and advances in medicine have distanced us from the observation of death, we have forgotten 'the weakness of our mortal nature'. We are designed to fear death, as beings conscious of the need to avoid danger, and as social animals it is natural that we should grieve for the loss of someone we knew. The modern project – better living conditions for all, better health and better life expectancy, together with the abandonment of formal mourning, the loss of heaven and hell, and the disintegration of traditional communities – have all helped to obscure the innate wisdom of fear and grief.

But, as Francis Bacon said, you can't order nature about: 'Nature is often hidden, sometimes overcome, seldom extinguished.'[12] We do need, and shall continue to need, to express our anguish and to locate death on a spectrum of purpose that begins with birth and passes through the other rites of life, such as sexual initiation, separation from parents, partnership and child-rearing. How we are to do this has become more and more difficult as religion and community have declined and atheism has lost its *raison d'être*. In the absence of God, it is immaterial to state that you have no belief in him. As Pat Jalland has argued, one of the defining moments of the twentieth century was the cessation of the conflict between faith and atheism. Its effect was to shred any remnant of meaning still attaching to death:

> Without a dominant Christianity against which to define unbelief, the meaning of death has largely been excluded from public culture, except from the inherited rituals of the burial or cremation service. But the loss in the meaning of death has also been a loss in the meaning of human life, a cultural problem which post-Christian societies seem unable to resolve.[13]

What Is To Be Done?

It remains true that there will be many people who face death with the substantial benefits of a religious faith. They may, through conviction, be able to bear physical suffering and the anxiety of loss without fear. For others, though, who have no religious beliefs to sustain them, death may prove to be the greatest test to which their inner strengths have ever been put, and they will rightly ask of their carers that they be looked after with consideration, tenderness and reassurance.

Death is the ultimate loss of control. Not only can the various functions of the physical body deteriorate and cease to work, but our minds may pack up and we may lose the ability to make decisions and conduct our affairs and relationships. Our experience of life has been to develop a sense of responsibility and the skills needed to manage our lives. Then we find ourselves confronting death, and all responsibility and management seem to pass from our hands. We are in the grip of disease, of doctors, of relatives, of institutions, of eternity. The fear of death is, in this respect, no different from the fear of attack, the fear of our plane dropping out of the sky, or the fear of a relationship ending. We would like to take control of the situation, but it is the other party that appears to be in charge.

That loss of control is a defining characteristic of dying is well known amongst those who work in palliative care. It is the reason so much is done to try and restore a degree of control to patients at an early stage. First, this means that pain, and any other distressing symptoms, must be eliminated or greatly reduced. It is only without pain that the dying can be expected to function with a modicum of autonomy. Once that has been achieved, the dying can be assisted to make a will, to imagine the kind of funeral they would wish and to settle their affairs with relatives and friends.

All of these are valuable and practical ways in which

dying can be improved. But the meaning and appreciation that the dying will attach to them will depend on the quality of trust that develops between patient and carers. The dying are empowered chiefly through information. Knowledge of what is happening to them and what options there are for their further care will enable them to make choices. It is one of the great disservices we do to the dying to disempower them by keeping them ignorant.

The dying will also want to find meaning in what they are going through, a sense that what is ending has had value. Apart from the more or less desperate efforts of patriots to dignify their war dead with the achievement of sacrifice, we have tended to make death into a pointless travesty of life: a burlesque of all we have tried to do, and have sometimes done, and we must either laugh or cry in the face of it. Dying is a mockery of living. It swipes the Queen of Hearts from the bottom row and the whole House of Cards collapses. It is hard to excavate meaning from the crumbling edifice. The possibility of finding meaning, then, is only credible if there is a relationship of trust between patient and carers. Meaning, in this context, is something communicated to and acknowledged by another, and we are much more likely to reveal our deepest thoughts and feelings if we believe that those who have charge of our care are doing their best to sustain our integrity when it is under attack.

Attempts are being made by the hospice movement and others to restore meaning to the lives of the dying by experiential storytelling. Even some who are fearful and dispirited can be encouraged to tell the tale of their childhood to a nurse willing to listen. The experience of hospice staff is that the dying substantiate their lives in this way. Their experience of love, friendship and adversity makes their history strong when their present is weak. This is all to the good and the fact that this kind of storytelling is a practical technique, rather than the basis of a universal truth, does not alter its power to lend significance to the individual's biography. Until there is a structure of belief that endows death with a new universal meaning, practical strategies of this kind are most likely to help us assuage the fear and the taboo of death.

Bereavement, equally, entails a terrifying loss of control. Someone we loved has been taken away from us and we can do nothing to recover them. The body we loved is supervised by doctors and a funeral director. Our minds and bodies are awash with a torrent of emotion, which leaves us weak, exhausted and without sleep or appetite. The mechanisms by which we regulate our lives break down. We do not know what the future holds, but fear that it will be both momentous and horrible. Plans are anathema, and yet we are faced with the need to bury our dead and to honour them with a ceremony that reflects the scale and quality of our loss.

Now that death is in the process of being cut loose from organized religion – the implication of any mass abandonment of faith – it is hard to imagine that the traditional framework of funerary ritual will continue to fulfil that need for very long. That said, much of a society's view of itself is illustrated in, and worked through, its death rituals. A society without death rituals, if such could exist, would be one which had no beliefs about death other than it being a void – not merely an end, but something beyond comment, 'meaningless and valueless', as Beckett said. It would also be a society that did not believe in its future, because it would have lost the opportunity to define a meaning for life itself. The evidence is, though, that we do want new ritual norms, and that finding meaning in the absence of God is one of the great – if largely tacit – endeavours of the twenty-first century. It remains to be seen what developed societies will put in the place of religious organizations, but the rapid adoption of alternative funerals suggests that whilst the bereaved do not necessarily need the supernatural, they do need a formal means to voice feelings of loss.

That alternative funeral companies such as Heaven on Earth have expanded so quickly is firstly because they provide a funeral which, if not unique, is highly individual in form. They help the bereaved to conceive and arrange a 'service' that suits their individual needs. To some extent, the churches have tried to adapt themselves in this direction as well, but their choices are constrained by theology and liturgy and to many people both are alien. But the logical conclusion to the seemingly irreversible secularization of society is that everyone will ask for an alternative funeral. Once that happens, of course, the departure from convention loses some of its point. Like the atheist railing against a long-vanished Christian establishment, alternative funerals will lose some of their meaning without their antithetical thrust. Take that away and it becomes an individual act, without any grounding system of belief to plagiarize or deny. The greater the number of individual acts of secular obsequy, the more we lose any collective means of honouring the dead. More disturbingly, we lose in the process any means to generate a collective understanding of death.

Yet that is what we must search for in this secular age if death is not to have the last word. We must construct rituals or ceremonies for our lives that are not contingent on supernatural redemption or mere imaginative idiosyncrasy. It seems to me that the key to some modern grief theory is not simply the emphasis that it places on the bereaved taking an active role, but that it encourages the sharing of memories *in the long run*. This is not ritual in the usual sense, but *ritualized* remembering can be attached to anniversaries in the form of, say, parties. To begin with, the bereaved can be encouraged to take a hand; they can design the funeral and share their memories; they can learn to look upon their grief as an act of remembrance rather than of separation. But then, in the months and even years that follow, they can continue the process of talking and writing about their experience and their recollections, freed from the fear that it is socially inappropriate to do so.

What I hope has emerged from this discussion is that activity is better than passivity, and that, in practice, means gaining as much control as possible over the experience. In the context of dying, control means that patients are able to express their needs, discuss hopes and fears, seek the truth of what is happening and, with the help of others, discover the substantial meaning that resides in the very achievement of having lived. In the context of funerals, control has two aspects: to decide or influence the form and content of the ritual, and to participate in telling the story of the life that is over. Here, as with bereavement, the problem is how to gain control over an emotional experience which is overwhelming and unpredictable. The very word 'control', in this context, evokes Canute and the rolling waves on the Kent coast. But the evidence from the hospice movement, from the increasing number of alternative funerals and from bereavement counsellors, should convince us that we can, even when transfixed by death, exert more influence over events than we might at first think.

The Need for 'Haptonomy'

An active role of this kind is only possible with the full co-operation of the rest of us and our agreement that it is an acceptable form of behaviour. The idea that the dying and the grieving should put on a brave face, in order to save the rest of us the pain of identifying too closely with what they are going through, has done much to undermine the quality of terminal and bereavement care. Worse, it has made death harder for us all. We do not treat the dying or the bereaved with anything like enough patience and kindness. We escape into a fearful evasion of the subject, afraid to discuss it because it is freighted with potential embarrassment. It is limitless and unknown. To talk intimately with the dying or bereaved is to jump into a conversational abyss; we have no idea what lies at the bottom and no idea what condition we will end up in when we get there. We also have the perverse idea that those who are suffering do not wish to dwell on death. This may be true at certain times and very definitely not true at others, but their apparent reluctance to speak could as easily be ascribed to an apprehension about the listener as a dislike of morbidity.

In place of silence, both the dying and the bereaved have need of active, concerned, patient, restorative care, or what Marie de Hennezel calls 'haptonomy'. Haptonomy is the word de Hennezel uses to describe the kind of emotional and physical care she practises at her hospice in Paris. 'One develops and tries to ripen one's human faculties of contact,' she writes, 'one learns to "dare" to encounter another human being by touch.'[14] The extent to which one human being offers to touch another has to be judged, but to conclude that since it is so sensitive it is best avoided, is to leave the dying isolated at a time when they need to be reassured that the last of their physical life is worthwhile.

If we take from 'haptonomy' its central idea of intimacy, it may have an application to bereavement as well. Of course, it is true that death can bring out the best in people. Family and friends do rally round after a death, trying to give whatever succour they can to the bereaved. Death can also elicit a public goodwill when disasters such as a famine in Ethiopia or a rail crash in Britain hit the headlines. But the limitation of most of the human kindness shown to the bereaved is that it is far too short-lived. The bereaved are expected to 'recover' too quickly and it is very often only a few days after the funeral that people begin to regard them as peculiar if they have not regained a semblance of normality. In this respect, the behaviour of developed societies has not changed very much at all. Geoffrey Gorer claimed in 1965 that mourning was treated 'as if it were a weakness, a self-indulgence, a reprehensible bad habit',[15] and in 1981 Philippe Ariès was describing it as a 'malady'.[16] Both statements are true today.

That we should be more attentive to the grieving is not merely a personal and civic duty; it might also preserve life. (There is a noticeable rise in the mortality rate amongst widows and widowers in the first year after the deaths of their spouses.) In particular, the bereaved complain about society's expectation that they will maintain a calm dignity during the weeks and months following their loss. Induced inhibition starts with the funeral. Whilst restraint may not be wrong for all mourners at all times, there is no doubt that seen in the context of other cultures, the western habit of keeping down strong emotions is highly deviant.

According to Pat Jalland, it was the public schools in the late nineteenth century that stifled the expression of feeling. Up until the 1870s, it was not unusual for a newly bereaved man to tug his hair and deliver long laments about his loss. As the public school ethos of self-control began to impose itself on what was already a rigorously formal society, families found themselves torn between the wishes of one relative not to comment on the death and the regrets of another that feelings were not adequately expressed. Death was becoming an event too shocking to witness and too indelicate to discuss.[17]

The result of accumulated inhibition has been a society that encounters the first shock of grief unprepared, without an inkling either of its power or of how to deal with it. We are not now familiar with what death is like and we have never been encouraged to think about it before it happens. On the contrary, such contemplation of death, in advance of one's first bereavement, has been deemed morbid. Of course, all people in all ages have in the end to quell the fear of death and find a way to memorialize the dead that is a salve for their grief and not a prompt to morbidity, but it was more common in the past to view life as a *preparation* for death. Indeed, as recently as a century ago, Henry James was speaking of life as the 'predicament before death'. In the absence of such an intimacy with death, modernity has given rise to diverse and contradictory attitudes.

There seems to be little doubt that with the growth of palliative care techniques and of the hospice movement, great strides have been made in understanding what it is to die. Developments in psychotherapy of all kinds have similarly improved our knowledge of grief and of the counselling techniques that are most effective in the treatment of the bereaved. There does, however, seem to be a lot further to go, which is partly due to the tardiness with which the medical profession has come to recognize that care of the dying is one of the primary responsibilities for which doctors should be trained. What sort of change is in the wind is, as yet, unclear. Medical schools are building into the curriculum courses in terminal care, but it remains to be seen how widespread they will be, how compulsory and how much trainee doctors learn.

There are signs, too, that some sections of society may be waking up to the wisdom of preparing for death, of accepting its inevitability and anticipating what bereavement may do to us. It is reported that bereavement studies are at last to play a part in the education of children, at least in Britain. In the year 2000, it was announced that the PHSE syllabus in secondary schools would, at some point in the future, include classes designed to prepare children for a family bereavement. Not surprisingly, doubts have been raised about inducing morbidness in young minds. Children under three cannot grasp what death implies or understand it to be anything other than a temporary separation, such as a shopping trip. But by nine or ten children have begun to realize that death happens to us all and is irreversible, and in their teens they know that death is, as Francesca Thompson and Sheila Payne put it, 'personal'; bereavement is something they expect to hurt.[18] Morbidness is a risk, as it is indeed a risk that a teacher, having failed to realize that a child in the class is newly bereaved, will conduct a lesson insensitively. What mitigates the danger is proper training. If bereavement studies becomes the responsibility of the 'least resistant' – as has previously happened when teachers of religious education were forced to take on sex – children could, in the hands of unskilled teachers, become disturbed or anxious. With skilled teaching, however, there is every reason to believe that children can both handle a discussion about death and benefit from it.

The general consensus amongst psychotherapists of all disciplines supports the idea articulated by Colin Murray Parkes that 'societies which encourage grief expression do better.'[19] Parkes agrees with the view taken by Gorer that those who are unable to express their grief early on are more likely to become 'disturbed' later.[20] This does not mean that we all give – or should give – expression to our grief in the same way, but rather that it is important for our psychological health that the feelings of grief are 'permitted to emerge into consciousness'.[21]

Remembrance

The test of any society that aspires to openness is whether thought and feeling customarily regarded as private can be admitted into general discourse. We shall be able to state confidently that there is no longer a taboo against death once people who are dying or grieving can speak out in routine circumstances about their condition, when they can feel able to return to the subject, and not feel inhibited, let alone prohibited, by their audience. As the broadcaster Libby Purves remarked in *The Times*, 'It is not the simple statement of facts that ushers in freedom, it is the constant repetition of them.'[22]

There is, however, one fact on which there already seems to be common agreement: we do not forget the dead. Much has been said and written in recent years, in sociological and psychotherapeutic circles, about whether it is better for the bereaved to 'let go' or to 'preserve' the image of the deceased. Do we move on in life only when we have surrendered our attachment to the dead loved one, or can we take him or her with us? The debate between supporters of these two theories is playing a valuable part in improving the counselling of the bereaved, but at a fundamental level, most of us know that we never let go.

The catalogue of ways in which we recall and stay close to the dead, whether we have beliefs in the supernatural or not, is huge. We have only to think of their faces in our memories, the photographs and diaries, the bequeathed books, the old letters and bits of furniture, the pieces of jewellery, the house they lived in, the family anecdotes and sayings they originated, and the jokes with friends who knew them, to realize that the dead linger on. They hang about, almost indefinitely. To suggest that we get over our grief by ceasing to think about them is wrong and colludes with the taboo against which we struggle to speak.

Instead, we strive to reach a point when contemplating the deceased can be done with an easy mind, when to do so is a source of sadness, but of joy and comfort as well. It may be the work of a lifetime, and to keep us from going mad, we need a new narrative about death and its meaning, and a new language of condolence, which is not emasculated by euphemism, cliché or incredible myth. We need to value the dead and keep them in our memories, to talk about them and share our stories. If our sense of identity, in life, is affirmed by the awareness that others have of us, then an afterlife for the dead is, in this way, possible.

End Notes

1 Why We Think as We Do

1 Philip Morgan, 'Of worms and war 1380–1558', in *Death in England: an Illustrated History*, ed. Jupp and Gittings, Manchester, 1999, p. 129.

2 Izaac Walton, 'Life of Dr Donne' (1640), in *Walton's Lives*.

3 Jeremy Taylor, *The Rule and Exercises of Holy Dying* (1651), London, 1845, pp. 194–6.

4 Ralph Houlbrooke, *Death, Religion and the Family in England 1480–1750*, Oxford, 1998, p. 185.

5 Clare Gittings, *Death, Burial and the Individual in Early Modern Britain*, London, 1984, p. 15.

6 See Pat Jalland, *Death in the Victorian Family*, Oxford, 1996, p. 320.

7 Jalland, p. 11.

8 Sigmund Freud, *Thoughts for the Times on War and Death* (1915), Penguin Freud Library, vol. 12, 1985, p. 79.

9 Alan Wilkinson, 'Changing Attitudes to Death in the Two World Wars', in *The Changing Face of Death*, ed. Jupp and Howarth, London, 1997, pp. 149–63.

10 Jalland, p. 379.

11 Thomas Kirkwood, *Time of Our Lives: the Science of Human Ageing*, London, 1999, p. 175.

12 Kirkwood, p. 8.

13 See Porter, *The Greatest Benefit to Mankind*, London, 1997.

14 Gorer, *Death, Grief and Mourning in Contemporary Britain*, London, 1965, p. 114.

15 Kirkwood, p. 33.

16 Walter, *The Eclipse of Eternity*, London, 1996, p. 30.
17 Gorer, p. 63.
18 Walter, *The Revival of Death*, London, 1994, p. 112.
19 Wittgenstein, *Tractatus Logico-Philosophicus*, trans. C. K. Ogden, 1918.
20 Dollimore, *Death, Desire and Loss in Western Culture*, London, 1998, p. xxviii.
21 Hitchins, Sewell, *Evening Standard*, 27 August 1998.
22 Lynda Lee Potter, *Daily Mail*, 1 September 1997.
23 *Today* programme, BBC Radio 4, 2 September 1997.
24 Merrin, 'Crash, bang, wallop! What a picture! The death of Diana and the media', *Mortality*, vol. 4, no. 1, March 1999, pp. 41–62.
25 *BMJ*, 18 November 2000.
26 'Controversy of the Week', *The Week*, 28 March 1998, p. 4.
27 Quoted by Dorothy Hewlett in *A Life of John Keats*, London, 3rd ed., 1970, p. 369. See also *Holy Dying*, p. vii.
28 Montaigne, *Essays*, vol. 1, trans. J. Florio, London, 1965, p. 79.
29 Ariès, *The Hour of Our Death*, London, 1981, p. 613.
30 'How to Rest in Peace', *Spectator*, 31 July 1999, p. 11.

2   Terminal Illness

1 Interview by Jeremy Paxman, *Start the Week*, BBC Radio 4, 2001.
2 *The Week*, 2 January 1999, p. 25.
3 Sally Cline, *Lifting the Taboo: Women, Death and Dying*, London, 1995, p. 198.
4 Elisabeth Lee, *A Good Death: a Guide for Patients and Carers Facing Terminal Illness at Home*, London, 1995, p. 11.
5 CancerBACUP is chiefly a phone helpline. Between 6 and 8 lines are open every weekday morning and evening (4 in the less busy afternoons) and they have a staff of 17 trained nurses, each of whom will do a shift of 4½ hours on the phones. They also reply to emails and letters during that time. The volume of enquiries increases every year. In 1998–9, they received 46,000 – the bulk of which were phone calls. (A similar service is run in the USA by the National Cancer Institute, although the nursing staff are not specifically trained in oncology.) All 52 of their booklets and their 70 factsheets are available on their website as well as by mail order from their London office.
6 Ruth Picardie, *Before I Say Goodbye*, London, 1998, p. 100.

7 Michael Young and Lesley Curren, *A Good Death: Conversations with East Londoners*, London, 1996, p. 152.
8 Picardie, p. 13.
9 Picardie, p. 58.
10 Picardie, p. 51.
11 Sontag, *AIDS and Its Metaphors*, London, 1989, p. 16.
12 *Today* programme, BBC Radio 4, 22 March 2000.
13 *Why Me?*, London, 1993, p. 11.
14 *World Health Report*, Geneva, 1998, p. 93.
15 *Why Me?*, p. 19.
16 *Living with Grief after Sudden Loss*, ed. Kenneth Doka, Washington, 1996, p. 14.
17 Marie de Hennezel, *Intimate Death*, trans. Jareway, London, 1997, p. 152.
18 de Hennezel, pp. 45–7.

3 The Gift of Hospice

1 Cicely Saunders and Mary Baines, *Living with Dying: the Management of Terminal Disease*, Oxford, 1983, p. 1.
2 'Spiritual Pain', *Journal of Palliative Care*, vol. 4, no. 3, 1988, pp. 29–32.
3 E Kübler-Ross, *Living with Death and Dying*, London, 1982, p. 19.
4 de Hennezel, p. 9.
5 Manning, *The Hospice Alternative: Living with Dying*, London, 1984, pp. 36–7.
6 See Clare Humphreys, 'Waiting for the last Summons: the Establishment of the First Hospices in England', *Mortality*, vol. 6, no. 2, July 2001, pp. 146–66.
7 Saunders and Baines, p. 11.
8 Saunders and Baines, p. 26.
9 Saunders and Baines, p. 26.
10 de Hennezel, p. 100.
11 *Living with Death and Dying*, pp. 25–47.
12 MacLeod and Carter, 'The significance of hope in the care of people who are dying', *Mortality*, vol. 4, no. 3, November 1999, p. 313.
13 Jalland, p. 110.
14 Quoted by David Clark in 'Originating a movement: Cicely Saunders and the development of St Christopher's Hospice, 1957–1967', *Mortality*, vol. 3, no. 1, March 1998, p. 45.
15 Stedeford, *Facing Death: Patients, Families and Professionals*, London, 1984, p. 18.

16 Saunders and Baines, p. 10.
17 *Living with Death and Dying*, pp. 3–4.
18 Seale and Cartwright, *The Year Before Death*, Aldershot, 1994, pp. 26, 35, 186.
19 Seale and Cartwright, pp. 47–8.
20 J. Andrew Billings, 'Palliative Care', *BMJ*, pp. 555–8, 2 September 2000.
21 Anne-Mei Thé *et al*, 'Collusion in doctor-patient communication about imminent death', *BMJ*, pp. 1376–81, 2 December 2000.
22 de Hennezel, p. 18.
23 Young and Curren, p. 161.
24 *Living with Death and Dying*, p. 10.
25 Saunders and Baines, p. 56.
26 Saunders and Baines, p. 58.
27 Saunders and Baines, p. 63.
28 Saunders and Baines, p. 63.
29 Elias, *The Loneliness of Dying*, trans. Jephcott, London, 1985, p. 62.
30 See Lawton, *The Dying Process: Experiences of Patients in Palliative Care*, London, 2000.
31 *The Revival of Death*, p. 75.
32 Quoted by Bethne Hart, Peter Sainsbury and Stephanie Short in 'Whose dying? A sociological critique of the "good death"', *Mortality*, vol. 3, no. 1, March 1998, p. 71.

4   Dying at Home – the Future of Palliative Care

1 Saunders and Baines, p. 66.
2 Lloyd, 'Dying in old age: promoting well-being at the end of life', *Mortality*, vol. 5, no. 2, July 2000, p. 175.
3 Lloyd, pp. 175–6.
4 Seale and Cartwright, p. 219.
5 Lloyd, p. 175.
6 Lee, *A Good Death*, p. 98.
7 Kübler-Ross, Postscript to Manning, *The Hospice Alternative*, p. 170.
8 Lee, p. 99.
9 Kübler-Ross, *Living with Death and Dying*, p. 14.
10 Billings, *BMJ*, 2 September 2000.
11 See Froggatt, 'Rites of passage and the hospice culture', *Mortality*, vol. 2, no. 2, July 1997, p. 131.

5 The Need for Ritual

1 Lynch, *The Undertaking: Life Studies from the Dismal Trade*, London, 1997, p. 106.
2 *The Undertaking*, p. 11.
3 *The Undertaking*, p. 8.
4 *The Dead Citizens Charter*, National Funerals College, London, 1996.
5 Gittings, *Death, Burial and the Individual*, p. 28.
6 Gittings, 'Sacred and Secular 1558–1660', in *Death in England*, pp. 159–60.
7 *Death in England*, p. 162.
8 Jalland, p. 371.
9 *The Churchyards Handbook*, London, 3rd ed., 1988, p. 106.
10 Samuel Johnson, 'An essay upon the epitaphs of Alexander Pope', *Gentleman's Magazine*, 1740.
11 Letter to Lucy Porter, 2 December 1784, *Faber Book of Letters*, ed. Pryor, London, 1988, p. 84.
12 'Essay Upon Epitaphs', *Wordsworth: Poetical Works*, ed. de Selincourt, Oxford, 1974, pp. 728–33.
13 See *World in Action*: 'What a Business', Granada Television, 1998; and Lynch, *Bodies in Motion and at Rest*, London, 2000, p. 159.
14 Gittings, *Death, Burial and the Individual*, pp. 105–6.
15 *Death, Burial and the Individual*, p. 140.
16 See J. B. Bradfield, *Green Burial: the D-I-Y Guide to Law and Practice*, London, 1994.
17 Lynch, *Bodies in Motion and at Rest*, pp. 64–6.
18 Osmond, *Changing Perspectives: Christian Culture and Morals in England Today*, London, 1993, p. 35.
19 *The Dead Citizens Charter*, p. 1.

6 Dealing with Grief

1 Colin Murray Parkes, *Bereavement: Studies of Grief in Adult Life*, new. ed., London, 1998, p. 6.
2 Jeannette Kupfermann, *When the Crying's Done*, London, 1992, p. 84.
3 Jalland, pp. 230–6.
4 Cline, p. 141.
5 *Death and Bereavement Across Cultures*, ed. Parkes, Laungani and Young, London, 1997, p. 5.
6 Parkes, *Bereavement*, p. 62.
7 *Bereavement*, p. 90.

8 Isabella Allende, *Paula*, London, 1995, p. 209.
9 Kupfermann, p. 2.
10 Some reservations have been expressed regarding child grief and the benefits of the Tasks model. (See Parkes, Laungani and Young, p. 198.)
11 Worden, *Grief Counselling and Grief Therapy*, London, 1991, p. 35.
12 Worden, p. 17.
13 *Essays*, vol. 1, p. 89.
14 Rando, 'Complications in Mourning Traumatic Death', *Living with Grief after Sudden Loss*, p. 145.
15 *Bereavement*, p. 6.
16 See *Information for Families of Homicide Victims*, Home Office Communications Directorate 1995.
17 See Victoria Cummock, 'Journey of a Young Widow: the Bombing of Pan Am 103', in *Living with Grief after Sudden Loss*, p. 7.
18 *Living with Grief after Sudden Loss*, p. 226.
19 *Bereavement*, p. 47.
20 Rhona Campbell, 'Trauma and Bereavement', a lecture given at the Findhorn Community, 6 April 1998.
21 Jalland, pp. 319–21.
22 Taylor, *Holy Dying*, p. 101.
23 Houlbrooke, p. 18.
24 Jalland, p. 120.
25 *Bereavement*, p. 122.
26 Letter to Sir Richard Browne, 14 February 1658.
27 *Faber Book of Letters*, p. 100.
28 Jalland, pp. 127–42.
29 *Love, Labour and Loss: stillbirth and neonatal death*, London, 1996, pp. 2–7.
30 Benson and Robinson-Walsh, p. 19.
31 Benson and Robinson-Walsh, p. 114.
32 Klass, 'The Deceased Child', in *Continuing Bonds: New Understandings of Grief*, ed. Klass, Silverman and Nickman, London, 1996, p. 202.
33 SAMM was originally part of the Compassionate Friends, but became an independent charity in 1990. It provides support, sympathy and an ear to listen, and campaigns to make society more aware of the devastating effects of these crimes on bereaved relatives.
34 Jalland, p. 335.
35 Quoted by Houlbrooke, p. 236.
36 Report of trial, *Daily Mail*, 12 November 1997.
37 *Talking Care*, BBC2, 7 December 1999.

38 *Taking a Stand*, BBC Radio 4, 8 January 2002.
39 *The Road to Golgotha*, BBC1, 6 April 1996.
40 Walter, 'A new model of grief: bereavement and biography', *Mortality*, vol. 1, no. 1, March 1996, p. 13.
41 Walter, 'Letting go and keeping hold: a reply to Stroebe', *Mortality*, vol. 2, no. 3, November 1997, p. 263.
42 Sogyal Rinpoche, *The Tibetan Book of Living and Dying*, ed. Gaffney and Harvey, London, 1992, p. 300.
43 Rinpoche, p. 309.
44 *Bereavement*, p. 172.
45 *Living with Grief after Sudden Loss*, p. 3.

Conclusion

1 Frankl, *Man's Search for Meaning* (1946), Washington, 1985, p. 77.
2 Sarah Webster Goodwin and Elisabeth Bronfen, *Death and Representation*, London, 1993, p. 4.
3 George Frederick Watts, quoted by Karl S. Guthke in *The Gender of Death*, Cambridge, 1999, p. 204.
4 *Death and Representation*, p. 9.
5 Quoted in *Big Issue*, 30 October 2000.
6 Beckett, *Proust* (1931), London, 1976, p. 17.
7 See James, *Varieties of Religious Experience* (1902).
8 *Beyond the Pleasure Principle* (1920), Penguin Freud Library, vol.11, 1984, p. 319.
9 Gittings, *Death, Burial and the Individual*, p. 10.
10 Elias, p. 35.
11 *Death, Burial and the Individual*, p. 10.
12 Bacon, *Of Nature in Man*.
13 Jalland, p. 357.
14 de Hennezel, p. 47.
15 Gorer, p. 113.
16 Ariès, p. 580.
17 Jalland, p. 5.
18 Thompson and Payne, 'Bereaved children's questions to a doctor', *Mortality*, vol. 5, no. 1, March 2000, p. 76.
19 *Bereavement*, p. 154.
20 *Bereavement*, p. 171.
21 *Bereavement*, p. 174.
22 Purves, 'Long live our queens,' *The Times*, 23 November 1999.

Recommended Reading

Historical Background

Philippe Ariès, *The Hour of Our Death* (1981)
Ariès' work is unsurpassed in its breadth and analysis of changing attitudes to death in Europe from the middle ages to the present day. It is a massive volume, dense with historial detail, but with a lovely sense of the bizarre. The central contention of the book, that we live in a society that denies death, has held good for twenty years.

Clare Gittings, *Death, Burial and the Individual in Early Modern Britain* (1984)
One of the first British studies to come out of the renewed academic interest in death, Clare Gittings' book remains an excellent account of burial and mourning rituals in the early modern period. It's accessible and entertaining, and recovers fascinating details about ornate funerals of the past, as well as pressing home a convincing argument that post-Reformation individualism lies at the heart of our modern anxieties about death.

Pat Jalland, *Death in the Victorian Family* (1996)
A feat of scholarship, Jalland's work draws on the diaries, letters and public writings of upper-class Victorians. The focus is on the idea of the 'good death'. Whilst fully aware of the frequent disparity between the reality of deaths as they were experienced and what the families chose to record about them afterwards, Jalland gives some very moving accounts of families riven by scarlet fever or TB. She also provides a clear overview of the

period and of how Victorian rituals changed and declined during the century.

P. Jupp and C. Gittings, (eds.) *Death in England: an Illustrated History* (1999)

For a shorter description of the evolution of our attitudes to death over 2,000 years of English history, this can't be beaten. The book assembles many of the first division now writing about death and together these authors create a rich and fascinating storehouse of information and analysis. *Death in England* is also very well illustrated, depicting the many faces of death from disinterred Iron Age skeletons to Renaissance bereavement portraiture to an extraordinary Victorian photograph of a dead baby that the photographer thought was asleep.

Dying and Bereavement

C. Saunders, M. Baines and R. Dunlop, *Living with Dying: the Management of Terminal Disease,* (3rd ed., 1995)

Cicely Saunders has written extensively on the subject of the hospice movement and its approach to care of the dying. All her work is worth reading, but this is a short book which sets out the key principles of the hospice and provides a clear introduction to the ideas of palliative care.

Marie de Hennezel, *Intimate Death: How the Dying Teach Us to Live* (1997)

François Mitterand said this book was 'dense with humanity'. Marie de Hennezel was the psychologist attached to the first palliative care unit in a Parisian hospital for the terminally ill, and this highly personal and remarkable book is the result of her work there. It is constructed as a series of vignettes, each advancing the story of one or other of the unit's patients. De Hennezel also cared for Mitterand in his last days, and his death, as indeed all those in the unit, comes across as not merely moving but, in Mitterand's own phrase, as 'an accomplishment'.

Elisabeth Lee, *A Good Death: a Guide for Patients and Carers Facing Terminal Illness at Home* (1995)

Elisabeth Lee, too, is a professional working with the dying. One of her concerns is our denial of death and she is frank about how as a doctor she has hurried past patients' beds rather than confront her own fears of death. This is not a book for the frail. It does not pull its punches and the reader is left in no doubt about how awful dying can be. But it also has very practical recommendations to make, particularly in relation to preparing children for a relative's death.

Julia Neuberger, *Caring for Dying People of Different Faiths* (1987)
This is a clear and concise account of what adherents of the six major world faiths believe, particularly in regard to dying and the afterlife, and what their requirements, and those of their relatives, are likely to be as death approaches. Reading this invaluable resource can avoid embarrassment and insensitivity, and help create the conditions for a good death.

Susan Hill, *In the Springtime of the Year* (1974)
This well-known novel provides a moving record of one young widow's bereavement. Susan Hill is particularly good at exploring the initial problem of denial and the widow's slow and painful acceptance that there remains a life for her that is worth living.

Jeannette Kupfermann, *When the Crying's Done* (1992)
Fact rather than fiction, this is a very frank account of one woman's experience of losing her husband and finding that she has then to support her family. It is raw stuff at times, and not always easy to read, because Jeannette Kupfermann is faithful to the details of what she went through. She describes very well the physical and emotional trauma, and the sense of insecurity and social awkwardness she felt. Ultimately, though, this is a tale of survival: it's about how you do get through.

Colin Murray Parkes, *Bereavement: Studies of Grief in Adult life* (3rd ed., 1998)
A much more formal study of bereavement, written by a consultant psychiatrist who works in hospices, this is a classic text on how people grieve. Parkes draws extensively on the large number of cases he has personally dealt with and provides a broad-ranging discussion that seeks to differentiate between the various kinds of customary grief and the more problematic, or chronic, kind. Although it is used in the training of professionals, this is a book that many people will find valuable.

Rituals and Ceremony

J. B. Bradfield, *Green Burial: the D-I-Y Guide to Law and Practice*
Originally published in 1994 and revised since, this is what the title suggests: a down-to-earth handbook for anyone planning an independent burial or funeral. Bradfield describes the legal and environmental issues involved, and provides guidance on registration and form-filling. Importantly, it makes clear that we have a far greater degree of choice in how we dispose of the dead than we might imagine.

Sue Gill and John Fox, *The Dead Good Funerals Book* (1996)
A more idiosyncratic volume, this is also a guide to alternative ceremonies for the dead. Over and above advice on minimizing

the bureaucracy and cost of funerals, Gill and Fox provide a range of anecdotes about individuals' funerals and how they were done, together with suggested poems, prayers, music and ideas about the form that alternative ceremonies can take.

General

Tony Walter, *The Revival of Death* (1994)
Tony Walter is a sociologist at the University of Reading, where he runs an MA course on Death and Society. He has written several fascinating studies of death and our attitudes to it. This is typical of his broad-ranging books and includes a good deal of historical interest as well as observations on contemporary experience of dying and bereavement.

Thomas Lynch, *The Undertaking: Life Studies from the Dismal Trade* (1997)
Lynch's first book was a runaway success when it came out. It is a collection of essays about his life as an American funeral director and, when time permits, poet. Lynch's skill in this and his subsequent volume, *Bodies in Motion and at Rest* (2000), is to combine moments of deep emotion with insight, humour and a Zolaesque whiff of the morgue. He remains in no doubt, though, that however enlightened our attitudes to death may become, his will always be the 'dismal trade'. As he says, 'random samplings of consumer preference almost never turn up "weeping and mourning" as things we want to do on our vacations.' Death will never be a popular destination.

Useful Contacts

CancerBACUP
3 Bath Place, Rivington Street, London EC2A 3DR. Tel: 020
7696 9003. Helpline: 0808 800 1234.
e-mail: info@cancerbacup.org.
website: www.cancerbacup.org.uk
Information about all forms of cancer for people with cancer and
their families and friends. Large number of publications available
on living with cancer, the nature of individual cancers and the
treatments provided for them.

Imperial Cancer Research Fund
P. O. Box 123, Lincoln's Inn Fields, London WC2A 3PX. Tel:
020 7242 0200.
website: www.canceresearchuk.org
Information and fact sheets about cancer can be obtained by
sending a stamped addressed envelope.

Macmillan Cancer Relief
UK Office, 89 Albert Embankment, London SE1 7UQ.
Tel: 020 7840 7840. Information line: 0845 601 6161
website: www.macmillan.org.uk
Information about all Macmillan services, including advice on
living with cancer, Macmillan nurses and doctors, cancer care
units for residential and day care and grants that can be awarded
to those in financial need.

Cancer Help Centre
Grove House, Cornwallis Grove, Clifton, Bristol BS8 4PG.
Tel: 0117 980 9500. Helpline: 0117 980 9505.
e-mail: info@ bristolcancerhelp.org
website: www.bristolcancerhelp.org
The Centre runs a number of residential programmes (two or five days) for people living with cancer and also provides educational courses for professionals.

London Lighthouse
111–117 Lancaster Road, London W11 1QT.
Tel: 020 7792 1200.
website: www.tht.org.uk
Residential and day care for people living with HIV/AIDS.

National AIDS Helpline
Healthwise, 85–89 Duke Street, Liverpool L1 5AP.
Tel: 0151 703 7777. Helpline: 0800 567 123.
e-mail: info@healthwise.org.uk
Confidential advice and support available to anyone affected by HIV/AIDS. Non-English language services and services for people with hearing problems available.

Motor Neurone Disease Association
P. O. Box 246, Northampton NN1 2PR.
Tel: 01604 250 505. Helpline: 08457 626 262.
e-mail: enquiries@mndassociation.org
website: www.mndassociation.org
Advice, information and publications for people with MND, those supporting them and professionals. National network of volunteers who will visit people in their homes and organize the loan of useful equipment.

Multiple Sclerosis National
372 Edgware Road, London NW2 6ND.
Tel: 020 8438 0700. Helpline: 0808 800 8000
e-mail: info@mssociety.org
website: www.mssociety.org.uk
Information for people with MS and those supporting them. Some financial assistance and welfare services also available. The society will send out information on receipt of a stamped addressed envelope.

National Council for Hospice and Specialist Palliative Care Services
1st Floor, Hospice House, 34–44 Britannia Street, London
WC1X 9JG. Tel: 020 7520 8299.
e-mail: enquiries@hospice-spc-council.org.uk
website: www.hospice-spc-council.org.uk
Coordinating organization for services in England, Wales and
Northern Ireland. Provides information about palliative care to
government, health authorities, the press and relevant agencies.
Meetings organized by network of local representatives. Details
from the National Council.

Hospice Information Service
St Christopher's Hospice, 51–59 Lawrie Park Road, London
SE26 6DZ. Tel: 020 8778 9252.
e-mail: his@stchris.ftech.co.uk
General information on the hospice movement worldwide. The
service also publishes a directory of all hospice and palliative care
services in the United Kingdom and the Republic of Ireland,
together with information about bereavement services and
complementary care.

The Natural Death Centre
6 Blackstock Mews, Blackstock Road, London N4 2BT.
Tel: 020 7359 8391.
e-mail: rhino@dial.pipex.com
website: www.naturaldeath.org.uk
Information and advice about organizing a funeral either through
a funeral director or on your own. Several publications available
on woodland burials, biodegradable coffins and inexpensive
funeral services.

Heaven on Earth
18 Upper Maudlin Street, Bristol BS2 8DJ.
Tel/Fax: 0117 926 4999.
Supplies a range of inexpensive coffins, which can also act as
pieces of furniture. Offers full funeral services (religious or
secular) tailored to the individual needs of the family.

Cruse Bereavement Care
Cruse House, 126 Sheen Road, Richmond, Surrey TW9 1UR.
Tel: 020 8940 4818. Helpline: 020 8332 7227.
Well-established counselling and support service for anyone who
has been bereaved. Provides home visits, together with useful
leaflets, newsletters and information about other support groups.

SANDS (Stillbirth and Neonatal Death Society)
28 Portland Place, London W1N 4DE.
Tel: 020 7436 5881.
Provides support through self-help groups run by bereaved
parents. A helpline, local meetings and occasional home visits are
offered, together with a range of publications and leaflets.

Child Death Helpline
Bereavement Services Department, Great Ormond Street Hospital
NHS Trust, Great Ormond Street, London WC1N 3JH.
Tel: 020 7813 8551. Helpline: 0800 282 986
The helpline is confidential and staffed by volunteers who are
bereaved parents themselves. It provides information and support
to anyone affected by the death of a child.

The Compassionate Friends
53 North Street, Bristol BS3 1EN.
Tel: 0117 966 5202. Helpline: 0117 953 9639.
e-mail: info@tcf.org.uk
Nationwide network of branches offering support and friendship
to parents and families affected by the loss of a child, plus
information for carers and professionals.

Index

acceptance 111, 112, 134
  active stance 134
  movement towards 109–11
Addison, Joseph 265
afterlife 3, 19–20, 166, 228
  belief in 20, 228, 229,
    231
  historic attitudes 3–4
  loss of faith in 20–1, 23
Age Concern 186
AIDS 44, 67–94
  causes 68
  children with 85
  common dysfunctions 69
  death rate 74
  demographic profile 75
  drug therapy 73, 74, 90, 92,
    93, 103
  epidemiologies 68–9
  global incidence of 76–7
  HIV virus 68, 69, 74, 75
  hospice patients 131
  inclusion of PWAs within
    our circle 91–2
  living with 67–94
  palliative care 73, 84
  personal experiences 70–2,
    77–82, 85–94

  preventative caution 91
  public perception of 75–6,
    84
  seen as form of punishment
    68
  social pressure to conceal
    69–70, 72, 84
  vaccines 73–4
Alder Hey Children's Hospital,
  Liverpool 246, 268
Allende, Isabel 200–1
anger and resistance 40, 110,
  129–30, 135, 139, 145,
  214, 221, 245
Anson, Caroline 113, 160
anti-anxiety drugs 213, 214
anticipatory bereavement xviii
Ariès, Philippe 1, 37, 167,
  278
*Arte and Crafte to know well
  to dye* 5
Ash, Arthur 82
atheism 272
autonomy, erosion of 65, 141

Bacon, Francis 97, 133, 272
the 'bad death' 135, 136
bargaining stance 110, 111

Baudrillard, Jean 206
Beckett, Samuel 269, 275
belief systems 193
    eclectic beliefs 193
    see also religious belief
Bennett, Ellie 114–15, 130,
        131–2, 148, 155
Benson, Jo 239
bereavement
    adjusting to new
        circumstances 204
    anticipatory bereavement
        xviii
    first months 60
    forming new attachments
        204–5
    and loss of control 275
    moving on 204, 205
    physical effects 199
    toleration and recognition of
        the bereaved 261
    see also grief; mourning
bereavement studies 280
Binns, Anita and Glenn 77–82,
        83, 85–94
biographical recovery 128
body
    ambivalent dimensions of
        269
    cultural attachment to the
        body 266
    denial of access to the body
        221
    laying out xix
    releasing the body 189
    viewing xix, 181–2, 250
body-snatching 267
Bond, Julian 204, 205, 227
Book of Common Prayer 163,
        169, 172–3
Book of the Dead 3
Bowler, John 202
Bronfen, Elisabeth 266, 267
Buddhism 259, 270
burial service 169

burials 167–72
    cemeteries 172, 173, 178
    Church of England control
        of 172–3, 174, 175–6
    in gardens and private land
        189
    gravestones 176
    green burials 186
    night burials 170
    nineteenth-century practices
        170–2
    non-conformist burials 173
    Victorian reforms 171–4

Campbell, Rhona 224, 225
cancer 18, 44
    anti-cancer pill 46
    avoidance and risk reduction
        45, 46
    breast cancer 47, 49
    chemotherapy 62
    combative stance 45–6, 66
    detection 46
    gene therapy treatments 47
    guilt and 45
    increasing incidence of 47–8,
        49
    issue of denial 50, 52
    living with 44–53
    lung cancer 46, 48
    misdiagnosis 62–3
    NHS *National Cancer Plan*
        158, 160
    pain alleviation 106
    palliative care 142–3
    personal experiences 53–9,
        63–6
    prognosis 117
    reponse to 49–50
    self-help 50–1
Cancer Help Centre, Bristol
        50, 123
cancerBACUP 52
carers 135, 136, 137, 147, 149
    help available to 137–8

respites 137, 149
shopping and patient-sitting
services 137
Carter, Helen 112
Cartwright, Ann 116, 117, 229
Cassidy, Sheila 75–6
cemeteries 172, 173
memorials 178
Chadlington, Lord 40–1
Chadwick, Edward 171
chantries 6
Chatwin, Bruce 69
Chaucer, Geoffrey 5
Child Death Helpline 246,
247–8, 257
child organs 268
children
adapting to loss of a parent
138, 139–40
with AIDS 79–82, 85–
94
classes in bereavement
studies 280
common exclusion from
dying process 140
coping with patterns of
home care 138–9
grieving children 21, 22,
139, 140
survival rates 238
child's death 38, 203, 233–55
babies 182
child's acceptance of 87
death of adult children
248–55
denial of access to the body
221
and divine retribution 237
individuation of the child's
personality and life 241,
245
irreplaceability 241
mortality rates 238, 239
neonatal deaths 239
perinatal deaths 239

personal experiences 241–7,
249–53
stillbirths 239–41
Sudden Infant Death
Syndrome (SIDS) 248
support groups 246–8
Victorian era 10, 234, 237
Chillis, Valerie 229–30
Church of England
control of burials 172–3,
174, 175–6
and cremations 173–4
strictures on gravestones
175–6
in times of crisis and
national mourning 21
Church of Scotland 22
The Churchyards' Handbook
176
Clement-Jones, Vicky 52
Cline, Sally 198
coffins 189–90
College of Arms 169–70
communication skills 120–1,
144, 158, 159
community, decline of 272
Compassionate Friends 248,
253, 257
compassionate leave 196
condolence letters 11
containment of feeling 260
control
bereavement and loss of 275
death as ultimate loss of 273
loss of physical control 105
over grief 205
over individual identity 140
retaining 39, 134–5, 273, 277
coroners 189
counselling
bereavement counselling 23,
121–2, 212–13, 260, 280
marriage guidance
counselling 122
Cowie, Richard 120, 130, 160

Crace, Jim 195
cremations 167, 173-4
  formulaic character 167
  theological conundrum
    173-4
Cummings, John 47
Curren, Lesley 60, 122

Dance with Death 133
danse macabre 5
Darwinism 21
Day of the Dead 192
de Hennezel, Marie 91, 99,
    108, 122, 278
Dead Citizens Charter 192-3
death
  accepting the reality of 203
  arbitrariness 4, 35
  collective understanding of
    276
  death-as-disease model 264
  definition of 18
  denial of 1, 109-10
  friendship with 133
  historic beliefs and practices
    3-13
  isolating effect xxi
  paradoxes 265-6
  progressive detachment
    from physical act of
    dying 136
  as rite of passage 109
  sudden death 206-15
  taboo xxi, xxii, 33, 36-7
  as a transition 109-11
  uncertainties 145
deathbed memoirs 11
deathbed scenes 9
denial 113, 115, 116, 203
  coping mechanism 50, 119
  of death 1, 109-10
  of diagnosis 52
  doctors' collusion in 109, 119
  hope rooted in 111
  informed denial 119

depression 110-11
  biological signs 146
  vulnerability to 146
detachment 31, 136
diagnosis
  patients' interpretations of
    118
  and prognosis distinguished
    117
  responses to 43
Diana, Princess of Wales
    25-30, 31
Dibley, Minnie 63-6
Didham, Laurie 246-7
dignity 140, 149
Dinnage, Rosemary 163
dishonouring the dead 267
doctors
  changes of 119
  collusion in denial 109, 119
  gateway to therapy 155-6
  and home care of the dying
    141
  lack of candour 113, 116,
    117, 118
  as life-savers 17, 104, 265
  paternalistic attitude 112
  relationship between GPs
    and hospices 151-2
Doka, Kenneth 83-4, 222
Dollimore, Jonathan 24
Donne, John 6-7
Dr Barnardo's 139
Dunblane 223-4

Egyptian beliefs and practices
    3, 258-9
Elias, Norbert 128, 271
Elizabeth I 169
Ellershaw, John 120-1
embalming 181-2
'End of Life' (BBC programme)
    33-4
epitaphs 176-7
Epstein, Fred 54-5

euphemistic language 13, 21
Evangelical movement 9, 11
Evelyn, John 235
Everett, Kenny 82
evil, problem of 3
existential anxieties of dying
      126, 127

Fairnie, Steve 178–80, 232–3
families
    accommodating to death 134
    changing character of 124–5
    hospices as extensions of
      121–2
    infantalization and
      idealization 124
    reconciliation 122, 125, 126
    working with 121–2
fear
    of death 271, 272
    of the dying process 39, 51
    of having failed 40
    of hopelessness 40
    of separation from family 40
    of what lies beyond death 40
Field, Jennifer 142
financial hardship 143
Frankl, Viktor 263–4
Frazer, Harriet 178
Freud, Sigmund 12, 271
Frogatt, Katherine 156–7
fundamentalist Christians
      230–1
funerals 166–8
    alternative funerals 168,
      188–92, 193, 275–6
    Anglican clergy and 172,
      173, 176
    burials 167–72
    commercial aspects 184–6
    costs 171–2, 184–6
    cremations 167, 173–4
    departures from custom 186
    dissatisfaction with 167–8
    DIY approach 191, 193

embalming 181–2
    green burials 186
    heraldic funerals 169, 170
    historic practices 169–75
    life-story of the deceased 193
    locations 189
    officiating at 168, 189
    participation 184, 190–2
    pre-paid funerals 185–6
    recording 183
    retaining control 277
    stillbirths 240

Garland, Caroline 254
genetic engineering 18–19
genocide 14
Gittings, Clare 8, 170, 186,
      271
God's punishment, death as 5
the 'good death' 8–9, 10, 35,
      36, 37–8, 60
    criteria 132, 161
    modern era 38, 39, 132
    reconciliation 122
    Victorian era 8–10, 11–12
Goodwin, Sarah 266, 267
Gordon, Vincent 198, 226
Gorer, Geoffrey 17, 22, 278
graves
    desecration 188, 266–7
    resistance to re-use of 266
    visiting xix, 188, 258–9
gravestones 176
    epitaphs 176–7
    public status of 176
    regulations 175–6, 178
graveyards 186–7, 188
Greek beliefs about death 3–4
green burials 186
grief 195–262
    accumulating grief 227
    after sudden death 208
    ambivalent feelings 201
    anticipatory grief 201
    constant flux 256

'disenfranchized grief' 83–4
early grief 200
effect of personal history on 225–7
emotional trauma of 204
etiquette of grief 261
global uniformity 199
goal 255
grief tasks 202–6
guilt 200–1
'imitation' feature 200
incremental grief 225
irrational symptoms 201
mourning dress and emblems 196
open expression of 196, 281
physical injury analogy 217
physical symptoms xx, 210
postponed grief 227
preserving and letting-go 257
psychotherapeutic model 201
sensation that the deceased is present 200
'staged' recovery 196, 202–3
staggered farewells 259–60
susceptibility to ill-health 199, 210
value of an active grief 260
widows 197–9
guilt 200–1, 212, 221, 252
allied to sense of worthlessness 127
at passing on a terminal infection 88
cancer and 45

Hades 3, 4
haptonomy 91, 278
hell and damnation 4
Hillier, Richard 96, 117, 157
Hindu beliefs and practices 192, 270
historical beliefs about death 3–15

Holocaust 30
Holy Dying (Jeremy Taylor) 36
home, dying at 134–49
care service providers 142–7
carers 135, 136, 137, 147, 149
GP care 141
hospice home care 137
ill-adapted home settings 136
integration of health and social services 141
key advantage of home care 138
resentment and counter-productive care 136
restorative care 137
Hooper, Edward 69
hope
applied to new objectives 111–12
confusion between recovery and 111
dynamic of relationship 112
false hope 113
function of acceptance 112
hospices 38, 65, 95–132
admissions profile 131, 135
availability 130–2
average patient stay 108
class and ethnic boundaries 131
commitment to individual's emotional welfare 109
criticisms of infantalization and idealization 124
day hospice 102, 148
empowerment of the patient 105
essential features 98
extension of the family 122
formulaic tendency 129, 153
growth of hospice movement 102

home care 137, 142
hospice approach 105–9
hospice–health service
   relationship 152–3, 161
influence on palliative care
   151
openness 114–15
origins 100–3, 156
outreach work 103
parent–child model 124,
   156–7
patient–staff relationships
   97, 105, 108, 109, 145–6
peace and tranquillity 97,
   129
personal experiences 99–100,
   107–8, 125–6
philosophy of care 97
referral 107
respite nursing 147–9
restitution of older practices
   97
staying close ethos 132
symptom control 97, 100,
   107, 152
in the United States 102–3,
   151–2
Hospital Palliative Care Teams
   142
hospitals
   assoication with features of a
      'bad death' 135
   death in 104, 134
   incorporation of hospice care
      teams 154–5, 156, 160
   palliative care 142–3, 151
Houghton, Clare and Simon
   207–15, 231–2
Houlbrooke, Ralph 234, 235
Howe, Jeremy and Lizzie
   215–20
Hudson, Rock 82
Huizinga, Johan 4
Hunt, Janice and Alan 53–9,
   66

immortality 18, 265
individualism 271
intimacy xx, xxi, 66, 139, 278
Islam 270

Jalland, Pat 13, 174, 198, 225,
   234, 236, 249, 272, 279
James I 170
James, Henry 279
James, William 269
Johnson, Malcolm 167
Johnson, Samuel 38, 176–7
Jones, James 179, 180

Keats, John 36
Keble, John 225
Kellaway, Kate 120
Kellehear, Allan 132
Kelly, Anthony-Noel 267
Kestenbaum, Matthew 135,
   151, 152
Kirkwood, Thomas 16, 17, 18
Kitson, Alison 39
Klass, Dennis 244
Knight, Andrew 98–9, 150,
   153, 154, 158
Knights Hospitallers of St John
   100
knowledge
   communication skills 120–1,
      144, 158, 159
   empowerment through 51,
      53, 67, 274
   ethical and compassionate
      reasons for disclosure 113
   patient's right to know xv,
      51, 120
Koster, Margje 83
Kübler-Ross, Elisabeth 109,
   111, 116, 122, 138, 139,
   140
Kupfermann, Jeannette 197, 201

Lane, Sir David 46
language of condolence 199

language of death 13
Laotian-Hmong 192
Larkin, Philip 263
Lawrence, Stephen 253
Lawton, Julia 129
Ledwick, Martin 52, 53
Lee, Elisabeth 51, 139
leukaemia 238
life expectancy 2, 4–5, 15,
    16–17, 265
  extension 18–19
  mediaeval period 4–5
  Victorian era 8, 16
Lindsay, Neil 267
literature of consolation 11,
    225, 234, 237
living wills 65
Lloyd, Liz 134, 135, 136
Lockerbie bombing 222, 253–4,
    255
loneliness of dying 128
Lynch, Thomas 165–6, 175,
    191, 266

McAfee, Margaret 163–4
McCullough, Dina and Stuart
    70–2
MacLeod, Rod 112
Macmillan Cancer Relief 143
Macmillan nurses 143–5, 146,
    160
Macmillan Support Service
    142
  helpline 143
  support groups 143
Manning, Margaret 100
Marie Curie nurses 143, 144
Mary Queen of Scots 170
mass killings 14–15, 30, 223–5,
    261–2
massage 123
media treatment of death 23–34
medical research
  child organs 268
  organ retention without

consent 268
  use of bodies for 172,
    267–8
medical science
  autocratic approach 104
  death-as-disease model 264
  faith in 20–1
  see also doctors
medical training 39, 157–8
  communication skills 120–1,
    158, 159
  ethics of decision-making
    157
  Higher Medical Training
    (HMT) 158–9
  palliative care 157–9
  terminal care courses 280
mediaeval beliefs about death
    4–5
memorials 13, 178
Memorials by Artists 178
memory store 139
Merrin, William 27–8, 29
Methodists 228
Mexican beliefs and practices
    192
Miller, Sara 50, 51, 104, 123
miscarriage 240
Montaigne, Michel Eyquem de
    xi, 36, 206, 234, 263
Moore, Oscar 82
morbidness 280
morphine 106–7
mortality rates 15, 238, 239
motor neurone disease (MND)
    201
  characteristics xvi
  hospice patients 130–1
  intellectual deterioration xiv
  physical deterioration xv
mourning
  accepted mourning periods
    261
  dress and emblems 196,
    252

induced inhibition 277–8, 279
mourning-as-malady model xx, 278
open display of 261
Victorian era 11, 234
see also grief
multiple sclerosis 130
murders 215–20, 221
denial of access to the body 221
mass killings 14–15, 30, 223–5, 261–2
police procedures 221, 222
Victim Support 221–2
Muslim practices 188

Nabokov 264
Natural Death Centre 189
neonatal deaths 239
New, Jo 228–9
NHS National Cancer Plan 158, 160

Oklahoma bombing 254, 259–60
Oliver, Gill 144
openness 67, 93
onus of disclosure 116
willingness to inform 116–17
within relationships 123
opium 7
Orthodox Jews 22, 228, 258
Osmond, Rosalie 191
Oz, Amos 45

pain
alleviation 7, 100, 106–7, 152, 273
cycle of pain 106
fear of 106
of grief 204
previous experiences of 106
spiritual/redemptive function 7, 106

palliative care 38, 96, 273
AIDS 73, 84
clinical research 160
future of 149–61
home care 142–7
hospice techniques 151
inclusiveness 121
medical training 157–9
respite nursing 148
rising costs 149
service providers 142–7
see also hospices
Pan Am 103 bombing 261–2
Paradise 270
Parkes, Colin Murray 199, 213, 217, 223, 234, 261, 281
Pask, Robin 215, 217–18
'passed away' 13
patient-assisted suicide 151–2
Patterson, Joan 107–8
Payne, Sheila 280
Peel, John 33
perinatal deaths 239
periodic observance of death 258
Peto, Richard 48
Picardie, Ruth 59–60, 62, 67
Plato 4
Poe, Edgar Allan 9
Porter, Roy 68–9
post-mortems 209
post-traumatic stress disorder 219, 220–1
Potter, Dennis 43, 44, 61–3
preparation for death xiv–xv, 2, 4, 36, 41
prognosis 117, 118
psychotherapy 260, 279–80
public school ethos of self-control 279
Purgatory 5–6, 167, 259
Purves, Libby 281
Pythagoras 4

Rainey Croft, Paula 189–90
Rando, Therese A. 211
Ray, Sandra 18
reconciliation 122, 125, 126
reincarnation 259, 270
relationships
  fears of parting 123
  honesty within 123
  survivor anxieties 122, 123
religious belief 4, 126, 227–33
  cessation of conflict between
    faith and atheism 272
  loss of 15, 19–23, 168, 191,
    272
  sustaining ideology 20, 232,
    233, 251
  theological crisis 127
  see also afterlife
remembering death 30, 253,
    281–2
  anniversaries 276
  periodic observance 258
  ritualized remembrance 258,
    276
  twelvemonths mind 258
  visits to the grave xix, 188,
    258–9
  Yahrzeit 258
Remembrance Day 30
respite nursing 147–9
resurrection 269–70
resuscitation practices 155
ritual 163–94
  abandonment of orthodoxy
    193
  culture-specific 192–3
  deprofessionalizing of 193–4
  inclusion of children 140
  loss of 23
  see also funerals
Robinson-Walsh, Dawn 239
Roman Catholicism 22, 173,
    228–9
Rowland-Jones, Sarah 77

Sage, Bev 178–80, 232–3, 260
St Christopher's Hospice,
    London 101–2, 116, 131,
    146, 149–50, 153–4, 158,
    160
St Nicholas's Hospice, Bury
    141–2, 155
St Paul 35
Saunders, Dame Cicely 34, 95,
    97, 100, 101–2, 104, 106–
    7, 112–13, 115, 116,
    123, 124, 127–8, 129–30,
    134, 145–8, 153, 156,
    157–8
scarlet fever 10, 236
Seale, Clive 116, 117, 229
searching 223
secularization of society xxii,
    276
sedation 96
self-esteem 137
selfhood 270, 271
sequestration of the dying 129
Service Corporation
    International (SCI) 185
Sherwood, Molly 106
shiva 228
Smith, Sue and Giles 249–53
Socrates 4
Sontag, Susan 67–8
soul
  departure from the body xix
  see also afterlife
Southampton University
    Hospital 157
Spinoza, Baruch 15–16, 37
staying close xxii, 39, 122–3,
    127, 132
Stedeford, Averil 113
Stephens, Simon 248
Stillbirth and Neonatal Death
    Society (SANDS) 240
stillbirths 239–41
  funerals 240
  taboo subject 239–40

stoicism in the face of death 234
storytelling 257–8, 274
Stroud, John 140, 141
Sudden Death Syndrome (SDS) 209
sudden death 206–15
  acute psychological disturbance 224
  inadequacy and powerlessness 224
  nightmares and flashbacks 223
  personal experiences 207–20
  post-traumatic stress disorder 219, 220–1
  see also murders
Sudden Infant Death Syndrome (SIDS) 248
suicide 84, 229
Sullivan, Andrew 73
Swire, Jane and Flora 255
Symptom Control Teams 142

Tait, Campbell 236–7
Taylor, Jeremy 7, 36, 133, 233, 249
Tell Me the Truth, Doctor (BBC programme) xx
Tennyson, Alfred, Lord 225
terminal illness xxi–xxii 43–94
  denial 50
  openness, need for 67, 83
  passing on a terminal infection 88
  see also AIDS; cancer
Thé, Anne-Mei 119
Thomas, Dylan 130
Thompson, Francesca 280
Tibetan beliefs 259, 270
traumatic death 38, 84, 217
  need to blame 253–4
  see also murders; suicide
Traumatic Incident Reduction (TIR) 257

trust 141
  between patient and carers 274
truth 44
  commitment to 112
tuberculosis (TB) 9, 10, 16, 101
twelvemonths mind 258

The Undertaking (Thomas Lynch) 165–6
Underwood, James 268–9
'unfinished business' 127, 212
United States 192, 257
  hospices 102–3, 151–2
  medical training 159
  openness with information 117
  religious belief 228
Unknown Warrior 13

vicarious experience of death 24
Victim Support 221–2
Victoria, Queen 8, 9, 225–6
Victorian era 5
  bereavement 10
  child death 10, 234, 237
  death and mourning rituals 8, 10–11
  doctor–patient relationship 112
  funerals 174–5
  the 'good death' 8–10, 11–12
  hospices 101
  life expectancy 8, 16
vigils and wakes 164, 165, 186–7, 228

Walker, George Alfred 171
Walter, Tony 20, 23, 129, 256
Walton, Izaac 6
Warton, Angela 231
Waterhouse, Dorothy 180–3, 184
Weatherell, Sue 144–5
Welsh, Bud and Julie 254

widows 11, 197–9
  as appendages 198
  mortality rate 278–9
  ostracization 197, 198, 199
Wilkinson, Alan 13
Winston, Robert 33, 34
Wittgenstein, Ludwig 24
Wootton, Julia 105, 142
Worden, J. William 202–3,
  204, 205

Wordsworth, William 177,
  187–8, 235–6
World Trade Center terrorist
  attacks 15, 21
World Wars 12–14, 30
Wythe, Jane 145

Yahrzeit 258
Young, Michael 60, 122